Study Guide

Advanced Accounting

NINTH EDITION

Paul Marcus Fischer, PhD, CPA

Professor of Accounting / University of Wisconsin, Milwaukee

William James Taylor, PhD, CPA, CVA

Assistant Professor of Accounting / University of Wisconsin, Milwaukee

Rita Hartung Cheng, PhD, CPA

Professor of Accounting / University of Wisconsin, Milwaukee

THOMSON

SOUTH-WESTERN

Australia · Brazil · Canada · Mexico · Singapore · Spain · United Kingdom · United States

Study Guide to accompany
Advanced Accounting, 9th edition tion

Paul M. Fischer, William J. Taylor, Rita H. Cheng

VP/Editorial Director
Jack W. Calhoun

Publisher:
Rob Dewey

Acquisitions Editor
Matthew Filimonov

Marketing Manager
Chris McNamee

Developmental Editor
Leslie Kauffman

Production Technology Project Manager
Peggy Buskey

Manufacturing Coordinator
Doug Wilke

Ancillary Coordinator
Erin M. Donohoe

Production Artist
Patti Hudepohl

Cover Photo
Stone/Robin Smith

Printer
Globus Printing
Minster, OH

For more information about our products,
contact us at:

Thomson Learning Academic Resource
Center

1-800-423-0563

Thomson Higher Education
5191 Natorp Boulevard
Mason, OH 45040
USA

Table of Contents

Chapter 1   Business Combinations: America's Most Popular Business Activity, Bringing an End to the Controversy

OUTLINE FOR REVIEW

A business combination occurs when two or more previously independent business entities are brought together into one accounting entity with one company acquiring control. Acquisitions may take the form of purchasing all of the assets of another company or buying a controlling interest in another company's voting common stock. In the past, the transaction could be accounted for as a purchase, which recorded fair values, or as a pooling of interests that recorded existing book values. Since July 2001, only the purchase method is allowed.

I.   There are two ways to achieve control of another company.
   A.   Direct method—*asset* acquisition.
      1.   The acquiring company buys the net assets (assets less liabilities) directly from the selling company and records the newly acquired assets and liabilities on its books.
      2.   All subsequent transactions of both companies are recorded in one remaining set of accounts. Therefore, combined financial statements automatically result for periods after the business combination.
   B.   Indirect method—*stock* acquisition.
      1.   The acquiring company purchases enough voting common stock (usually over 50%) of the acquired company to obtain control. This type of acquisition is covered in Chapter 2.
      2.   Both companies remain separate legal entities with their own accounting records. In order to present the real economic substance of the single economic entity, the separate financial statements are combined into one set of consolidated statements using worksheet procedures discussed in Chapters 2–8.

II.   Alternative accounting models.
   A.   Purchase accounting brings over the accounts of the acquired company at fair values (to the extent the price paid allows it). Income statement accounts of the acquired company are added only after the purchase date. No retained earnings are carried over.
   B.   Pooling of interest accounting (allowed prior to July 1, 2001) brought over the accounts of the acquired company at book value. Typically, this meant that income would be enhanced as a result of lower depreciation and amortization charges, which would be based on book values. Income statement accounts were combined for the entire year, no matter when during the year the acquisition occurred. Retained earnings of the acquired firm were added to that of the acquirer

III.   The purchase method treats the acquisition as a mass purchase of assets at fair value.
   A.   The total value assigned to the net assets acquired includes direct acquisition costs. These are amounts paid to outside parties to complete the purchase transaction. Indirect costs are expensed. Issue costs of securities that might be used as consideration are deducted from the value assigned to the debt or stock issue.
   B.   If the total price paid exceeds the sum of the assets' values, less liabilities at fair value, goodwill is recorded. Goodwill is not amortized; rather, it is subject to annual impairment testing. A price below the sum of the net assets at fair value requires careful evaluation.
      1.   Priority accounts include all current assets and all liabilities plus the following accounts that would not otherwise qualify as current assets: all investments except those maintained under the equity method, assets to be disposed of, deferred tax assets, and prepaid assets relating to pension plans or other postretirement benefit plans. These accounts are always recorded at fair value. If the price paid is less than their total, an extraordinary gain is recorded and no value is assigned to nonpriority accounts.
      2.   If after the priority accounts are recorded at fair value, the remaining unallocated price is less than the sum of the fair values of the nonpriority accounts, the transaction is considered a "bargain." The remaining price is allocated to the nonpriority accounts proportionate to their individual fair values.
   C.   There may be tax loss carryovers. To the extent realization is expected, this is an asset, which is recorded. Goodwill, once recorded, is subject to impairment testing and possible adjustment.

1. Impairment testing is done annually. Goodwill is considered to be impaired if the estimated fair value of the business unit is less than the sum of the net assets (including goodwill).
2. If goodwill is impaired, it must be remeasured. The new amount would be the fair value of the business unit less the sum of its identifiable assets (excluding goodwill) at their fair values.
3. The excess of the newly measured goodwill over the existing recorded goodwill is the goodwill impairment loss (it is not extraordinary).

   D. Some purchases may be structured as a "nontaxable exchange." The purchasing firm will then record a deferred tax liability applicable to each asset recorded at more than book value (including goodwill).

IV. A purchase agreement may require that additional assets or securities be paid to the seller, contingent upon future events or transactions. During the contingency period, the contingent liability is disclosed in a footnote to the financial statements.

   A. Contingent consideration based on future earnings—When the additional consideration is paid, the recorded cost of the company increases. The additional cost is recorded as additional goodwill.
   B. Contingent consideration based on issuer's security prices—When this contingency is resolved, the amount originally assigned to the securities issued is adjusted, and the total cost is not changed.

PART 1

Instructions: Use a check mark to indicate whether each of the following statements is true or false.

	True	False
1. Return on assets was lower in a pooling than in a purchase transaction.		
2. When control is obtained through a stock acquisition, combined financial statements automatically result for future periods.		
3. Tax loss carryovers are generally transferable in a business combination and may be recorded as an asset.		
4. In all business combinations, one company gains control over the assets and liabilities of another company.		
5. Regardless of the purchase price, the current assets, liabilities, and long-term investments (not including equity method investments) are recorded at fair market value in a business combination recorded as a purchase.		
6. Resolution of a contingency based on security prices of shares used as consideration changes the overall price paid for a company.		
7. Tax loss carryovers of a company purchased are not recorded unless it is certain that they will reduce future tax liability of the purchasing company.		
8. When a purchase occurs during a reporting period, income from the purchased company is included in financial statements for the entire period.		
9. An extraordinary gain is recorded if the price paid for a company is less then its total net assets at fair value.		
10. Direct acquisition costs are added to the price paid for a company and often result in additional goodwill.		
11. Goodwill can be increased as the result of an additional payment made pursuant to an earnings contingency agreement.		
12. If a price is paid for a company that is far below the amount required to record goodwill, fixed assets will still be recorded at full fair value.		
13. If a price is paid for a company that is far below the amount required to record goodwill, inventory will still be recorded at full fair value.		

14. After a purchase occurs, it is likely that the income of the unit purchased will be less than it
     would have been had it not been purchased.   _____ _____

15. In a nontaxable exchange, a machine with a book value of $100 and a market value of $150
     will result in recording a deferred tax liability of $50.   _____ _____

16. Goodwill is considered impaired if the market value of the business is less than the recorded
     book values (including goodwill of the net assets).   _____ _____

PART 2

Instructions: Circle the letter that identifies the best response to each question. (Items 1, 2, and 5–13 are AICPA adapted.)

1.   On February 15, 20X8, Saxe Corp. paid $3,000,000 for all the issued and outstanding common stock of Carr, Inc., in
     a business combination properly accounted for as a purchase. The carrying amounts and fair values of Carr's assets
     and liabilities on Febru**ary 15, 20X8, were as follows:

	Carrying Amount	Fair Value
Cash	$ 320,000	$ 320,000
Receivables	360,000	360,000
Inventory	580,000	540,000
Property, plant, and equipment	1,740,000	1,920,000
Liabilities	(700,000)	(700,000)
Stockholders' equity	$2,300,000	

     What is the amount of goodwill resulting from the business combination?
     a. $700,000   b. $560,000   c. $140,000   d. $0

2.   On August 31, 20X0, Wood Corp. issued 100,000 shares of its $20 par value common stock for the net assets of Pine,
     Inc., in a business combination accounted for by the purchase method. The market value of Wood's common stock
     on August 31 was $36 per share. Wood paid a fee of $160,000 to a consultant who arranged this acquisition. Costs of
     registering and issuing the equity securities amounted to $80,000. No goodwill was involved in the purchase. What
     amount should Wood capitalize as the cost of acquiring Pine's net assets?
     a. $3,600,000   b. $3,680,000   c. $3,760,000   d. $3,840,000

3.   Kelly Corporation purchased the net assets of Frye Company in a business combination accounted for as a purchase.
     For tax purposes, this combination was considered to be a tax-free exchange. Kelly purchased a machine from Frye
     with an appraised value of $85,000 at the date of the business combination. This asset had a cost of $50,000, which
     was net of accumulated depreciation and which was based on accelerated depreciation for accounting purposes. The
     machine had an adjusted tax basis to Frye (and to Kelly as a result of the exchange) of $56,000. Assuming a 40%
     income tax rate, at what amount should Kelly record this machine on its books after the purchase?
     a. $56,000   b. $71,000   c. $73,400   d. $85,000

4.   Which of the following expenses related to effecting the business combination may enter into the determination of
     net income of the combined corporation for the period in which the expenses are incurred?

	Fees of Finders and Consultants	Stock Registration Fees
a.	Yes	Yes
b.	Yes	No
c.	No	No
d.	No	Yes

5.   Kiwi executed a business combination with Mori prior to July 1, 2001. The fair value of the stock issued by Kiwi
     exceeded the book value of Mori's net identifiable net assets. These book values are less than fair values. Mori's
     assets consist of current assets and depreciable noncurrent assets. Ignoring costs required to affect the combination

and income tax expense, how would the combined entity's net income under purchase accounting compare to that under pooling of interests accounting?
   a.   Less than pooling
   b.   Equal to pooling
   c.   Greater than pooling
   d.   Not determinable from information given

6. Company P purchased the net assets of Company S on July 1, 20X1, at a price high enough to result in goodwill. Fixed assets have fair values in excess of book values. What is the best statement to describe Company P's reported income for 20X1?
   a.   Sum of P + S for entire year
   b.   Sum of P + ½S
   c.   Less than sum of P + S for entire year
   d.   Less than sum of P + ½S

Common information for Items 7–9
Company S had the following net assets at fair value on the day it was purchased by Company P:

Inventory	$ 150,000
Land	80,000
Machinery	50,000
Building	150,000
Patents	40,000
Note payable	(100,000)

7. Assuming the price paid was $400,000, which prices would be assigned to the following assets?

	Inventory	Machinery	Patents	Goodwill
a.	$150,000	$50,000	$0	$70,000
b.	150,000	50,000	40,000	0
c.	150,000	50,000	40,000	30,000
d.	150,000	50,000	0	0

8. Assuming the price paid was $300,000, which prices would be assigned to the following assets?

	Inventory	Machinery	Patents	Goodwill
a.	$150,000	$50,000	$0	$0
b.	150,000	50,000	40,000	−70,000
c.	150,000	39,063	31,250	0
d.	150,000	50,000	0	−30,000

9. Assuming the price paid was $30,000, which prices would be assigned to the following assets?

	Inventory	Machinery	Patents	Goodwill
a.	$150,000	$50,000	$0	$0
b.	150,000	0	0	−20,000
c.	150,000	50,000	40,000	0
d.	150,000	0	0	0

PART 3

1. Summarize the assignment of value to an acquired company's accounts based on alternative prices paid.

   _____

   _____

   _____

2. What were the major advantages of pooling of interest accounting that made it worth trying to structure the transaction to allow pooling methods to be used?

   _____

   _____

   _____

3. Explain the situation that creates the need to record a deferred tax liability in a purchase. What happens to the deferred tax liability that is recorded as a part of a purchase?

   _____

   _____

   _____

4. Prior to July 1, 2001, goodwill was amortized over a period not to exceed 40 years. How does that differ from the current accounting method for goodwill that arises from a purchase?

   _____

   _____

   _____

PART 4

Gail Berry, the owner of Berry Corporation, has informed you that she is interested in acquiring one of her suppliers, Neske Company, at the end of this fiscal year. Berry has expressed her concerns over the impact that purchase accounting will have on future income statements. She is interested in learning how much more favorably the previously allowed pooling method would have recorded the transaction. The following balance sheet has been estimated for January 1, 20X1, the expected date of combination:

Neske Company
Balance Sheet
January 1, 20X1

Assets		Liabilities and Equity		
Current assets	$ 75,000	Current liabilities		$ 90,000
Inventory	50,000			
Property, plant, and equipment:				
Building	250,000	Stockholders' equity:		
Accum. depreciation	(80,000)	Common stock ($20 par)	$160,000	
Equipment	175,000	Retained earnings	195,000	355,000
Accum. depreciation	(25,000)			
Total assets	$445,000	Total liabilities and equity		$445,000

The appraised fair values of the buildings and equipment are $210,000 and $185,000, respectively. The inventory has a current market value of $60,000 and is expected to be sold this year. Straight-line depreciation is used for all plant assets. Given the condition of the assets, the equipment has a remaining useful life of 6 years and the building a remaining life of 15 years. Berry Corporation will issue 15,000 shares of its $10 par common stock, which has a current market value of $40, as consideration for the net assets of Neske. Direct acquisition costs are $10,000.

Instructions: Given the estimated combined revenues and expenses for 20X1, complete the following estimated income statement.

Berry Corporation and Neske Company
Comparison of Income
For Year Ending December 31, 20X1

	Purchase Method	**Pooling Method**
Revenue	$650,000	$650,000
Less: All expenses except depreciation and other adjustments resulting from business combination	(215,000)	(215,000)
Depreciation of buildings:		
Purchase		—
Pooling	—	
Depreciation of equipment:		
Purchase		—
Pooling	—	
Other adjustments:		
Net income		

PART 5

Monty Company is about to purchase the net assets of Halgo Inc. On December 31, 20X6, Halgo had the following balance sheet:

Assets		Liabilities and Equity	
Current assets	$120,000	Liabilities	$ 80,000
Land	50,000		
Buildings (net)	150,000	Common stock ($10 par)	200,000
Equipment (net)	40,000	Retained earnings	140,000
Goodwill	60,000		
Total assets	$420,000	Total liabilities and equity	$420,000

Monty has obtained the following fair values for certain accounts of Halgo Inc.:

Current assets	$100,000
Land	50,000
Buildings	100,000
Equipment	100,000
Liabilities	85,000

Instructions:

1. Prepare a zone analysis:

    a. Above what price would goodwill be recorded?

    b. Below what price would an extraordinary gain be recorded?

2. Prepare the entry by Monty Company to record the purchase of the net assets of Halgo Inc. on December 31, 20X6, for $215,000 in cash.

Allocation:

Consideration (cash)		$215,000
Less market value of net current assets:		
Current assets		
Liabilities	_____	_____
Value available for plant assets		=========

Asset	Fair Value	Percent of Nonpriority Total	X	Value Available	=	Assigned Value
Land	$ 50,000					
Buildings	100,000					
Equipment	100,000	_____				_____
Total	$250,000	=========				0

PART 6

Rocky Company has the following summarized balance sheet on January 1, 20X1:

Assets		Liabilities and Equity	
Accounts receivable	$ 20,000	Accounts payable	$ 60,000
Inventory	50,000	Bonds payable	100,000
Marketable investments	120,000		
Land	80,000		
Building (net)	200,000		
Equipment (net)	50,000		
Patents	25,000	Common stock, no par	200,000
Goodwill	15,000	Retained earnings	160,000
Total	$520,000	Total	$520,000

Fair values that differ from book values are as follows:

Inventory	$ 80,000
Marketable securities	100,000
Land	110,000
Building	275,000
Equipment	82,500
Patents	44,000
Employee training	38,500

Instructions:
1. Prepare a zone analysis for the Rocky Company.

	Group Amount	Cumulative Total
Priority accounts		
Nonpriority accounts		

2. Prepare the entry to record the purchase for $600,000.

3. Prepare the entry to record the purchase for $400,000.

Allocation:

Price paid	$400,000
Priority accounts	
Available	————

Asset	Fair Value	Percent of Nonpriority Total X	Amount Available =	Assigned Value
Land	$110,000			
Buildings	275,000			
Equipment	82,500			
Patents	44,000			
Employee training	38,500			
Total	$550,000			

4. Prepare the entry to record the purchase for $20,000.

PART 7

The Barns Company purchased the Farm Company on January 1, 20X1, for $800,000. All assets were recorded at fair value, which exceeded each accounts book value on the purchase date. There were no liabilities.

The following values apply to Farm accounts:

Account	Fair Value, Jan. 1, 20X1	Remaining Book Value, Dec. 31, 20X3	Fair Value, Dec. 31, 20X3
Inventory	$100,000	$100,000	$100,000
Marketable investments	200,000	250,000	250,000
Land	50,000	50,000	70,000
Building (net)	250,000	200,000	220,000
Goodwill			
Estimated value of business entity	800,000		700,000

Instructions:

1. What was the goodwill recorded on the purchase date?

2. If there have been no prior adjustments to goodwill, is goodwill impaired as of December 31, 20X3?

3. If goodwill is impaired, what is the impairment loss recorded on December 31, 20X3?

PART 8

Blinka Corporation expanded its operations by purchasing King Corporation on December 31, 20X7. The exchange was structured so that it was nontaxable. Blinka issued 14,000 shares of its $2 par stock, having a $30 market value, for the net assets of King and paid cash for the following costs related to the acquisition:

Direct acquisition costs	$13,000
Indirect acquisition costs	9,800
Issue costs	22,000

The following balance sheet was prepared for King Corporation on the date of purchase.

King Corporation
Balance Sheet
December 31, 20X7

Assets		Liabilities and Equity		
Current assets	$150,000	Accounts payable		$90,000
Inventory	35,000	Bonds payable		85,000
Property, plant, and equipment:		Stockholders' equity:		
Land	28,000	Common stock		
Building	165,000	($10 par)	$ 40,000	
Accum. depreciation	(80,000)	Retained earnings	153,000	193,000
Equipment	95,000			
Accum. depreciation	(25,000)			
Total assets	$368,000	Total liabilities and equity		$368,000

The companies agreed that the following market values should replace the above book values for the purpose of the purchase:

Building	$200,000
Equipment	78,000

Instructions:

Assume that the price paid is high enough to allow goodwill. Prepare the journal entries to record the purchase on the books of the Blinka Corporation. Assume a tax rate of 30%. Use the supporting schedule that follows to organize your calculations.

Computation of Assigned Values for Long-Lived Assets

Total consideration:		
Market value of securities issued		
Direct acquisition costs		
Total price		
Less assignment to identifiable assets and liabilities:		
Current assets		
Inventory		
Accounts payable		
Bonds payable		
Land		
Buildings		
DTL		
Equipment		
DTL		
Available for goodwill net of DTL		
Goodwill		
DTL		

Entries to Record the Purchase of the King Corporation:

Chapter 2   Consolidated Statements: Date of Acquisition

OUTLINE FOR REVIEW

Control of another company may be accomplished by acquiring a controlling interest in its voting common stock. This type of business combination requires preparation of consolidated financial statements. Chapter 2 concentrates on balance sheet presentation the day that control is achieved.

I.   A parent company is a company that acquires a controlling interest in the voting common stock of another company, the subsidiary. Each company is still a separate legal entity and will prepare its own financial statements. Consolidation of these statements is required to show the affiliated group as one economic entity.

II.   Control is presumed if the parent owns over 50% of the subsidiary's voting common shares.

III.   On the purchase date, the price paid is compared to the equity purchased to determine the adjustments needed to subsidiary accounts in order to consolidate the accounts with those of the parent.
   A.   Zone analysis is used to sum the total priority and nonpriority accounts as defined in Chapter 1. Zone totals are the fair values of the appropriate subsidiary accounts multiplied by the parent ownership percentage.
   B.   The comparison of the price paid to the cumulative zone totals will determine the amounts available for nonpriority accounts (priority accounts are always adjusted to the parent's percentage of fair value). Allocation to nonpriority assets is needed when there is an amount available for the assets but not enough to raise each asset to the parent's share of fair value.
   C.   The determination and distribution of excess schedule (D&D) will summarize the adjustments need to each account when consolidating.

IV.   Worksheet procedures will replace the investment account with subsidiary accounts and will eliminate any stockholders' equity that is owned by the parent and, thus, is not held by outside interests.
   A.   Entry "EL" will eliminate the parent's percentage of each subsidiary equity account against the investment accounts. The remaining excess should agree with the excess on the D&D schedule.
   B.   Entry "D" will distribute the excess as shown on the D&D schedule. This will adjust assets for the disparity between the parent's share of book versus fair value, to the extent the price paid allows it.
   C.   Where the parent owns less than a 100% interest, a portion of the subsidiary equity accounts will not be eliminated. The remaining portion of subsidiary equity is referred to as the noncontrolling interest (NCI). The NCI portion of each subsidiary equity account is summarized in the NCI column of the worksheet, and the total is extended as the NCI line in the consolidated balance sheet column.

V.   The consolidated balance sheet will be derived from the worksheet.
   A.   Assets and liabilities will be those of the parent (at recorded book value) plus the assets and liabilities of the subsidiary at adjusted fair value to the extent allowed by the price paid.
   B.   Stockholders' equity will include detailed equity accounts for the parent company and a one-line summary for the noncontrolling interest.

VI.   Push-down accounting may be used. Under this approach, the subsidiary adjusts its accounts to reflect the fair values assigned by the parent. This means that the accounts of the subsidiary are already at fair value when they enter the trial balance column of the worksheet. No adjustment to fair value is made in the consolidation process.

PART 1

Instructions: Use a check mark to indicate whether each of the following statements is true or false.

		True	False
1.	Consolidation adjustments and eliminations are recorded on the books of both the parent and subsidiary companies.	_____	_____
2.	In the consolidation process, the investment account is eliminated and replaced with the parent company's share of underlying assets and liabilities.	_____	_____
3.	A write-up of current assets, land, liabilities, and long-term investments in marketable securities is permitted only when there is sufficient excess of cost over book value.	_____	_____
4.	The excess available for long-lived assets decreases when the market value of subsidiary debt increases.	_____	_____
5.	The noncontrolling interest (NCI) should be presented by means of footnotes to the consolidated balance sheet.	_____	_____
6.	When the acquiring company purchases over 50% of the outstanding voting common stock from the stockholders of a company, it gains control over the assets indirectly.	_____	_____
7.	The price paid in a bargain purchase might exceed the recorded book value of the subsidiary's assets.	_____	_____
8.	So long as the price paid is high enough, all subsidiary assets are adjusted 100% of the way to fair value regardless of the parent ownership percentage.	_____	_____
9.	It is possible that a parent would have to consolidate a company even if it owned less than 50% of the voting common stock.	_____	_____
10.	In a 100% purchase, goodwill can only exist if all other accounts are first adjusted to full fair value.	_____	_____
11.	A piece of production equipment has a clear fair value; the fair value of the land is less certain. The equipment can be adjusted to full fair value and any remaining excess, if any, can be used to adjust the land.	_____	_____
12.	The noncontrolling interest (NCI) can be shown between liabilities and equity.	_____	_____

PART 2

Instructions: Circle the letter that identifies the best response to each question. (Items 1–7, 10, and 11 are AICPA adapted.)

1. On December 31, 20X8, Saxe Corporation was merged into Poe Corporation. In the business combination, Poe issued 200,000 shares of its $10 par common stock, with a market price of $18 a share, for all of Saxe's common stock. The stockholders' equity section of each company's balance sheet immediately before the combination was

	Poe	Saxe
Common stock	$3,000,000	$1,500,000
Additional paid-in capital	1,300,000	150,000
Retained earnings	2,500,000	850,000
	$6,800,000	$2,500,000

The merger qualifies as a purchase of saxe. In the December 31, 20X8, consolidated balance sheet, additional paid-in capital should be reported at:

   a. $950,000   b. $1,300,000   c. $1,450,000   d. $2,900,000

Items 2 through 6 are based on the following:

On January 1, 20X8, Polk Corp. and Strass Corp. had condensed balance sheets as follows:

	Polk	Strass
Current assets	$ 70,000	$ 20,000
Noncurrent assets	90,000	40,000
Total assets	$160,000	$ 60,000
Current liabilities	$ 30,000	$ 10,000
Long-term debt	50,000	—
Stockholders' equity	80,000	50,000
Total liabilities and stockholders' equity	$160,000	$ 60,000

On January 2, 20X8, Polk borrowed $60,000 and used the proceeds to purchase 90% of the outstanding voting common shares of Strass. This debt is payable in 10 equal annual principal payments, plus interest, beginning December 31, 20X8. The excess cost of the investment over Strass's book value of acquired net assets should be allocated 60% to inventory and 40% to goodwill.

On Polk's January 2, 20X8, consolidated balance sheet,

2. Current assets should be:
   a. $99,000   b. $96,000   c. $90,000   d. $79,000

3. Noncurrent assets should be:
   a. $130,000   b. $134,000   c. $136,000   d. $140,000

4. Current liabilities should be:
   a. $50,000   b. $46,000   c. $40,000   d. $30,000

5. Noncurrent liabilities should be:
   a. $115,000   b. $110,000   c. $104,000   d. $50,000

6. Stockholders' equity, controlling interest, should be:
   a. $80,000   b. $85,000   c. $90,000   d. $130,000

7. Which of the following is the best theoretical justification for consolidated financial statements?
   a. In form the companies are one entity; in substance they are separate.
   b. In form the companies are separate; in substance they are one entity.
   c. In form and substance the companies are one entity.
   d. In form and substance the companies are separate.

8. P's cost of investment in S exceeded its equity in the book value of S's stockholders' equity on the acquisition date. The excess is not attributable to specific accounts. On the consolidated statements, this excess should be:
   a. Eliminated
   b. Allocated proportionately to the subsidiary's plant assets
   c. Shown on the balance sheet as surplus from consolidation
   d. Shown on the balance sheet as goodwill

9. Company J acquired all of the outstanding voting common stock of Company K in exchange for cash. The acquisition price exceeds the fair value of net assets acquired. How should Company J determine the amounts to be reported for the plant and equipment and long-term debt acquired from company K?

	Plant and Equipment	Long-Term Debt
a.	K's carrying amount	K's carrying amount
b.	K's carrying amount	Fair value

   c.   Fair value   K's carrying amount
   d.   Fair value   Fair value

10. What is the theoretically preferred method of presenting noncontrolling interest on a consolidated balance
     sheet?
     a.   As a separate item in the deferred credits section
     b.   As a deduction from (contra to) goodwill from consolidation, if any
     c.   By means of notes or footnotes to the consolidated balance sheet
     d.   As a separate item within the stockholders' equity section

PART 3

Stinson Enterprises is considering the acquisition of Williams Corporation on January 1, 20X4. Williams
Corporation provided Stinson Enterprises with the following balance sheet on December 31, 20X3:

Williams Corporation
Balance Sheet
December 31, 20X3

Assets		Liabilities and Equity	
Cash	$ 80,000	Accounts payable	$ 80,000
Accounts receivable	45,000	Common stock	100,000
Inventory	50,000	Paid-in capital in excess of par	150,000
Equipment	220,000	Retained earnings	95,000
Goodwill	30,000		
	$425,000		$425,000

The following fair values have been estimated for the assets of Williams Corporation:

Inventory	$ 60,000
Equipment	250,000

Stinson Enterprises is contemplating making several different offers for the net assets of Williams. They are also
uncertain what percentage interest they want to acquire. You, as the staff accountant, have been asked to complete the
following zone analyses and alternative determination and distribution of excess schedules for the different offers
made, and percentage interests acquired.

100% Interest

1. a. Zone analysis

	Group Total	Cum. Total
Priority accounts	$105,000	$105,000
Nonpriority accounts	250,000	355,000

b. D&D of excess

Price paid		$650,000		$360,000		$295,000		$100,000
Less interest acquired:								
Common stock	$100,000		$100,000		$100,000		$100,000	
Paid-in capital in excess of par	150,000		150,000		150,000		150,000	
Retained earnings	95,000		95,000		95,000		95,000	
Total equity	$345,000		$345,000		$345,000		$345,000	
Ownership interest	100%	345,000	100%	345,000	100%	345,000	100%	345,000
Excess of cost (book)		$305,000		$ 15,000		$(50,000)		$(245,000)
Adjustments:								
Inventory								
Equipment								
Goodwill (net adjustment)								
Extraordinary gain								
Total adjustments								

80% Interest

2. a. Zone analysis

	Group Total	Ownership Portion	Cum. Total
Priority accounts	$105,000	$ 84,000	$ 84,000
Nonpriority accounts	250,000	200,000	284,000

b. D&D of excess

Price paid		$650,000		$360,000		$295,000		$100,000
Less interest acquired:								
Common stock	$100,000		$100,000		$100,000		$100,000	
Paid-in capital excess of par	150,000		150,000		150,000		150,000	
Retained earnings	95,000		95,000		95,000		95,000	
Total equity	$345,000		$345,000		$345,000		$345,000	
Ownership interest	80%	276,000	80%	276,000	80%	276,000	80%	276,000
Excess of cost (book)								
Adjustments:								
Inventory								
Equipment								
Goodwill (net adjustment)								
Extraordinary gain								
Total adjustments								

PART 4

Black Company is contemplating the purchase of 8,000 shares of the outstanding stock of Wright Company, which just prior to acquisition has the following balance sheet:

Assets		Liabilities and Equity	
Cash	$ 20,000	Current liabilities	$250,000
Inventory	200,000	Common stock ($5 par)	50,000
Land	80,000		
Plant and equipment (net)	400,000	Paid-in capital in excess of par	130,000
Goodwill	100,000	Retained earnings	370,000
Total assets	$800,000	Total liabilities and equity	$800,000

Black Company believes that the inventory has a market value of $300,000; the land, 100,000; and that the plant and equipment are worth $500,000.

Instructions:

1.   Prepare a zone analysis.

Zone Analysis:

	Group Total	Ownership Portion	Cumulative Total
Priority accounts			
Nonpriority accounts			

2.   For each of the following alternative fair values per share of Black Company stock, complete the determination and distribution of excess schedules:

   a. $90

   b. $74

   c. $42

		a. $720,000	b. $592,000	c. $ 336,000
Price paid		$720,000	$592,000	$ 336,000
Less book value of interest purchased:				
Common stock	$ 50,000			
Paid-in capital in excess of par	130,000			
Retained earnings	370,000			
Total stockholders' equity	$550,000			
Ownership interest	80%	440,000	440,000	440,000
Excess cost over book value (book value over cost)		$280,000	$152,000	$(104,000)
Adjustments: Land				
Inventory				
Plant and equipment				
Goodwill (adjustment)				
Total adjustments				

3.   Prepare the worksheet entries:

   a.   To eliminate 80% of the stockholders' equity against the investment:

_____

_____

_____

_____

b.   To distribute the excess of cost over book value:

(1) For $280,000 Excess	(2) For $152,000 Excess

c.   To eliminate the excess of book value over cost:

_____

_____

_____

_____

_____

PART 5

Lobell Company purchased 80% of the outstanding stock of Wren Inc. for $380,000 when Wren Inc. had the following balance sheet:

Assets		Liabilities and Stockholders' Equity	
Current assets	$ 80,000	Liabilities	$100,000
Land	20,000	Common stock ($5 par)	50,000
Buildings	180,000	Paid-in capital in excess of par	150,000
Equipment	210,000	Retained earnings	190,000
Total assets	$490,000	Total liabilities and equity	$490,000

Lobell obtained the following fair values for the accounts of Wren Inc.:

Current assets	$110,000
Land	50,000
Buildings	250,000
Equipment	200,000

Instructions: Complete the following zone analysis, price analysis, and determination and distribution of excess and allocation schedules.

Zone Analysis:

	Group Total	Ownership Portion	Cumulative Total
Priority accounts			
Nonpriority accounts			

Price Analysis:

Price paid (including any direct acquisition costs)	$380,000	
Assign to priority accounts, controlling share		
Assign to nonpriority accounts, controlling share		
Goodwill		
Extraordinary Gain		

D&D of Excess:

Price paid		$380,000
Less book value of interest purchased:		
Common stock	$ 50,000	
Paid-in capital in excess of par	150,000	
Retained earnings	190,000	
Total stockholders' equity	$390,000	
Ownership interest	_____	_____
Excess of cost over book value		=======
Adjustments:		
Current assets	_____	
Land	_____	
Buildings	_____	
Equipment	_____	
Goodwill	_____	
Total adjustments		=======

Allocation Schedule

Asset	Fair Value	Percent	Amount to Allocate	Allocated Amount	Book Value (80%)	Adjustment Increase (Decrease)
Land	$ 50,000					
Buildings	250,000					
Equipment	200,000					
Total	$500,000			_____	_____	_____

PART 6

Yankee Corporation acquired 80% of the outstanding stock of Gary Corporation in December 31, 20X6, for $735,000 cash. The acquisition occurred on the last day of the fiscal year for both companies. Yankee paid an additional $15,000 in direct acquisition costs to consummate the purchase. The following balance sheets of the parent and subsidiary were prepared immediately subsequent to the investment:

	Yankee	Gary
Cash	$ 115,000	$ 60,000
Accounts receivable	290,000	160,000
Inventory	520,000	80,000
Land	1,000,000	100,000
Building (net)	700,000	230,000
Equipment (net)	1,500,000	400,000
Investment in Gary	750,000	
Goodwill	—	—
Current liabilities	$ 500,000	$ 85,000
Bonds payable		400,000
Common stock ($1 par)	600,000	100,000
Paid-in capital in excess of par	1,400,000	110,000
Retained earnings	2,375,000	335,000
Total	$ 0	$ 0

On the purchase date, some of Gary Corporation's assets were recorded at book values not consistent with fair values. The following fair values were obtained:

Inventory	$120,000
Land	185,000
Building	350,000
Equipment	465,000

Instructions:

1. Prepare a zone analysis.

	Group Total	Ownership Portion	Cumulative Total
Priority accounts			
Nonpriority accounts			

Price Analysis:

Price paid (including any direct acquisition costs)
Assign to priority accounts, controlling share
Assign to nonpriority accounts, controlling share
Goodwill
Extraordinary gain

2. Prepare a determination and distribution of excess schedule.

Price paid for investment in subsidiary (including direct acquisition costs)		$750,000
Less book value of interest purchased:		
Common stock	$100,000	
Paid-in capital in excess of par	110,000	
Retained earnings	335,000	
Total stockholders' equity	$545,000	
Ownership interest		
Excess of cost over book value		
Adjustments:		
Inventory		
Land		
Buildings		
Equipment		
Goodwill		
Total adjustments		

3. Complete the worksheet for a consolidated balance sheet on December 31, 20X0.

Yankee Corporation and Subsidiary Gary Corporation
Worksheet for Consolidated Balance Sheet
December 31, 20X0

	Trial Balance		Eliminations and Adjustments		NCI	Consolidated Balance Sheet	
	Yankee	Gary	Dr.	Cr.		Dr.	Cr.
Cash	115,000	60,000					
Accounts receivable	290,000	160,000					
Inventory	520,000	80,000					
Land	1,000,000	100,000					
Buildings	700,000	230,000					
Equipment	1,500,000	400,000					
Investment in Gary	750,000						
Goodwill							
Current liabilities	(500,000)	(85,000)					
Bonds payable		(400,000)					
Common stock—Yankee	(600,000)						
Paid-in capital in excess—Yankee	(1,400,000)						
Retained earnings—Yankee	(2,375,000)						
Common stock—Gary		(100,000)					
Paid-in capital in excess—Gary		(110,000)					
Retained earnings—Gary		(335,000)					
Total	0	0					
Total NCI							

4. Complete the formal consolidated balance sheet for December 31, 20X0.

Yankee Corporation and Subsidiary Gary Corporation
Consolidated Balance Sheet
December 31, 20X0

Assets

Current assets:

  Cash $

  Accounts receivable

  Inventory

  Total current assets   _____

Property, plant, and equipment:

  Land

  Buildings

  Equipment

Goodwill   _____   _____

Total assets   _____   _____

Liabilities and Stockholders' Equity

Current liabilities

Bonds payable

Total liabilities   _____

Stockholders' equity:

  Noncontrolling interest

  Controlling interest:

    Common stock

    Paid-in capital in excess of par

    Retained earnings   _____   _____

Total liabilities and stockholders' equity   _____   _____

Chapter 3   Consolidated Statements: Subsequent to Acquisition

OUTLINE FOR REVIEW

When an investment in a subsidiary is consolidated subsequent to its acquisition, additional adjustments are necessary on the worksheet for consolidated financial statements. The consolidation procedures depend on whether the parent uses the equity method or the cost method to account for its investment.

I.   Two basic methods may be used to account for an investment in a subsidiary on the parent's books.

    A.   Under the equity method, the parent records as income (loss) the ownership percentage of subsidiary income or loss and adjusts the investment account by the same amount. Dividends reduce the investment account.

       1.   The simple equity method does not adjust the investment for amortizations of excess required by the determination and distribution of excess schedule; this is done on the consolidated worksheet. Consolidation procedures are as follows:

          a.   (CY) Eliminate current-year adjustments to the investment account against the parent's subsidiary income account and the subsidiary's dividends declared account.

          b.   (EL) Eliminate parent ownership portion of subsidiary equity against investment.

          c.   (D) Distribute excess according to the determination and distribution of excess schedule.

          d.   (A) Amortize excess (for those requiring it) for current and past periods.

       2.   The sophisticated equity method does adjust the investment for amortizations of excess. Consolidation procedures are as follows:

          a.   (CY) Eliminate the current-year adjustments to the investment account (net of amortizations) against subsidiary income (net of amortizations) and dividend accounts.

          b.   (EL) Eliminate parent ownership portion of subsidiary equity against investment.

          c.   (D) Distribute the beginning-of-the-period unamortized excess.

          d.   (A) Amortize excess (for those requiring it) for current period only. (Previous period's amortizations have been recorded by the parent.)

    B.   Under the cost method, the parent records income only when dividends are declared by the subsidiary. The investment is maintained at its original cost and is converted to the simple equity method during the consolidation process. Consolidation procedures are as follows:

       1.   Convert to the simple equity method as of the beginning of the period.

          a.   It is not necessary to convert to the equity method during the first year of combined operations.

          b.   (CV) The conversion step used in subsequent periods is:

Ownership interest	X	Change in retained earnings from date of acquisition to the beginning of the current year

       2.   (CY) Eliminate current-year intercompany dividends.

       3.   Follow the simple equity method for remaining procedures.

II.   Consolidation eliminations and adjustments are made every year on the consolidated worksheet. Current-year amortizations of excess are charged to expense, and amortizations for past years (except sophisticated equity method) are charged to controlling retained earnings, since asset and liability revaluations pertain only to the controlling interest.

III.   There are two options for consolidating an intraperiod purchase of a subsidiary investment.

    A.   Parent company requires the subsidiary to close its books as of the purchase date. The determination and distribution of excess schedule is based on subsidiary equity on the intraperiod acquisition date, since nominal accounts are closed. The consolidated income statement includes only subsidiary operations subsequent to the purchase date.

    B.   Parent company does not require the subsidiary to close its books as of the purchase date. The modified determination and distribution of excess schedule is based on subsidiary equity at the beginning of the year, plus undistributed income for the portion of the year prior to the purchase. The consolidated income statement includes the subsidiary's operations for the entire fiscal year. Under this option, income earned by outside interests prior to the parent's acquiring control (purchased income) is subtracted to arrive at consolidated net income.

C. Added disclosure is required due to an intraperiod purchase. The income statement or notes to the financial statements must include what consolidated income would have been if the combination had occurred at the beginning of the period.

Appendix A: Vertical Worksheet

I.   There is no change in elimination procedures. The differences are:

A. The order of accounts on the trial balance is changed. First come nominal accounts, then retained earnings accounts, and then balance sheet accounts.

B. Adjustments are to be made to beginning retained earnings, not ending.

C. Income is carried down to the retained earnings statement. The ending NCI and controlling retained earnings balances are carried down to the balance sheet.

D. This approach has been used on the CPA Exam. It is unlikely to be used in practice.

Appendix B: Tax-Related Adjustments

I.   In a tax-free exchange, the purchasing company may only deduct book value depreciation or amortization in periods after the purchase.

A. DTLs (deferred tax liabilities) should be recorded in an amount equal to the tax rate times the fair value adjustment.

B. The goodwill balance that emerges at the bottom of a determination and distribution of excess schedule is the amount available for goodwill, net of tax. The amount, say $70,000, has to be divided by the net of tax rate (assume 70%) to determine the gross amount of goodwill ($100,000, in this example).

II.   The purchased company may have tax loss carryovers.

A. They may only offset income taxes payable for the current and future periods. There are limitations on the amount available in any period.

B. The tax loss carryovers are recorded as priority items.

PART 1

Instructions: Use a check mark to indicate whether each of the following statements is true or false.

	True	False
1. Under the equity method, the parent debits the investment in the subsidiary account and credits subsidiary income for its pro rata share of the subsidiary's income.	_____	_____
2. Consolidated financial statements are not affected by whether the parent uses the simple equity, sophisticated equity, or cost method to record its investment in the subsidiary.	_____	_____
3. Dividends reduce the investment account under the equity method and increase the investment account under the cost method.	_____	_____
4. At the end of the first year of operations, it is not necessary to convert a cost method investment to the equity method.	_____	_____
5. Amortizations of excess affect both the NCI share and the parent share of subsidiary income.	_____	_____
6. When a subsidiary's plant assets are revalued, the depreciation method and remaining life used by the subsidiary must be continued by the parent.	_____	_____
7. Previous years' consolidation adjustments and eliminations are reflected in the current-year trial balances of the parent and subsidiary.	_____	_____
8. Using the cost method to record an investment assures that every dollar of change in subsidiary equity is recorded on a pro rata basis in the investment account.	_____	_____

9. When the sophisticated equity method is used, only current-year amortizations of excess are made on the consolidated worksheet.   _____ _____

10. In an intraperiod purchase when the subsidiary's books are not closed, the NCI receives a share of subsidiary income for the entire year.   _____ _____

11. Under intraperiod purchase accounting, consolidated net income includes the parent's interest in the subsidiary income earned prior to the purchase date and therefore requires adjustment.   _____ _____

12. Consolidated net income is synonymous with the controlling share of income.   _____ _____

13. Under the cost method, dividends received reduce the investment account.   _____ _____

PART 2

Instructions: Circle the letter that identifies the best response to each question. (All items except 1 are AICPA adapted.)

1. Peel Co. received a cash dividend from a common stock investment. Should Peel report an increase in the investment account if it uses the cost method or the equity method of accounting?

	Cost	Equity
a.	No	No
b.	Yes	Yes
c.	Yes	No
d.	No	Yes

Items 2 through 5 are based on the following:

The separate condensed balance sheets and income statements of Dean Corp. and its wholly owned subsidiary, Kay Corp., are as follows:

Balance Sheets
December 31, 20X1

Assets	Dean	Kay
Current assets	$ 430,000	$300,000
Property, plant, and equipment (net)	360,000	400,000
Investment in subsidiary (equity method)	690,000	
Total assets	$1,480,000	$700,000

Liabilities and Stockholders' Equity	Dean	Kay
Current liabilities	$ 130,000	$140,000
Stockholders' equity:		
Common stock ($10 par)	320,000	80,000
Additional paid-in capital	370,000	200,000
Retained earnings	660,000	280,000
Total stockholders' equity	1,350,000	560,000
Total liabilities and stockholders' equity	$1,480,000	$700,000

Income Statements
For Year Ended December 31, 20X1

	Dean	Kay
Sales	$1,100,000	$600,000
Cost of goods sold	770,000	400,000
Gross profit	330,000	200,000
Other operating expenses	120,000	100,000
Operating income	210,000	100,000
Equity in earnings of Kay	100,000	—
Net income	$ 310,000	$100,000

Additional information:

- On January 1, 20X1, Dean purchased all of Kay's $10 par voting common stock for $600,000. On that date, the fair value of Kay's assets and liabilities equaled their carrying amount of $660,000 and $160,000, respectively. The remaining excess is attributable to a patent with a 10-year life.
- During 20X1, Dean and Kay paid cash dividends of $50,000 and $10,000, respectively.
- There were no intercompany transactions, except for Dean's receipt of dividends from Kay and Dean's recording of its share of Kay's earnings.
- On June 30, 20X1, Dean sold 12,000 shares of its common stock for $17 per share. There were no other changes in either Dean's or Kay's common stock during 20X1.

2. In Dean's 20X1 consolidated income statement, what amount should be reported as consolidated net income?

   a. $200,000   b. $210,000   c. $300,000   d. $310,000

3. In Dean's December 31, 20X1, consolidated balance sheet, what amount should be reported as total consolidated assets?

   a. $2,140,000   b. $1,580,000   c. $1,490,000   d. $1,440,000

4. In Dean's December 31, 20X1, consolidated balance sheet, what amount should be reported as total retained earnings?

   a. $678,000   b. $688,000   c. $650,000   d. $660,000

5. In Dean's 20X1 consolidated income statement, what amount should be reported for patent amortization expense?

   a. $0   b. $6,000   c. $9,000   d. $10,000

Items 6 and 7 are based on the following:

On January 1, 20X1, Ritt Corp. purchased 80% of Shaw Corp.'s $10 par common stock for $975,000. On this date, the carrying amount of Shaw's net assets was $1,000,000. The fair values of Shaw's identifiable assets and liabilities were the same as their carrying amounts except for plant assets (net), which were $100,000 in excess of the carrying amount. For the year ended December 31, 20X1, Shaw had net income of $190,000 and paid cash dividends totaling $125,000.

6. On the January 1, 20X1, consolidated balance sheet, goodwill should be reported at:

   a. $0   b. $75,000   c. $95,000   d. $175,000

7. In the December 31, 20X1, consolidated balance sheet, NCI should be reported at:

   a. $200,000   b. $213,000   c. $220,000   d. $233,000

8.   On June 30, 20X1, Post Inc. issued 630,000 shares of its $5 par common stock, for which it received 200,000 shares of Ship Corp.'s $10 par common stock. The market value of a Post share was $20. The stockholders' equities immediately before the combination were:

	Post	Ship
Common stock	$ 6,500,000	$ 2,000,000
Additional paid-in capital	4,400,000	1,600,000
Retained earnings	6,100,000	5,400,000
	$ 17,000,000	$ 9,000,000

Any excess of cost over book value is attributable to goodwill.

Both corporations continued to operate as separate businesses, maintaining accounting records with years ended December 31. For 20X1, net income and dividends paid from separate company operations were:

Net Income	Post	Ship
Six months ended 6/30/X1	$1,000,000	$300,000
Six months ended 12/31/X1	1,100,000	500,000

Dividends Paid		
April 1, 20X1	130,000	—
October 1, 20X1	—	350,000

Ship Corp.'s books are not closed midyear.
In the 20X1 consolidated income statement, net income should be reported at:

a. $2,540,000   b. $2,420,000   c. $2,600,000   d. $2,900,000

9.   On January 1, 20X1, Prim Inc. acquired all the outstanding common shares of Scarp Inc. for cash equal to the book value of the stock. The carrying amounts of Scarp's assets and liabilities approximated their fair values, except that the carrying amount of its building was more than fair value. In preparing Prim's 20X1 consolidated income statement, which of the following adjustments would be made?

a.   Depreciation expense would be decreased and goodwill amortization would be recognized.
b.   Depreciation expense would be increased and goodwill amortization would be recognized.
c.   Depreciation expense would be decreased and no goodwill amortization would be recognized.
d.   Depreciation expense would be increased and no goodwill amortization would be recognized.

PART 3

Instructions: Explain the meaning of the following terms and how they are computed.

1.   Purchased income

2.   Noncontrolling share of consolidated net income

3.   Consolidated net income

4.   Controlling interest in net income

PART 4

Nitro Corporation purchased an 80% interest in Mars Company on January 1, 20X5. The following determination and distribution of excess schedule was prepared on the purchase date:

Price paid for investment in Mars		$160,000
Less book value of interest purchased:		
Common stock	$ 24,000	
Paid-in capital in excess of par	41,600	
Retained earnings	93,400	
Total stockholders' equity	$159,000	
Ownership interest	80%	127,200
Excess of cost over book		$32,800
Adjustments:		
Equipment (80% x $20,000)		
(8-year amortization, $2,000 per year)		$16,000 Dr.
Goodwill		16,000 Dr.
Total adjustments		$32,800

Income and dividends for Mars Company during 20X5 and 20X6 were as follows:

	20X5	20X6
Income	$45,000	$52,000
Dividends	12,000	18,000

Instructions:

1. Complete the following entries on the books of Mars Company under each of the methods indicated.

Event		(A) Simple Equity Method	(B) Sophisticated Equity Method	(C) Cost Method
20X5 To record investment in Mars Company	Investment in Mars Company .... Cash			
Subsidiary income of $45,000 reported to parent	Investment in Mars Company .... Subsidiary income.................			
Dividends of $12,000 paid by Mars	Cash .... Investment in Mars Company			
20X6 Subsidiary income of $52,000 reported to parent	Investment in Mars Company .... Subsidiary income.................			
Dividends of $18,000 paid by Mars	Cash .... Investment in Mars Company			

2. Assuming the same facts applicable to the acquisition as used in Part 4(1), fill in the investment account balance and prepare the eliminations and adjustments on the partial December 31, 20X6, worksheets here and on page SG 3-9.

Nitro Corporation and
Partial Worksheets
For Year Ended

| | (a) Simple Equity Method | | | |
| | Trial Balance | | Eliminations and Adjustments | |
	Nitro	Mars	Dr.	Cr.
Equipment (net)	640,000	320,000		
Investment in Mars Company				
Goodwill				
Common stock—Nitro	(60,000)			
Paid-in capital in excess—Nitro	(185,000)			
Retained earnings—Nitro (1/1/X6)	(703,500)			
Common stock—Mars		(24,000)		
Paid-in capital in excess—Mars		(41,600)		
Retained earnings—Mars (1/1/X6)		(126,400)		
Expenses	250,000			
Subsidiary income*	(41,600)			
Dividends declared	45,000	18,000		
Totals				

*"Dividend income" under the cost method.

Eliminations and Adjustments:
CV Convert to simple equity (if needed).
CY_1 Eliminate current-year equity income (if needed).
CY_2 Eliminate intercompany dividends.
EL   Eliminate 80% of Mars' beginning-of-the-year equity balances.
D   Distribute excess as required by the determination and distribution of the excess schedule.
A   Amortize equipment for the current and prior year (not under sophisticated equity method).

Subsidiary Mars Company
Under Three Methods
December 31, 20X6

(b) Sophisticated Equity Method				(c) Cost Method			
Trial Balance		Eliminations and Adjustments		Trial Balance		Eliminations and Adjustments	
Nitro	Mars	Dr.	Cr.	Nitro	Mars	Dr.	Cr.
640,000	320,000			640,000	320,000		
(60,000)				(60,000)			
(185,000)				(185,000)			
(701,500)				(677,100)			
	(24,000)				(24,000)		
	(41,600)				(41,600)		
	(126,400)				(126,400)		
250,000				250,000			
(39,600)				(14,400)			
45,000	18,000			45,000	18,000		

PART 5

On January 1, 20X5, Payrol Company purchased 80% of the outstanding common stock of Johnson Company for $1,500,000. The determination and distribution schedule prepared on the date of the purchase was as follows:

Price paid for investment in Johnson		$1,500,000
Less book value of interest purchased:		
Common stock	$1,000,000	
Paid-in capital in excess	300,000	
Retained earnings	400,000	
Total stockholders' equity	$1,700,000	
Ownership interest	80%	1,360,000
Excess of cost over book (debit balance)		$ 140,000
Adjustments:		
Inventory (80% x $10,000)		$ 8,000 Dr.
Patents (80% x $100,000)		
(10-year amortization, $8,000 per year)		80,000 Dr.
Equipment (80% x $50,000)		
(8-year amortization, $5,000 per year)		40,000 Dr.
Goodwill		12,000 Dr.
Total adjustments		$ 140,000

During 20X5, all of the inventory was sold by Johnson Company.

Instructions: Complete the following consolidated worksheet for the year ending December 31, 20X7, and the income distribution schedules. Payrol Company uses the cost method to account for its investment in Johnson Company.

Eliminations and Adjustments:
CV　Convert from the cost to the equity method as of January 1, 20X7.
CY$_2$ Eliminate intercompany dividends.
EL　Eliminate subsidiary equities.
D　　Distribute the excess cost as given by the determination and distribution schedule:
　　(1)　Decrease parent's retained earnings for inventory sold.
　　(2)　Increase equipment.
　　(3)　Increase patents.
　　(4)　Increase goodwill.
A　　Record amortizations resulting from the revaluations:
　　(1)　No amortization necessary.
　　(2)　Record annual increase in equipment depreciation for the current and past two years.
　　(3)　Record annual increase in patent depreciation for the current and past two years.

Payrol Company and Subsidiary Johnson Company
Worksheet for Consolidated Balance Sheet
For Year Ended December 31, 20X7

	Trial Balance		Eliminations and Adjustments		Consolidated Income		Controlling Retained	Consolidated Balance
	Payrol	Johnson	Dr.	Cr.	Statement	NCI	Earnings	Sheet
Cash	654,000	505,000						
Equipment (net)	1,290,000	940,000						
Patents	195,000	35,000						
Other assets	1,720,000	730,000						
Investment in Johnson Company	1,500,000							
Goodwill								
Accounts payable	(550,000)	(205,000)						
Common stock— Payrol ($5 par)	(2,000,000)							
Paid-in capital in excess—Payrol	(1,200,000)							
Retained earnings— Payrol 1/1/X7	(1,255,000)							
Common stock— Johnson		(1,000,000)						
Paid-in capital in excess—Johnson		(300,000)						
Retained earnings— Johnson 1/1/X7		(580,000)						
Sales	(1,100,000)	(425,000)						
Costs of goods sold	470,000	170,000						
Other expenses	250,000	100,000						
Dividend income	(24,000)							
Dividends declared	50,000	30,000						
Total	0	0						
Consolidated net income								
To NCI								
To controlling interest								
Controlling retained earnings, December 31, 20X7								

Subsidiary Johnson Company Income Distribution

	Internally generated net income
	Adjusted income
	NCI
	NCI

Parent Payrol Company Income Distribution

Equipment depreciation	Internally generated net income
Patent amortization	80% x Johnson Company adjusted income
	Controlling interest

PART 6

Liberty Inc. paid $148,500 for an 85% interest in Ripley Company on September 1, 20X5. Liberty had access to the following Ripley trial balance on the purchase date, but Ripley did not close its books.

Current assets	$ 95,500	
Equipment	154,000	
Accumulated depreciation		$ 38,500
Liabilities		59,000
Common stock ($10 par)		10,000
Paid-in capital in excess of par		40,000
Retained earnings		84,000
Sales		112,000
Cost of goods sold	66,000	
Expenses	28,000	
Total	$ 343,500	$ 343,500

Any discrepancy between the price paid and the underlying book value is attributable to equipment, which had a 10-year remaining life on September 1, 20X5.

Instructions:

1. Prepare a determination and distribution of excess schedule for the investment.

2.   Complete the following consolidated worksheet for the year ended December 31, 19X5. Liberty uses the simple equity method to account for its investment in Ripley.

Eliminations and Adjustments:
CY$_1$ Eliminate subsidiary income recorded.
EL   Eliminate 85% of subsidiary equity including "purchased income."
D   Distribute excess cost.
A   Amortize excess.

Liberty Inc. and Subsidiary Ripley Company
Worksheet for Consolidated Financial Statements
For Year Ended December 31, 20X5

	Trial Balance		Eliminations and Adjustments		Consolidated Income Statement	NCI	Controlling Retained Earnings	Consolidated Balance Sheet
	Liberty	Ripley	Dr.	Cr.				
Current assets	427,000	118,000						
Land	62,000							
Equipment	285,000	154,000						
Accumulated depreciation	(145,000)	(41,000)						
Investment in Ripley Company	160,400							
Liabilities	(126,500)	(65,000)						
Common stock—Liberty	(100,000)							
Paid-in capital in excess of par —Liberty	(250,000)							
Retained earnings— Liberty	(180,000)							
Common stock— Ripley		(10,000)						
Paid-in capital in excess of par —Ripley		(40,000)						
Retained earnings— Ripley		(84,000)						
Sales	(460,000)	(156,000)						
Cost of goods sold	216,000	82,000						
Expenses	123,000	42,0000						
Subsidiary income	(11,900)							
Purchased income*								
Consolidated net income								
To NCI								
Consolidated net income								
Total NCI								
Retained earnings, controlling interest								

*This is subsidiary income that had been earned as of the purchase date.

Subsidiary Ripley Company Income Distribution

	Internally generated net income (entire year)
	Adjusted income
	NCI share
	NCI

Parent Liberty Inc. Income Distribution

Equipment depreciation	Internally generated net income
Purchased income	80% x Ripley Company adjusted income of $32,000
	Controlling interest

PART 7 (APPENDIX A)

Paxton purchased an 80% interest in the Saxton Company on January 1, 20X4, for $692,000. On that date, Saxton had the following balance sheet:

Assets		Liabilities and Equity	
Current assets	$190,000	Current liabilities	$100,000
Land	100,000		
Building	300,000		
Accumulated depreciation	(60,000)	Common stock (par)	100,000
Equipment	300,000	Paid-in capital in excess of par	200,000
Accumulated depreciation	(30,000)	Retained earnings	400,000
Total assets	$800,000	Total liabilities and equity	$800,000

Fair values that differ from book values on the purchase date are:

Buildings	$400,000, 20-year remaining life, straight line
Equipment	$250,000, 10-year remaining life, straight line

Any remaining excess is attributed to goodwill.

The following worksheet is being prepared as of December 31, 20X6. That is 3 years after the purchase.

1.   Prepare a price analysis and a determination and distribution of excess schedule and income distribution schedules.

2. Complete the following worksheet. Be sure to number your entries and provide a brief description in the space provided below the income distribution schedules.

Worksheet for Paxton Company

	Trial Balance		Eliminations and Adjustments		NCI	Consolidated
	Paxton	Saxton	Dr.	Cr.		
Sales	(250,000)	(200,000)				
Cost of goods sold	150,000	120,000				
Expenses	50,000	40,000				
Dividend income	(8,000)					
Net income	(58,000)	(40,000)				
NCI						
Controlling interest						
Retained earnings Jan. 1, Paxton	(670,000)					
Retained earnings Jan. 1, Saxton		(500,000)				
Dividends declared		10,000				
Net income (from above)	(58,000)	(40,000)				
Retained earnings, Dec. 31	(728,000)	(530,000)				
Current assets	246,000	230,000				
Investment in Saxton	692,000					
Land	100,000	100,000				
Building	300,000	400,000				
Accumulated depr. (building)	(100,000)	(90,000)				
Equipment	150,000	300,000				
Accumulated depr. (equipment)	(60,000)	(90,000)				
Goodwill						
Current liabilities	(300,000)	(20,000)				
Common stock, par—Paxton	(300,000)					
Common stock, par—Saxton		(100,000)				
Paid-in capital in excess—Saxton		(200,000)				
Retained earnings Dec. 31—Paxton (from above)	(728,000)					
Retained earnings Dec. 31—Saxton (from above)		(530,000)				
Total NCI						
Total	0	0				

Subsidiary Saxton Company Income Distribution

	Internally generated net income	
	Adjusted income	
	NCI share	_____
	NCI	===========

Parent Paxton Company Income Distribution

Building depreciation	Internally generated net income	
	Equipment depreciation	
	80% x Saxton adjusted net income of $	
	Controlling interest	===========

Eliminations and Adjustments (numbered and keyed to the worksheet):

PART 8 (APPENDIX B)

The Alk Company purchased 100% ownership interest in the Barter Company by issuing 20,000 shares of its $5 par common stock, which has a market value of $36 per share. Direct acquisition costs were $16,000, and the cost of issuing the shares was $10,000. Prior to issuing the new shares, Alk had the following stockholders' equity:

Common stock, $1 par	$ 100,000
Paid-in capital in excess of par	1,900,000
Retained earnings	2,000,000

Barter had the following balance sheet on the date of acquisition:

Inventory	$ 50,000	Current liabilities	$ 75,000
Land	100,000		
Building (net)	200,000	Common stock, $2 par	200,000
Equipment (net)	300,000	Paid-in capital in excess of par	300,000
Goodwill	25,000	Retained earnings	100,000
Total assets	$ 675,000	Total liabilities and equity	$675,000

Fair values, which differ from book values, are:

Inventory	$ 60,000
Building	250,000
Equipment	400,000

The transaction will qualify as a tax-free exchange. The tax rate of both firms is 30%.

Prepare a price analysis and a determination and distribution of excess schedule.

Chapter 4   Intercompany Transactions: Merchandise, Plant Assets, and Notes

OUTLINE FOR REVIEW

After the investment is eliminated, additional adjustments due to intercompany transactions are necessary to produce consolidated statements. From a consolidated viewpoint, such transactions occur within a single company and should not appear on consolidated statements.

I.   Merchandise sales between a parent and a subsidiary are recorded in the normal manner on the books of the separate companies. The consolidation process eliminates the intercompany sale/purchase and defers any profit until the goods are sold to parties outside the affiliated group.

    A.   Intercompany goods in the purchaser's beginning inventory are reduced to their cost to the consolidated company: debit retained earnings and credit cost of goods sold (beginning inventory if periodic method is used) for the amount of sales profit in the beginning inventory.

        1.   When the parent company is the seller, only the controlling interest in retained earnings is decreased.

        2.   When the subsidiary company is the seller, the retained earnings decrease is shared by the NCI and the controlling interest.

    B.   Eliminate intercompany merchandise sales to avoid double counting: debit sales and credit cost of goods sold (purchases if periodic inventory is used).

    C.   When the perpetual inventory method is used (or a cost of goods sold account exists):
Intercompany goods in the purchaser's ending inventory are inventoried at their cost to the consolidated entity: debit cost of goods sold (the original credit is overstated) and credit inventory for the amount of sales profit in the ending inventory. All adjustments for unrealized profit due to intercompany merchandise sales are shown on the selling company's income distribution schedule.

    D.   When the periodic inventory method is used (and purchases and inventories have not been closed to a cost of goods sold account):
Intercompany goods should be reduced to cost. The trial balance inventory debit (carried to income statement) is overstated and must be reduced for the intercompany profit. The trial balance inventory credit (carried to the income statement) is also overstated and must be reduced for the intercompany profit.

    E.   The purchaser may write down intercompany goods due to a lower of cost or market adjustment. It is then necessary to defer only the remaining profit if any still exists.

    F.   Trade balances due to intercompany credit sales are eliminated: debit payables and credit receivables.

II.   Fixed asset sales between members of an affiliated group are recorded on the books of the separate companies at the agreed price. A gain on the sale of a nondepreciable asset is deferred until the asset is sold to an outside party. The selling company's income distribution schedule reflects the deferral of the gain.

    A.   In the year of the sale, eliminate the gain and adjust the asset.

    B.   In subsequent years, adjust the asset and remove the gain from consolidated retained earnings.

        1.   When the parent company is the seller, only the controlling interest in retained earnings is decreased.

        2.   When the subsidiary company is the seller, the retained earnings decrease is shared by the NCI and the controlling interest.

    C.   Sale of the asset to an outside party allows the intercompany gain to be realized. The intercompany gain is removed from consolidated retained earnings and adjusts the gain or loss on the asset sale to an outside party.

III.   A gain on the intercompany sale of a depreciable asset usually is realized as the asset is used. The selling company's income distribution schedule reflects the profit deferment and recognition entries.

    A.   In the year of the sale, eliminate the gain and adjust the asset. Also debit accumulated depreciation and credit depreciation expense for the amount of the realized profit. The profit realized each period is the depreciation absorbed by the buyer minus depreciation for consolidated purposes.

    B.   In subsequent years, adjust the asset and accumulated depreciation as of the beginning of the year and remove the unrealized gain from consolidated retained earnings.

        1.   When the parent company is the seller, only the controlling interest in retained earnings is decreased.

2. When the subsidiary company is the seller, the retained earnings decrease is shared by the NCI and the controlling interest.

C. Adjust depreciation expense and accumulated depreciation for profit realized each period. Adjust the income distribution schedule of the seller for the realized profit.

D. Sale of the asset to an outside party allows the remaining intercompany gain to be recognized. Current-year depreciation expense is adjusted, and any remaining gain is removed from consolidated retained earnings and is used to offset the gain or loss on the sale to the outside party.

IV. Losses on intercompany transactions are recorded at the time of sale if the sales price approximates fair market value. All other losses are deferred until realized through use or final sale to the outside party.

V. Intercompany long-term construction necessitates consolidation adjustments. The procedures depend on the method used to record the contract by the affiliate constructing the asset.

A. Completed-contract method. Intercompany billings are eliminated: debit billings on long-term contracts and credit cost of construction in progress. Any intercompany contracts receivable/payable are also eliminated.

B. Percentage-of-completion method. Intercompany construction costs are reduced to their cost to the consolidated entity: debit earned income on long-term contracts and credit construction in progress for the amount of profit recorded by the constructing affiliate. Intercompany billings are eliminated, and any unbilled costs are added to the asset under construction: debit assets under construction and billings on construction in progress; credit construction in progress. Any intercompany contracts receivable/payable are also eliminated.

VI. Intercompany loans and related interest amounts are legitimate accounts on the books of the separate companies but do not appear on the consolidated statements. The consolidation process eliminates the following intercompany accounts: notes receivable/payable, interest expense/income, and interest receivable/payable.

VII. The sophisticated equity method becomes complicated when there are intercompany profits.

A. The current year subsidiary income would be based on the adjusted income of the subsidiary as determined on the current year income distribution schedule (rather than reported income as under the simple equity method).

B. The retained earning of the subsidiary would reflect the adjusted income from prior years' income distribution schedules rather than the reported retained earnings of the subsidiary.

VIII. (Appendix) The vertical worksheet format does not use the trial balances of the parent and subsidiary. Instead, it uses the income statement, retained earning statement, and balance sheet.

A. Adjustments to income statement accounts are used to calculate a consolidated income amount.

B. The consolidated income is carried down to the retained earnings statement, which also reflects adjustment to beginning retained earnings.

C. The consolidated retained earnings are carried down to the balance sheet, which also reflects adjustments to balance sheet accounts.

PART 1

Instructions: Use a check mark to indicate whether each of the following statements is true or false.

	True	False
1. Intercompany gains and losses are never eliminated; only the period of recognition is changed.	_____	_____
2. Elimination procedures due to intercompany transactions depend on whether the parent uses the equity method or the cost method to record the investment.	_____	_____
3. Adjustments made in the subsidiary income distribution schedule are allocated to both the NCI and controlling interests.	_____	_____
4. If intercompany merchandise sales are not eliminated, the gross profit is understated.	_____	_____
5. From a consolidated viewpoint, intercompany goods in the purchaser's beginning inventory imply premature profit recognition by the seller.	_____	_____
6. Consolidated net income increases upon eliminating sales profit on intercompany goods in the ending inventory.	_____	_____

7. Intercompany transfer prices can be viewed as agreements between the NCI and controlling interests as to how income will be distributed.   _____ _____

8. Profit is eliminated when consolidating not-yet-completed intercompany long-term construction contracts recorded under the completed-contract method.   _____ _____

9. A parent that discounts a note received from a subsidiary records a gain or loss, which is eliminated when consolidating.   _____ _____

10. Intercompany debt and interest expense/income have no effect on consolidated net income distribution.   _____ _____

11. Intercompany plant asset sales, though eliminated, do affect distribution of consolidated net income.   _____ _____

12. Recognition of an intercompany gain on the sale of a depreciable asset must await sale of the asset to an outside party.   _____ _____

13. All losses on intercompany plant asset sales must be deferred until realized through use or sale.   _____ _____

14. The parent's and subsidiary's separate income statements are the sole determinant of the controlling and minority shares of income.   _____ _____

15. Use of the LIFO method for inventories could cause a given period's inventory profit to be deferred indefinitely.   _____ _____

PART 2

Instructions: Circle the letter that identifies the best response to each question. (Items 1, 3, and 7 are AICPA adapted.)

1. Perez Inc. owns 80% of Senior Inc. During 20X2, Perez sold goods with a 40% gross profit to Senior. Senior sold all of these goods in 20X2. For 20X2 consolidated financial statements, how should the summation of Perez and Senior income statement items be adjusted?
    a. Sales and cost of goods sold should be reduced by the intercompany sales.
    b. Sales and cost of goods sold should be reduced by 80% of the intercompany sales.
    c. Net income should be reduced by 80% of the gross profit on intercompany sales.
    d. No adjustment is necessary.

2. Eltro Company acquired a 70% interest in Samson Company in 20X2. For the years ended December 31, 20X3 and 20X4, Samson reported net income of $80,000 and $90,000, respectively. During 20X3, Samson sold merchandise to Eltro for $10,000 at a profit of $2,000. The merchandise later was resold by Eltro to outsiders for $15,000 during 20X4. For consolidation purposes, what is the NCI's share of Samson's net income for 20X3 and 20X4, respectively?
    a. $23,400 and $27,600   c. $24,600 and $26,400
    b. $24,000 and $27,000   d. $26,000 and $25,000

3. On January 1, 20X0, Poe Corp. sold a machine for $900,000 to Saxe Corp., its wholly owned subsidiary. Poe paid $1,100,000 for this machine, which had accumulated depreciation of $250,000. Poe estimated a $100,000 salvage value and depreciated the machine on the straight-line method over 20 years, a policy that Saxe continued. In Poe's December 31, 20X0, consolidated balance sheet, this machine should be included in cost and accumulated depreciation as:

	Cost	Accumulated Depreciation
a.	$1,100,000	$300,000
b.	$1,100,000	$290,000
c.	$ 900,000	$ 40,000
d.	$ 850,000	$ 42,500

4. On July 1, 20X6, Master Corp. sold a building to its 90%-owned subsidiary, Hadit Company, at a gain of $24,000. The building had a remaining life of 6 years on the sale date. What is the decrease due to this transaction in the

January 1, 20X7, retained earnings for the controlling and noncontrolling interests, respectively, on the worksheet for consolidated financial statements?
a. $20,000 and $0
c. $22,000 and $0
b. $18,000 and $2,000
d. $19,800 and $2,200

5. Bonanza Inc. is an 85%-owned subsidiary of Percy & Associates. During 20X8, Bonanza sold land to Percy at a gain of $3,600. How does the land sale affect Bonanza's income distribution schedule?
a. It has no effect.
b. Income is lowered by $540.
c. Income is lowered by $3,600.
d. Income is lowered, but only for the amount of a permanent lower of cost or market adjustment.

6. What is the adjustment to cost of goods sold as a result of $65,000 of intercompany goods in a subsidiary's (purchaser) ending inventory? The goods were sold to yield a gross profit of 30%, and a $7,000 lower of cost or market adjustment was made by the subsidiary at year end.
a. $12,500 debit
b. $17,400 debit
c. $19,500 debit
d. $65,000 debit

7. Wright Corp. has several subsidiaries that are included in its consolidated financial statements. In its December 31, 20X2, trial balance, Wright had the following intercompany balances before eliminations:

	Debit	Credit
Current receivable due from Main Co.	$ 32,000	
Noncurrent receivable from Main	114,000	
Cash advance to Corn Corp.	6,000	
Cash advance from King Co.		$ 15,000
Intercompany payable to King		101,000

In its December 31, 20X2, consolidated balance sheet, what amount should Wright report as intercompany receivables?
a. $152,000
b. $146,000
c. $36,000
d. $0

PART 3

Instructions: During 20X6, Von Corporation purchased 80% of the outstanding common stock of Gary Company. For each of the following intercompany transactions, give the elimination entries that would be made on the trial balance worksheet for consolidated financial statements.

1. Current-year merchandise sales of $60,000 by Gary Company to Von Corporation at a price to realize a 20% gross profit.

2. $10,000 of intercompany goods sold last year by Gary Company is in Von Corporation's beginning inventory. Gary Company sold these goods at a price to realize a 20% gross profit.

3. Von Corporation's ending inventory contains $15,000 of intercompany goods that were sold by Gary Company at a price to realize a 20% gross profit.

4. $40,000 of intercompany trade balances at year end resulting from merchandise sales by Gary Company to Von Corporation.

5. $20,000 gain on sale of land by Von Corporation to Gary Company two years ago. The land is still owned by Gary.

PART 4

On January 1, 20X7, Mannix Corporation purchased 80% of the outstanding common stock of Raun Company. No excess of cost or book value resulted from the acquisition. The following information has been gathered pertaining to the two years of operation since Mannix's purchase of Raun Company stock.

(a) Intercompany merchandise sales by Raun to Mannix were as follows:

Year	Sales	Gross Profit	Purchases Remaining in Mannix Ending Inventory
20X7	$40,000	30%	$10,000
20X8	50,000	40%	15,000

(b) Mannix wrote down the merchandise purchased from Raun and remaining in its ending inventory to $13,000 on December 31, 20X8.

(c) On December 31, 20X8, Mannix owed $10,000 pertaining to intercompany sales.

Instructions: Complete the following partial worksheet and income distribution schedules for 20X8. Key your eliminations to the explanations shown. Also prepare income distribution schedules for Mannix and Raun.

Mannix Corporation and Subsidiary Raun Company
Partial Worksheet
For Year Ended December 31, 20X8

	Trial Balance		Eliminations and Adjustments		Consolidated Income Statement
	Mannix	Raun	Dr.	Cr.	
Accounts receivable (net)	200,000	71,000			
Inventory	281,000	175,000			
Accounts payable	(230,800)	(102,000)			
Retained earnings—Mannix	(827,000)				
Retained earnings—Raun		(260,000)			
Sales	(1,800,000)	(700,000)			
Cost of goods sold	750,000	400,000			
Other expenses	240,000	98,000			
Consolidated net income					
To NCI					
To controlling interest					

Eliminations and Adjustments:
(BI) Eliminate intercompany profit from beginning inventory.
(IS) Eliminate intercompany sales.
(EI) Eliminate intercompany profit from ending inventory.
(IA) Eliminate intercompany trade balances.

Subsidiary Raun Company Income Distribution

Unrealized profit in ending inventory	Internally generated net income
	Realized profit in beginning inventory
	Adjusted income
	NCI share
	NCI

Parent Mannix Corporation Income Distribution

	Internally generated net income
	80% x Raun Company adjusted income
	Controlling interest

PART 5

Barney Company is an 80%-owned subsidiary of Hayes Inc. During 20X2, Hayes sold land to Barney for $60,000, based upon an independent appraisal of the land's value. The land originally cost $40,000. On July 1, 20X2, Barney sold machinery to Hayes for $20,000. The machinery was carried on Barney's books at a $30,000 cost, with accumulated depreciation of $17,000. The machinery had a remaining life of 5 years at the sale date. Both companies use the straight-line method of depreciation.

Instructions: Complete the following partial worksheet for 20X3, the year subsequent to the asset sales. Key and explain all eliminations and adjustments.

Hayes Inc. and Subsidiary Barney Company
Partial Worksheet
For Year Ended December 31, 20X3

	Trial Balance		Eliminations and Adjustments	
	Hayes	**Barney**	**Dr.**	**Cr.**
Land	103,000	95,000		
Machinery	317,000	190,000		
Accumulated depreciation	(185,000)	(73,000)		
Retained earnings—Hayes	(921,000)			
Retained earnings—Barney		(219,000)		
Depreciation expense	15,600	7,100		

Eliminations and Adjustments:

_____

_____

_____

_____

_____

_____

PART 6

Park Corporation is constructing an office building for its wholly owned subsidiary, May Corporation. The contract price of construction of the building is $1,000,000. At December 31, 20X6, Park's estimate of costs to complete the building is $480,000. Park uses the percentage-of-completion method to account for long-term construction contracts. To date, $320,000 of costs have been incurred.

Instructions: The following partial worksheet contains accounts relevant to the construction contract. The account balances reflect journal entries for 20X6. Use the information shown here to prepare the eliminations for Park Corporation and its subsidiary, May Corporation, for the year ended December 31, 20X6. Key and explain all eliminations and adjustments.

	Trial Balance		Eliminations and Adjustments	
	Park	**May**	**Dr.**	**Cr.**
Assets under construction		250,000		
Contracts receivable	250,000	190,000		
Construction in progress	400,000	(73,000)		
Payables (to outsiders)	(230,000)			
Contracts payable		(250,000)		
Billings on construction in progress	(250,000)			
Earned income on long-term contracts	(80,000)			

Eliminations and Adjustments:

_____

_____

_____

_____

_____

_____

_____

PART 7

Paul Company purchased 80% of the shares of Sara Inc. on December 31, 20X3, for $120,000. The following determination and distribution of excess schedule was prepared on the date of purchase.

Price paid		$120,000
Less interest acquired:		
Common stock	$100,000	
Retained earnings	30,000	
Total stockholders' equity	$130,000	
Interest acquired	80%	104,000
Goodwill		$ 16,000

Paul Company sells merchandise to Sara Inc. at the same price and terms as it sells to other customers. During 20X7, Paul's sales to Sara totaled $100,000. Sara had $30,000 of the merchandise purchased from Paul in its December 31, 20X7, inventory, which was an increase of $10,000 over the previous year. Invoices of $21,000 for intercompany purchases remained unpaid at year end.

Paul advanced $10,000 to Sara for a future advertising campaign. The advance is outstanding at year end.

On July 1, 20X4, Sara purchased real estate from Paul for $115,000. Of that amount, $15,000 was allocated for land, and $100,000 for the building. The land had cost Paul $15,000, and the building cost Paul $80,000 to build. The building has a 20-year life and is depreciated using the straight-line method of depreciation. The purchase was financed in part by an $80,000 mortgage note held by the Paul Company. Principle payments of $20,000 are made on each 1-year anniversary of the sale. Interest is also to be paid on each payment date at the rate of 10% annual. Paul Company credits its expenses account for interest earned.

Sara Inc. paid a cash dividend of $9,000 on December 1, 20X7.

Subsidiary Sara Inc. Income Distribution

	Internally generated net income	$25,000
	Adjusted income NCI share	
	NCI	

Parent Paul Company Income Distribution

Unrealized gross profit in ending inventory	Internally generated net income	$40,000
	Realized gross profit in beginning inventory	
	Gain realized through use of building sold to Sara	
	Share of subsidiary income	
	Controlling interest	

Instructions: Complete the worksheet for December 31, 20X7. Also complete the income distribution schedules, which follow the worksheet. Provide explanations for entries below the income distribution schedules.

Paul Company and Subsidiary Sara Inc.
Worksheet for Consolidated Financial Statements
For Year Ended December 31, 20X7

	Trial Balance		Eliminations and Adjustments		Consolidated Income Statement	NCI	Controlling Retained Earnings	Consolidated Balance Sheet
	Paul	Sara	Dr.	Cr.				
Cash	21,400	18,700						
Accounts receivable	80,000	76,000						
Inventories	54,800	85,600						
Other current assets	15,000	10,200						
Investment in Sara Inc.	120,000							
Notes receivable	20,000							
Land	25,000	15,000						
Building and equipment	200,000	100,000						
Accumulated depreciation	(102,000)	(17,500)						
Goodwill								
Accounts payable	(35,500)	(81,000)						
Dividends payable		(12,000)						
Other current liabilities	(24,500)							
Notes payable		(20,000)						
Common stock—Paul	(300,000)							
Retained earnings, Jan. 1, 20X7—Paul	(27,000)							
Common stock—Sara		(100,000)						
Retained earnings—Sara		(59,000)						

(Worksheet continued on next page.)

	Trial Balance		Eliminations and Adjustments		Consolidated Income Statement	NCI	Controlling Retained Earnings	Consolidated Balance Sheet
	Paul	Sara	Dr.	Cr.				
Sales	(420,000)	(300,000)						
Cost of goods sold	315,000	240,000						
Expenses	65,000	35,000						
Dividend income	(7,200)							
Dividends declared		9,000						
	0	0						
Consolidated net income								
To NCI		}See distribution schedule						
To controlling interest		}See distribution schedule						
Total NCI								
Retained earnings—Controlling interest, Dec. 31, 20X7								

Eliminations and Adjustments:

CV　Convert to simple equity.

CY$_2$　Eliminate intercompany dividends.

EL　Eliminate pro rata share of Sara's equity balances.

D　Distribute excess cost according to determination and distribution of excess schedule.

BI　Eliminate intercompany profit from beginning inventory.

IS　Eliminate intercompany sales.

EI　Eliminate profit in ending inventory.

IS　Eliminate intercompany trade balances resulting from the intercompany sales.

LN1　Eliminate cash advance.

LN2　Eliminate intercompany mortgage and interest due to sale of building.

F1　Eliminate gain on sale of building remaining at the beginning of the period.

F2　Reduce depreciation for current year.

Chapter 5   Intercompany Transactions: Bonds and Leases

OUTLINE FOR REVIEW

Subsequent to the elimination of the investment account, further adjustments and eliminations are needed for intercompany bond and lease transactions.

I.   When a member of the consolidated group purchases the outstanding bonds of an affiliate, the bond liability is treated as retired, from a consolidated viewpoint. This retirement must be reflected in the consolidated statements.

    A.   In the year the bonds are acquired:

        1.   In a single entry, eliminate the interest expense recorded by the issuer on the intercompany bonds against the interest revenue recorded by the purchaser and eliminate the intercompany bonds payable and the applicable discount/premium against the investment in bonds.

        2.   The net difference in the above entry is the gain or loss on retirement that is entered into the worksheet.

        3.   Eliminate the intercompany interest payable and receivable.

        4.   The income distribution schedule of the issuer will reflect:

            a.   The gain or loss on retirement of the debt.

            b.   An interest adjustment equal to the difference between the interest expense of the issuer and the interest revenue of the purchaser.

    B.   Subsequent to the year of acquisition:

        1.   In a single entry, eliminate the interest expense recorded by the issuer on the intercompany bonds against the interest revenue recorded by the purchaser and eliminate the intercompany bonds payable and the applicable remaining discount/premium against the investment in bonds.

        2.   The net difference in the above entry is the remaining gain or loss on retirement at the start of the year. It is carried to beginning retained earnings. If the issuer was the subsidiary, the gain or loss is allocated to the controlling and NCI retained earnings by the applicable ownership percentages. If the bonds were issued by the parent, the controlling retained earnings receives the entire adjustment.

        3.   Eliminate the intercompany interest payable and receivable.

        4.   The income distribution schedule of the issuer will reflect an interest adjustment equal to the difference between the interest expense of the issuer and the interest revenue of the purchaser.

II.   In an operating lease situation, the lessor has recorded the purchase of the asset, is depreciating it, and is recording the rent revenue while the lessee records the rent expense.

    A.   Eliminate the intercompany rental expense and the rental revenue.

    B.   Eliminate any rent receivable and payable.

    C.   Reclassify the leased asset and related accumulated depreciation as a normal productive asset with the corresponding accumulated depreciation.

    D.   The income distribution schedule will show no adjustments as a result of the operating lease.

III.   Direct-financing leases are transfers of an asset to the lessee by the lessor, who accepts a long-term receivable from the lessee as consideration for the asset.

    A.   Eliminate the intercompany interest expense and revenue.

    B.   Eliminate the intercompany obligation under the capital lease plus accrued interest payable against the minimum lease payments receivable less unearned interest income.

    C.   Reclassify the asset under capital lease and related accumulated depreciation as a normal, productive asset.

    D.   The income distribution schedules will reflect no adjustments when all payments are made by the original lessee, since the recorded interest expense and revenue are equal.

    E.   If a portion of the annual rent is designated as applicable to executory costs incurred by the lessor, that portion is excluded from the minimum lease payments receivable of the lessor and the obligation of the lessee. This portion of the payment is recorded as rental expense and income and is to be eliminated.

IV.   Under the sales-type lease, the lessor records a sales profit or loss at the inception of the lease. Consolidation procedures disallow the immediate recognition of that profit or loss but require that it be recognized over the useful life of the leased asset. Procedures in addition to those for a direct-financing lease are as follows:

   A. In the year of inception of the lease:
      1. Eliminate the sales profit or loss against the property, plant, and equipment.
      2. Adjust the accumulated depreciation and depreciation expense to eliminate the current year's recognition of the sales profit or loss.
      3. The income distribution schedule of the lessor will reflect the deferral of the sales profit or loss and the recognition of the current portion of that profit or loss.
   B. In subsequent periods, the asset and accumulated depreciation are adjusted at the beginning of the year. The net adjustment is carried to retained earnings. The current year's depreciation expense and addition to accumulated depreciation also are adjusted to remove the profit (loss) element.

Appendix

I.   A direct-financing or sales-type lease with an unguaranteed residual value differs from that with a guaranteed residual value because the lessee and lessor are applying interest to different present values. The value of the obligation recorded by the lessee will exclude the amount pertaining to the unguaranteed residual value, whereas the value of the minimum lease payments receivable recorded by the lessor will include the unguaranteed residual value.
   A. Eliminate the intercompany interest expense and revenue as recorded by the lessee and lessor.
      1. The disparity between the interest expense and interest revenue is that portion of interest that applies to the unguaranteed residual value. It is returned to unearned interest income.
   B. Eliminate the intercompany debt, unearned income, unguaranteed residual value, and the asset under capital lease. Record the owned asset, which is equal to the original purchase price.
   C. Reclassify and adjust the accumulated depreciation as that applicable to a normal productive asset.

PART 1

Instructions: Use a check mark to indicate whether each of the following statements is true or false.

	True	False
1. In preparing consolidated statements subsequent to the year of acquisition of intercompany bonds, a gain or loss on retirement of bonds is recognized as a separate line item.	_____	_____
2. When the purchaser of intercompany debt amortizes its premium or discount upon purchase, it adjusts both the investment in bonds and interest income accounts.	_____	_____
3. The purchaser of intercompany debt absorbs the gain or loss on retirement of bonds.	_____	_____
4. The gain or loss on retirement of bonds is the difference between the book value of the bonds and the price paid by the purchaser.	_____	_____
5. The income distribution schedules of a parent will show no adjustments as a result of its purchase of subsidiary bonds at a loss.	_____	_____
6. Operating lease elimination procedures involve only the elimination of intercompany rent expense and revenue.	_____	_____
7. Under a direct-financing lease with guaranteed residual value, there is no adjustment to consolidated net income.	_____	_____
8. Payments for executory costs are included in the obligation of the lessee and the receivables of the lessor.	_____	_____
9. The lessee's incremental borrowing rate typically is used for leases between members of a consolidated firm.	_____	_____
10. All interest expense in a direct-financing lease with a guaranteed residual value is eliminated.	_____	_____
11. The sales profit in a sales-type lease must be deferred and amortized over the life of the leased asset on the consolidated worksheet.	_____	_____

PART 2

Instructions: Circle the letter that identifies the best response to each question. (Items 6 and 7 are AICPA adapted.)

1. Camden Company is an 85%-owned subsidiary of Greale Inc. Camden is leasing equipment from Greale under an operating lease. The appropriate valuation of the operating lease on the balance sheet of Camden is:
   a. Zero
   b. The absolute sum of the lease payments
   c. The present value of the sum of the lease payments discounted at an appropriate rate
   d. The market value of the asset at the date of the inception of the lease

2. In a lease that is recorded as a sales-type lease by the lessor, the difference between the sale price of the lease and the sum of the present values of the rent and residual value should be recorded as:
   a. Unearned income
   b. Manufacturer's or dealer's profit
   c. Rental income
   d. Deferred charge

3. The present value recorded as a net receivable by the lessor equals the present value recorded as a payable by the lessee under an intercompany:
   a. Operating lease
   b. Direct-financing lease with a guaranteed residual value
   c. Direct-financing lease with an unguaranteed residual value
   d. Sales-type lease with an unguaranteed residual value

4. Commerce Company is a 90%-owned subsidiary of Metro Industries. Metro leases a $200,000 asset (8-year life) to Commerce under a valid operating lease of $2,500 a month. What effect does elimination of the intercompany operating lease have on consolidated income?
   a. Consolidated income is unchanged by the eliminations.
   b. Consolidated income increases because depreciation expense of $25,000 is eliminated.
   c. Consolidated income decreases because yearly rental income ($2,500 x 12 = $30,000) exceeds the cost to the consolidated entity ($25,000 depreciation expense) and must be deferred.
   d. 90% of Commerce Company's leasing rental expense is eliminated and only the minority interest's share (10%) is extended to the consolidated income statement.

5. Maxwell Inc. owns a 95% interest in Empire Corporation. On January 1, 20X2, Maxwell entered into a 4-year leasing agreement with Empire; the leased asset had a remaining life of 10 years. The following entries were made:

   MaxwellInc.

Minimum lease payments receivable	10,000	
Cash	3,000	
Unearned interest income		3,198
Asset (cost of asset leased)		8,802
Sales profit on leases		1,000

   Empire Corporation

Assets under capital lease	9,802	
Obligations under capital lease		$6,802
Cash		3,000

   20X2 intercompany interest expense/revenue as a result of the lease was $1,360. What is the net adjustment to consolidated net income that results from eliminating this transaction?
   a. $0
   b. $1,838 decrease
   c. $1,360 decrease
   d. $900 decrease
   e. $750 decrease

6. P Co. purchased term bonds at a premium on the open market. These bonds represented 20% of the outstanding class of bonds issued at a discount by S Co., P's wholly owned subsidiary. P intends to hold the bonds until maturity. In a consolidated balance sheet, the difference between the bond carrying amounts in the two companies would be
    a. Included as a decrease to retained earnings.
    b. Included as an increase to retained earnings.
    c. Reported as a deferred debit to be amortized over the remaining life of the bonds.
    d. Reported as a deferred credit to be amortized over the remaining life of the bonds.

7. Wagner, a holder of a $1,000,000 Palmer, Inc., bond, collected the interest due on March 31, 20X2, and then sold the bond to Seal, Inc., for $975,000. On that date, Palmer, a 75% owner of Seal, had a $1,075,000 carrying amount for this bond. What was the effect of Seal's purchase of Palmer's bond on the retained earnings and NCI interest amounts reported in Palmer's March 31, 20X2, consolidated balance sheet?

	Retained Earnings	NCI
a.	$100,000 increase	$0
b.	$ 75,000 increase	$25,000 increase
c.	$0	$25,000 increase
d.	$0	$100,000 increase

PART 3

Instructions: Prepare skeleton year-end elimination entries for each of the following intercompany transactions. Skeleton entries include account titles organized as debits and credits but without amounts.

1. In a prior year, Parent loaned money to Sub to retire its outstanding bonds. The loan is still outstanding.

2. During the current year, Parent purchased Sub Company's outstanding bonds. The bonds were issued below face, and Parent paid above face.

3. Case (b), the following year.

4. During the current year, Sub leased a machine to Parent under an operating lease.

5.   In a prior period, Parent leased Sub a machine under a direct-financing lease. The lease contains a bargain purchase option.

6.   On December 31 of the current year, Parent leased Sub a machine under a sales-type lease. There is a bargain purchase option.

PART 4

Pat Inc. purchased the $100,000 face value outstanding bonds of Slinger Company, its 80%-owned subsidiary, for $97,000 on January 1, 20X3. The bonds mature on January 1, 20X6. The bonds have a stated interest rate of 8% and were sold for $101,000 on January 1, 20X1. The bonds pay interest each January 1. Amortization of the issue premium and/or discount will be on the straight-line basis.

Instructions:

1.   Record the entries Slinger Company would make on its books for 20X3.

2.   Record the entries Pat Inc. would make on its books for 20X3.

3. Complete the following partial worksheet for Pat Inc. and subsidiary Slinger Company for the year of acquisition of intercompany bonds, 20X3.

Pat Inc. and Subsidiary Slinger Company
Partial Consolidated Worksheet
For Year Ended December 31, 20X3

| | Trial Balance | | Eliminations and Adjustments | | | |
	Pat	Slinger	Dr.		Cr.	
Interest receivable	8,000					
Investment in Slinger bonds	98,000					
Interest payable		(8,000)				
Bonds payable		(100,000)				
Premium on bonds payable		(400)				
Interest income	(9,000)					
Interest expense		7,800				

Eliminations and Adjustments:
(B1) Eliminate the intercompany bonds and the applicable interest revenue and expense. Record the gain or loss on retirement.
(B2) Eliminate the intercompany interest payable and receivable.

4. Complete the following partial worksheet for Pat Inc. and subsidiary Slinger Company for the first year subsequent to acquisition of intercompany bonds, 20X4.

Pat Inc. and Subsidiary Slinger Company
Partial Consolidated Worksheet
For Year Ended December 31, 20X4

| | Trial Balance | | Eliminations and Adjustments | | | |
	Pat	Slinger	Dr.		Cr.	
Interest receivable	8,000					
Investment in Slinger bonds	99,000					
Interest payable		(8,000)				
Bonds payable		(100,000)				
Premium on bonds payable		(200)				
Retained earnings—Pat						
Retained earnings—Slinger						
Interest income	(9,000)					
Interest expense		7,800				

Eliminations and Adjustments:
(B1) Eliminate the intercompany bonds and the applicable interest revenue and expense. Record the adjustment to retained earnings.
(B2) Eliminate the intercompany interest payable and receivable.

PART 5
(Part 4 with effective interest)

Pat Inc. purchased the $100,000 face value outstanding bonds of Slinger Company, its 80%-owned subsidiary, for $101,300 (to yield 7.5% annual interest) on January 1, 20X3. The bonds have a stated nominal interest rate of 8% annual. The bonds were sold on January 1, 20X1, for $101,005 to yield 7.75% annual interest. The bonds mature on January 1, 20X6. The bonds pay interest each January 1. Amortizations of premiums are done using the effective interest amortization method.

Instructions:

1.   Prepare the 5-year amortization schedule for the bonds issued by Slinger.

Date	Payment	7.75% Interest	Amortization	Balance
1/1/X1				101,005
1/1/X2	8,000			
1/1/X3	8,000			
1/1/X4	8,000			
1/1/X5	8,000			
1/1/X6	8,000			

2.   Prepare the 3-year amortization schedule for the bonds purchased by Pat Inc.

Date	Payment	7.5% Interest	Amortization	Balance
1/1/X3				101,300
1/1/X4	8,000			
1/1/X5	8,000			
1/1/X6	8,000			

3.   Record the entries made by Slinger in 20X3 relative to the bonds.

4.   Record the entries made by Pat Inc. in 20X3 relative to the bonds.

5. Complete the following partial worksheet for Pat Inc. and subsidiary Slinger Company for the year of acquisition of intercompany bonds, 20X3.

Pat Inc. and Subsidiary Slinger Company
Partial Consolidated Worksheet
For Year Ended December 31, 20X3

	Trial Balance		Eliminations and Adjustments	
	Pat	Slinger	Dr.	Cr.
Interest receivable	8,000			
Investment in Slinger bonds	100,898			
Interest payable		(8,000)		
Bonds payable		(100,000)		
Premium on bonds payable		(448)		
Interest income*				
Interest expense*				

*To be entered.

Eliminations and Adjustments:
(B1) Eliminate the intercompany bonds and the applicable interest revenue and expense. Record the gain or loss on retirement.
(B2) Eliminate the intercompany interest payable and receivable.

6. Complete the following partial worksheet for Pat Inc. and subsidiary Slinger Company for the first year subsequent to acquisition of intercompany bonds, 20X4.

Pat Inc. and Subsidiary Slinger Company
Partial Consolidated Worksheet
For Year Ended December 31, 20X4

	Trial Balance		Eliminations and Adjustments	
	Pat	Slinger	Dr.	Cr.
Interest receivable	8,000			
Investment in Slinger bonds	100,465			
Interest payable		(8,000)		
Bonds payable		(100,000)		
Premium on bonds payable		(233)		
Retained earnings—Pat				
Retained earnings—Slinger				
Interest income*				
Interest expense*				

*To be entered.

Eliminations and Adjustments:
(B1) Eliminate the intercompany bonds and the applicable interest revenue and expense. Record the adjustment to retained earnings.
(B2) Eliminate the intercompany interest payable and receivable.

PART 6

Kovcic Inc., a subsidiary of Gorski Inc., leases assets from Gorski that are properly recorded as operating leases.

Instructions: On the following partial consolidated worksheet, complete the necessary eliminations and adjustments for the intercompany lease.

Gorski Inc. and Subsidiary Kovcic Inc.
Partial Consolidated Worksheet
For Year Ended December 31, 20X4

| | Trial Balance | | Eliminations and Adjustments | |
	Gorski	Kovcic	Dr.	Cr.
Rent receivable	2,000			
Equipment	700,000	200,000		
Accumulated depreciation—equipment	(350,000)	(50,000)		
Rent payable		(2,000)		
Rent income	(12,000)			
Rent expense		12,000		
Depreciation expense	30,000			

Eliminations and Adjustments:

(OL1)   Eliminate the intercompany rent expense and revenue.
(OL2)   Eliminate the accrued rent payable and receivable.

PART 7

Miller Corporation, a subsidiary of Jo Company, leased a computer from Jo on January 2, 20X0, that is properly recorded as a sales-type lease under the following terms:

Cost of the asset to the lessor: $20,119.
Lease payments: The lessee will pay five equal installments of $6,000 at the beginning of each year.
Bargain purchase option for the lessee is $4,000 at the end of the lease (to be included in minimum lease payments).
Lessor's implicit interest rate: 15%.
Depreciation is taken over the 7-year lease life, using straight-line amortization.
PV of annuity due for 5 years at 15% = 3.85498.
PV of 1 for 5 years at 15% = 0.49718.

Instructions:

1. Complete the following amortization schedule.

Amortization Schedule

	Annual Lease Payment	Interest	Reduction of Principal	Principal Balance
Jan. 1, 20X0	6,000	—	6,000	19,119
Jan. 1, 20X1	6,000	2,868	3,132	15,987
Jan. 1, 20X2	6,000			
Jan. 1, 20X3	6,000			
Jan. 1, 20X4	6,000			
Jan. 1, 20X5	6,000			

2. Record all entries on the books of the lessor for 20X0 (initial recording and year-end adjustments).

3. Record all entries on the books of the lessee for 20X0 (initial recording and year-end adjustments).

4.   Make all the necessary eliminations and adjustments on the following partial consolidated worksheet.

Jo Company and Subsidiary Miller Corporation
Partial Consolidated Worksheet
For Year Ended December 31, 20X0

	Trial Balance		Eliminations and Adjustments	
	Jo	Miller	Dr.	Cr.
Minimum lease payments receivable	28,000			
Unearned interest income	(6,013)			
Assets under capital lease		25,119		
Accumulated depreciation—assets under capital lease		(3,588)		
Property, plant, and equipment	680,000	320,000		
Accumulated depreciation—property, plant, and equipment	(240,000)	(160,000)		
Obligations under capital lease		(19,119)		
Interest payable		(2,868)		
Interest income	(2,868)			
Interest expense		2,868		
Sales profit on lease	(5,000)			
Depreciation expense	19,000	10,500		

Eliminations and Adjustments:
(CL1)   Eliminate intercompany interest expense and revenue.
(CL2)   Eliminate intercompany debt including accrued interest.
(CL3)   Reclassify asset and accumulated depreciation on leased assets.
(F1)   Eliminate intercompany profit on fixed asset sale.
(F2)   Adjust current-year depreciation for profit on fixed asset sale.

PART 8

On December 31, 20X1, Steady Winds Inc. purchased 90% of the common stock of Rigging Ltd. for $250,000. On that date, there was no difference between the book value and market value of Rigging's net assets. Since then, Steady Winds has maintained its investment in the subsidiary using the simple equity method.

Rigging issued $100,000, 10-year bonds on January 2, 20X3, for $105,500 cash. The bonds pay annual interest of 10% and were sold to yield 9%. Straight-line amortization is used by Rigging.

On October 31, 20X5, Steady Winds purchased all of Rigging's bonds for $97,850. Steady Winds is using the straight-line amortization method.

Instructions: Complete the worksheet on the following page and prepare income distribution schedules.

Eliminations and Adjustments:
(CY₁) Eliminate the entry recording the parent's share of the subsidiary net income.
(EL) Eliminate the parent's investment in the subsidiary and the parent's share of the subsidiary equity as of the beginning of the year.
(B) Eliminate intercompany interest revenue and the expense. Eliminate the balance in the investment in bonds against the bonds payable. The gain on retirement at the start of the year is calculated as follows:

Gain remaining at year end:		
Carrying value of bonds at Dec. 31, 20X6	$	
Investment in bonds at Dec. 31, 20X6	_____	$
Gain amortized during the year:		
Interest revenue eliminated	$	
Interest expense eliminated	_____	_____
Remaining gain at Jan. 1, 20X6		$ 5,950

Subsidiary Rigging Ltd. Income Distribution

Interest adjustment	Internally generated net income	$ 27,550
	Adjusted net income	
	NCI share	
	NCI	

Parent Steady Winds Income Distribution

	Internally generated net income	$185,300
	90% x Rigging adjusted income	
	Controlling interest	

Steady Winds Inc. and Subsidiary Rigging Ltd.
Worksheet for Consolidated Balance Sheet
For Year Ended December 31, 20X6

	Trial Balance		Eliminations and Adjustments		Consolidated Income Statement	NCI	Controlling Retained Earnings	Consolidated Balance Sheet
	Steady Winds	Rigging	Dr.	Cr.				
Cash	105,000	45,000						
Accounts receivable	87,500	78,000						
Inventory	88,000	58,860						
Investment in bonds	98,200							
Plant and equipment (net)	642,000	345,990						
Investment in Rigging	326,295							
Accounts payable	(102,500)	(62,000)						
Bonds payable (10%)		(100,000)						
Premium on bonds payable		(3,300)						
Common stock—Steady (no par)	(450,650)							
Paid-in capital—Steady								
Retained earnings—Steady 1/1/X6	(683,750)							
Common stock—Rigging (no par)		(75,000)						
Paid-in capital—Rigging								
Retained earnings—Rigging 1/1/X6		(260,000)						
Sales	(800,000)	(305,000)						
Cost of goods sold	525,000	183,000						
Selling and general expense	100,000	85,000						
Interest income	(10,300)							
Interest expense		9,450						
Subsidiary income	(24,795)							
Dividends declared	100,000							
Total	0	0						
Consolidated net income								
To NCI								
To controlling interest								
Total NCI								
Retained earnings, controlling interest, Dec. 31, 20X6								

Chapter 6   Cash Flow, EPS, Taxation, and Unconsolidated Investments

OUTLINE FOR REVIEW

The application of consolidation procedures to the following additional areas is explored: cash flow statements, earnings per share, taxation, and unconsolidated investments.

I.   The consolidated statement of cash flows begins with the use of the already consolidated income statement and balance sheet.

     A.   In the year of the purchase, a comparison of this year's consolidated balance sheet with the prior year's parent-only balance sheet is required. Special procedures are necessary for the period in which an acquisition occurs.

         1.   When a controlling interest is purchased for cash:

            a.   The cash paid for the interest is included as a cash outflow under investing activities.

            b.   The schedule of noncash activities includes the liabilities assumed and the NCI.

         2.   When a controlling interest is acquired in a noncash purchase transaction:

            a.   The cash of the subsidiary received is shown as a cash inflow under investing activities.

            b.   The stock issued and/or the bonds issued, along with the liabilities assumed and the NCI, are shown in the schedule of noncash transactions.

     B.   The amortization of excesses that are designated in the determination and distribution of excess schedule and that are reflected in consolidated net income do not require the use of cash and must be added back to consolidated net income to arrive at cash from operations. Cash from operating activities also must be adjusted for depreciation and amortization of book value recorded by the parent and the subsidiary on their separate books.

     C.   Additional subsidiary shares may have been purchased by the parent.

         1.   When additional subsidiary shares are purchased directly from the subsidiary:

            a.   No cash flows exist for the consolidated company.

            b.   The transfer of cash between the parent and the subsidiary would not appear in the consolidated cash flow statement.

         2.   When additional subsidiary shares are purchased from the NCI shareholders:

            a.   An outflow of cash to the NCI shareholders results.

            b.   From a consolidated viewpoint, this is a treasury stock purchase. The acquisition cost of the shares is an application of funds under financing activities.

     D.   Subsidiary dividends paid to the NCI shareholders appear as a financing application of funds in the consolidated cash flow statement. The portion of subsidiary dividends paid to the parent is only a transfer of cash within the consolidated entity and not an inflow or outflow of cash.

II.   Consolidated earnings per share are computed according to the usual guidelines regarding income and share adjustments.

     A.   Basic earnings per share (BEPS) is calculated by dividing consolidated net income (that is, only the controlling interest under current methods) by parent company outstanding shares.

     B.   The parent includes subsidiary income in its diluted earnings per share (DEPS) numerator by including the number of shares owned times subsidiary DEPS.

         1.   All subsidiary DEPS calculations start with subsidiary income adjusted for any intercompany profits applicable to the subsidiary.

         2.   The parent also includes, in its DEPS numerator, its ownership interest in subsidiary dilutive securities times subsidiary DEPS.

         3.   Adjustments to parent DEPS include adjustments for dilutive subsidiary securities, which are satisfied by issuing parent company shares of common stock.

     C.   The parent's internally generated net income used in calculating the consolidated EPS must be adjusted for unrealized profits resulting from parent company–generated intercompany transactions.

     D.   When an acquisition occurs during the current period in a purchase, subsidiary income (for BEPS) and shares (for DEPS) are included only from the purchase date to the end of the period.

III.   Consolidated companies that qualify as an affiliated group (80% ownership tests) may elect to be taxed as a single consolidated entity.

     A.   Affiliated companies that elect taxation as a single entity do not record a provision for income tax based on their separate incomes. The basis for the tax calculation is the consolidated net income shown on the worksheet. The provision for income tax, on the consolidated worksheet, is calculated by applying the corporate tax rate to the consolidated taxable income.

     B.   The income distribution schedules are used to allocate the income tax expense according to the member's adjusted income before tax.

     C.   Each member company must record its share of the consolidated income on its separate books.

        1.   The subsidiary records its full share of taxes.

        2.   The parent records its allocated portion of consolidated income tax expense as calculated in the parent's income distribution schedule. This tax is based on the parent's internally generated net income adjusted for intercompany profits.

        3.   The parent's share of subsidiary net income is based on subsidiary income net of tax.

        4.   The parent also adjusts subsidiary income and the investment account for its controlling percentage of the subsidiary income tax recorded.

IV.   When members of the consolidated group file separate tax returns, each member must base its tax calculations on its separate income. Each company's trial balance will include a provision for income tax and the related tax liability.

     A.   Corporations are generally taxed on only 20% of subsidiary dividends received (for 20%–79% ownership; 30% for less than 20% ownership). For affiliated companies (over 80% ownership) electing to file separate returns, 100% of the dividends are excluded.

     B.   Since the tax expense is calculated prior to the application of consolidation adjustment and eliminations, intercompany gains and losses are included in each company's tax calculation. The majority of the intercompany transactions will create timing differences. This leads to a need for interperiod tax allocation.

        1.   Calculate the member companies' individual tax liabilities and record the tax liability and provision for income tax on each company's books prior to consolidating.

        2.   Where the companies are not affiliated companies, the parent company must provide for tax expense on 20% of the subsidiary net income. If the parent's share of income has not yet been received, the tax on that share is not yet payable and that portion of income tax usually is deferred.

        3.   Worksheet eliminations must include an adjustment, to the beginning retained earnings balances and deferred tax balance, for the tax impact of profit and loss deferments made in previous consolidated worksheets.

        4.   Worksheet eliminations also must include an adjustment to the provision for income tax and the deferred tax account for the expiration of prior years' tax deferrals and for the current year's tax provision on current intercompany profit (loss) transactions.

     C.   Income distribution schedules are prepared on a net-of-tax basis. Internally generated net incomes and adjustments are shown before tax, and tax is calculated based on adjusted income.

V.   The basic mechanics for application of the rules of the APB Opinion No. 18 equity method were discussed in Chapter 3. Only the complications are discussed here.

     A.   A determination and distribution of excess schedule is prepared as with a consolidated investment; however, the amortizations designated in the determination and distribution of excess schedule are made as an adjustment to the investment and investment income accounts.

     B.   The investor's share of the investee's gain or loss on intercompany transactions must be deferred until the goods are sold or the benefit is realized over the life of the asset. This means that the investee's income should be adjusted for gains and losses on transactions with the investor prior to applying the investor's ownership percentage.

     C.   Twenty percent of the investee's dividends to the investor are taxable to the investor.

        1.   Tax allocation procedures are applied. Provision for income tax is based on the investor's net investment income after adjustments for nontax deductible amortizations. The current tax liability reflects only income received as dividends.

        2.   A deferred tax liability must be created for undistributed investment income.

     D.   In the absence of consolidation, an investment in preferred stock is not eliminated. The investor's common stock equity adjustment must, however, be based on investee earnings available to common stockholders.

     E.   If the investee corporation engages in transactions with its common shareholders, the investor must calculate the transaction's effect on its investment and adjust the investment and investment income accounts.

F. The investment in an investee is written down to market value only if that decline in market value is perceived as relatively permanent. There can be no future write-ups other than those resulting from normal equity adjustments.

G. The investment balance may not have a negative balance. If the investee suffers losses and the investor's share of those losses exceeds its investment account balance, the excess losses are recorded only as a memo entry. If the investee becomes profitable later, the investor will not record income on the investment until its share of income exceeds its prior unrecorded losses.

H. The following procedures are applied when there is a gain or loss of influence:

1. If the investor company subsequently purchases additional shares to have its total interest equal or exceed 20%, the investor must apply retroactively the equity method to the total holding period of the investment. This results in an adjustment to the investor's retained earnings and retroactive restatement of prior years' comparative statements. Adjustments for the amortization of excess are based on the price paid for the prior interest.

2. If the investor company subsequently sells a portion of its shares so that it owns less than 20% of the shares, the equity method is discontinued as of the sale date.

I. The investor must defer its ownership share of profits made on sales to the investee. This adjustment is made to a separate deferred profit account rather than to the investment account, since it does not pertain to investee actions.

J. Disclosure of the following is required:

1. Name of each investee.

2. Percentage of ownership in each investee.

3. Disparity between the cost and underlying book value for each investment.

4. The reasons the equity method is not being used if it is not being applied.

PART 1

Instructions: Use a check mark to indicate whether each of the following statements is true or false.

		True	False
1.	The analysis of cash flows for consolidated companies begins with consolidated statements.		
2.	The purchase of a subsidiary for cash is considered a financing activity.		
3.	The assumption of long-term debt in a purchase of a subsidiary is considered a cash flow under financing activities.		
4.	The amortizations of excess resulting from a purchase will be listed as an adjustment under the cash flows from operating activities section.		
5.	When a consolidated statement of cash flows is prepared in the period a subsidiary is acquired, the NCI is treated as a source of cash.		
6.	The purchase of additional subsidiary stock from the noncontrolling shareholders is simply a transfer of funds within the consolidated entity and would not appear in the consolidated statement of cash flows.		
7.	The portion of subsidiary DEPS included in the consolidated DEPS is equal to the parent's ownership interest of each type of the subsidiary securities that were used to compute subsidiary DEPS.		
8.	The income used to compute subsidiary DEPS must be adjusted for intercompany transactions.		
9.	Consolidated companies that meet the definition of an affiliated group may elect to be taxed as either a single entity or as separate entities.		
10.	When an affiliated group elects taxation as a single entity, the affiliated companies should not calculate a separate provision for income tax based on their own separate incomes.		

11. Deferred tax liabilities are created when separately taxed affiliates have unrealized intercompany profits.   _____   _____

12. With taxation calculated separately for companies within a consolidated entity, the parent must make a provision for its share of subsidiary income.   _____   _____

13. When an influential investor purchases a depreciable asset from an investee and the investee has a gain, the entire gain must be deferred over the remaining life of the asset.   _____   _____

14. For influential investments, the provision for tax must be based on equity income, while a deferred tax liability must be created for undistributed investment income.   _____   _____

PART 2

Instructions: Circle the letter that identifies the best response to each question. (All are AICPA adapted.)

1. On July 1, 20X2, Denver Corp. purchased 3,000 shares of Eagle Co.'s 10,000 outstanding shares of common stock for $20 per share. On December 15, 20X2, Eagle paid $40,000 in dividends to its common stockholders. Eagle's net income for the year ended December 31, 20X2, was $120,000, earned evenly throughout the year. In its 20X2 income statement, what amount of income from this investment should Denver report?
   a. $36,000   b. $18,000   c. $12,000   d. $6,000

2. An investor uses the equity method to account for an investment in common stock. After the date of acquisition, the investment account of the investor would:
   a. Not be affected by its share of the earnings or losses of the investee.
   b. Not be affected by its share of the earnings of the investee, but be decreased by its share of the losses of the investee.
   c. Be increased by its share of the earnings of the investee, but not be affected by its share of the losses of the investee.
   d. Be increased by its share of the earnings of the investee, and decreased by its share of the losses of the investee.

3. When the equity method is used to account for investments in common stock, which of the following affects the investor's reported investment income?

	Amortizations of Excess Related to Purchase	Cash Dividends from Investee
a.	Yes	Yes
b.	No	Yes
c.	No	No
d.	Yes	No

4. Green Corp. owns 30% of the outstanding common stock and 100% of the outstanding noncumulative, nonvoting preferred stock of Axel Corp. In 20X1, Axel declared dividends of $100,000 on its common stock and $60,000 on its preferred stock. Green exercises significant influence over Axel's operations. What amount of dividend revenue should Green report in its income statement for the year ended December 31, 20X1?
   a. $0   b. $30,000   c. $60,000   d. $90,000

5. On January 1, 20X1, Mega Corp. acquired 10% of the outstanding voting stock of Penny Inc. On January 2, 20X2, Mega gained the ability to exercise significant influence over financial and operating control of Penny by acquiring an additional 20% of Penny's outstanding stock. The two purchases were made at prices proportionate to the value assigned to Penny's net assets, which equaled their carrying amounts. For the years ended December 31, 20X1 and 20X2, Penny reported the following:

	20X1	20X2
Dividends paid	$200,000	$300,000
Net income	600,000	650,000

   In 20X2, what amounts should Mega report as current-year investment income and as an adjustment, before income taxes, to 20X1 investment income?

	20X2 Investment Income	Adjustment to 20X1 Investment Income
a.	$195,000	$160,000
b.	195,000	100,000
c.	195,000	40,000
d.	105,000	40,000

6. Bart Inc., a newly organized corporation, uses the equity method of accounting for its 30% investment in Rex Co.'s common stock. During 20X1, Rex paid dividends of $300,000 and reported earnings of $900,000. In addition:
   - The dividends received from Rex are eligible for the 80%-dividends-received deduction.
   - All the undistributed earnings of Rex will be distributed in future years.
   - There are no other temporary differences.
   - Bart's income tax rate is 30%.

   In Bart's December 31, 20X1, balance sheet, the deferred income tax liability should be:
   a. $10,800   b. 0   c. $5,400   d. $4,500

7. In its financial statements, Pulham Corp. uses the equity method of accounting for its 30% ownership of Angles Corp. At December 31, 20X1, Pulham has a receivable from Angles. How should the receivable be reported in Pulham's 20X1 financial statements?
   a. None of the receivable should be reported, but the entire receivable should be offset against Angles' payable to Pulham.
   b. Seventy percent of the receivable should be separately reported, with the balance offset against 30% of Angles' payable to Pulham.
   c. The total receivable should be disclosed separately.
   d. The total receivable should be included as part of the investment in Angles, without separate disclosure.

8. Pare Inc. purchased 10% of Tot Co.'s 100,000 outstanding shares of common stock on January 2, 20X2, for $50,000. On December 31, 20X2, Pare purchased an additional 20,000 shares of Tot for $150,000. There was no goodwill as a result of either acquisition, and Tot had not issued any additional stock during 20X2. Tot reported earnings of $300,000 for 20X2. What amount should Pare report in its December 31, 20X2 balance sheet as an investment in Tot?
   a. $170,000   b. $200,000   c. $230,000   d. $290,000

PART 3

Money Inc. acquired for cash an 80% interest in the outstanding stock of Fastbuck Company on January 1, 20X2. At the time, the following information was available:

Fastbuck Company
Balance Sheet
December 31, 20X1

Assets		Liabilities and Equity	
Cash	$ 60,000	Current liabilities	$ 50,000
Inventory	90,000	Bonds payable	100,000
Property, plant, and equipment (net)	250,000	Common stock	100,000
		Retained earnings	150,000
Total	$400,000	Total	$400,000

Money Inc.
Balance Sheet
December 31, 20X1

Assets		Liabilities and Equity	
Cash	$ 400,000	Current liabilities	$ 150,000
Inventory	200,000	Common stock	300,000
Property, plant, and equipment (net)	400,000	Additional paid-in capital	150,000
		Retained earnings	400,000
Total	$1,000,000	Total	$1,000,000

Determination and Distribution of Excess Schedule

Price paid			$275,000
Less interest acquired:			
Common stock		$100,000	
Retained earnings		150,000	
Total stockholders' equity		$250,000	
Interest acquired		80%	200,000
Excess of cost over book value (debit balance)			$ 75,000
Attributable to property, plant, and equipment			
[10-year life (80% x $50,000)]			40,000 Dr.
Goodwill			$ 35,000 Dr.

Results for 20X2 are summarized in the following statements:

Money Inc. and Subsidiary Fastbuck Company
Consolidated Income Statement
For Year Ended December 31, 20X2

Sales		$800,000
Less cost of goods sold		500,000
Gross profit		$300,000
Less expenses:		
General and administrative	$75,000	
Depreciation	50,000	125,000
Consolidated net income		$ 175,000
To NCI		21,000
To controlling interest		$ 154,000

Money Inc. and Subsidiary Fastbuck Company
Consolidated Balance Sheet
December 31, 20X2

Assets		Liabilities and Equity	
Cash	$ 130,000	Current liabilities	$ 100,000
Inventory	400,000	Bonds payable	100,000
Property, plant, and equipment (net)	710,000	NCI	71,000
Goodwill	35,000	Controlling interest:	
		Common stock	300,000
		Additional paid-in capital	150,000
		Retained earnings	554,000
Total	$1,275,000	Total	$1,275,000

Additional information:
Money Inc. purchased additional equipment during 20X2 for $50,000.
No dividends were paid during 20X2.

Instructions:

1. Calculate the change in cash.

2. Prepare the consolidated statement of cash flows, including a schedule of noncash activities.

   Cash flows from operating activities:

   Net cash provided by operating activities: _____

   Cash flows from investing activities:

                                                _____

   Net cash used for investing activities: _____

   Net decrease in cash:*   _____

   Cash at beginning of year: _____

   Cash at year end: _____ 0

*There are no cash financing transactions.

Schedule of noncash investing and financing activity:

PART 4

Wond Company owns 90% of the outstanding common stock of Ellen Company. The income statements for Wond and Ellen for 20X3 are as follows:

	Wond	Ellen
Sales	$600,000	$350,000
Less cost of goods sold	300,000	200,000
Gross profit	300,000	150,000
Less operating expenses	175,000	110,000
Operating income	125,000	40,000
Subsidiary income	36,000	—
Income before tax	$161,000	$ 40,000

The following information pertains to intercompany sales made by Ellen:

Intercompany sales in the beginning inventory of Wond	$42,000
Intercompany sales in the ending inventory of Wond	50,000
Sales to Wond	88,000
Gross profit rate	25%
Tax rate	30%

On January 1, 20X2, Wond sold Ellen a packaging machine at a profit of $30,000. The machine is depreciated over 6 years using the straight-line method. Depreciation is included in operating expenses.

Patents, as designated on the determination and distribution of excess schedule, are $80,000, with a 10-year life. The original purchase was a taxable exchange.

Instructions:

1. Assume that a consolidated tax return will be filed. Compute the consolidated income and the tax provision for the consolidated company and complete the income distribution schedules.

Consolidated Income Statement Worksheet

	Wond	Ellen	Adjustments			Consolidated Income Statement
			Dr.		Cr.	
Sales	(600,000)	(350,000)				
Cost of goods sold	300,000	200,000				
Gross profit	(300,000)	(150,000)				
Less: Operating expenses	175,000	110,000				
Operating income	(125,000)	(40,000)				

Consolidated Tax Provision

	Consolidated Income Statement
Consolidated income before tax	
Consolidated tax liability (30%)	
Consolidated income after tax	

Subsidiary Ellen Company Income Distribution

Ending inventory profit	Internally generated net income
	Beginning inventory profit
	Adjusted income before tax
	Ellen's share of taxes
	Ellen's net income
	NCI (10%)

Parent Wond Company Income Distribution

Patent amortization	Internally generated income
	Gain realized on equipment through use
	Adjusted income before tax
	Wond's share of taxes
	Wond's net income
	Share of Ellen's net income
	Controlling interest

2. Based on Part (a), record the tax provision on each company's books, and record Wond's entry to adjust subsidiary income for the tax provision by Ellen.

Ellen's Books:

Wond's Books:

3.   Assume that the companies are affiliated companies for tax purposes but choose to be taxed separately. Record the provision for tax on each company's books.

Ellen's Books:

Wond's Books:

PART 5

The Paxton Company purchased a 60% interest in the Saxton Company on January 1, 20X5, for $481,000. The equity of the Saxton Company on January 1, 20X5 was:

Common stock	$100,000
Paid-in capital in excess	300,000
Retained earnings	235,000
Total	$ 635,000

Any excess cost was attributed to patents with a 20-year life.

Saxton sold Paxton a machine on January 1, 20X6, at a $60,000 profit. The machine has a 10-year depreciable life.

Paxton sells merchandise to Saxton at a gross profit rate of 40%. Intercompany sales during 20X7 were $80,000. Saxton had $10,000 of Paxton's goods in its beginning inventory and $20,000 of Paxton's goods in its ending inventory. The inventory values reflect Paxton's selling price.

The companies are taxed separately at a 30% tax rate. Income earned from the subsidiary is subject to the 80% exclusion. Paxton has provided for the tax on its full share of subsidiary income in both the current and prior periods.

Instructions:

1. Confirm the balance in the following accounts on the trial balance worksheet that follows on page SG 6–14:
    • Paxton deferred tax asset (liability)

    • Paxton provision for tax

Notice: All intercompany profits recorded by the separate companies have been taxed.

2.   Prepare the determination and distribution of excess schedule.

	Total	Controlling
Price paid	_____	_____
Interest acquired:		
Common stock	_____	_____
Paid-in excess	_____	_____
Retained earnings	_____	_____
Total equity	_____	_____
Ownership interest	_____	_____
Excess	_____	_____

3. Complete the December 31, 20X7 (3 years after the purchase), trial balance worksheet that follows. Provide short explanations for each elimination. Provide tax allocation schedules. Number each adjustment on the worksheet to correspond to the following explanations:
    (CY$_1$) Eliminate subsidiary income.
    (CY$_2$) Eliminate intercompany dividends.
    (EL) Eliminate 60% of subsidiary equity on January 1, 20X7.
    (D)   Distribute excess to patents.
    (A)   Amortize patents.
    (IS) Eliminate intercompany sales.
    (BI) Eliminate beginning inventory profit from cost of goods sold and parent beginning retained earnings.

(EI)   Eliminate ending inventory profit from cost of goods sold and inventory account.
 (F)   (1)   Eliminate remaining fixed-asset profit at start of year.
        (2)   Reduce current-year depreciation.

(T1)   Adjust the beginning retained earnings balances and create a deferred tax asset (DTL) on prior period adjustments as follows:

DTA/DTL adjustments	Total Tax	Parent	Sub.
To beginning retained earnings	_____	_____	_____	_____
Subsidiary transactions:			
Beginning inventory	_____	_____	_____	_____
Remaining fixed asset profit	_____	_____	_____	_____
Total	_____	_____	_____	_____
First tax	_____	_____	_____	_____
Second tax	_____	_____	_____	_____
Parent transactions:			
Beginning inventory	_____	_____	_____	_____
Remaining fixed asset profit	_____	_____	_____	_____
Amortizations of excess	_____	_____	_____	_____
Total	_____	_____	_____	_____
First tax	_____	_____	_____	_____
Total increase in retained earnings and DTA	_____	_____	_____	_____

(T2)   Adjust current-year tax provision and adjust deferred tax asset (DTA) for the tax effects of current year income adjustments:

Subsidiary transactions:	Total Tax	Parent	Sub.
Beginning inventory	_____	_____	_____	_____
Ending inventory	_____	_____	_____	_____
Fixed asset sale	_____	_____	_____	_____
Realized fixed asset	_____	_____	_____	_____
Total	_____	_____	_____	_____
First tax	_____	_____	_____	_____
Second tax	_____	_____	_____	_____
Parent transactions:			
Beginning inventory	_____	_____	_____	_____
Ending inventory	_____	_____	_____	_____
Fixed asset sale	_____	_____	_____	_____
Remaining fixed asset profit	_____	_____	_____	_____
Amortization of excess	_____	_____	_____	_____
Total	_____	_____	_____	_____
First tax	_____	_____	_____	_____
Increase (decrease) in DTA	_____	_____	_____	_____

Subsidiary Saxton Company Income Distribution

			Internally generated income (before tax) Realized gain on fixed asset		
			Total income before tax Tax provision (30%)		
			Net income NCI share (40%)		
			Controlling share (60%)		

Parent Paxton Company Income Distribution

Ending inventory profit Amortization of patents			Internally generated income (before tax) Realized beginning inventory profit		
			Total income before tax		
			Tax provision (30%) Net income		
			Controlling share of subsidiary income (net of first tax) Second tax on share of controlling subsidiary income		
			Total controlling interest		

Paxton Company and Subsidiary Saxton Company
Worksheet for Consolidated Financial Statements
For the Year Ended December 31, 20X7

	Trial Balance		Eliminations and Adjustments		Consolidated Income Statement	NCI	Controlling Retained Earnings	Consolidated Balance Sheet
	Paxton	Saxton	Dr.	Cr.				
Cash	166,360	91,000						
Accounts receivable	188,000	145,000						
Inventory	150,000	120,000						
Investment in Saxton	517,600							
Land	100,000	50,000						
Building and equipment	430,000	450,000						
Accum. depreciation, bldg. & equip.	(160,000)	(180,000)						
Patents		20,000						
Deferred tax asset (liability)	(2,196)							
Common stock—Paxton	(900,000)							
Retained earnings—Paxton	(428,920)							
Common stock—Saxton		(100,000)						
Paid-in capital in excess of par—Saxton		(300,000)						
Retained earnings—Saxton		(285,000)						
Dividends declared		10,000						
Sales	(400,000)	(250,000)						
Cost of goods sold	230,000	160,000						
Expenses	100,000	60,000						
Subsidiary income	(12,600)							
Provision for tax	21,756	9,000						
	0	0		0				
Consolidated net income								
To NCI								
To controlling interest								
Total NCI								
Retained earnings, controlling interest,								
December 31, 20X7								

PART 6

Rick Company acquired a 70% interest in the outstanding stock of Plann Inc. on January 1, 20X3. At that time, the following determination and distribution of excess schedule was prepared:

Price paid		$320,000
Less interest acquired:		
Common stock	$200,000	
Retained earnings	220,000	
Total stockholders' equity	$420,000	
Interest acquired	70%	294,000
Patents (10-year life)		$ 26,000

Plann sold inventory to Rick as detailed:

	20X3	20X4
Intercompany sales	$ 80,000	$100,000
Intercompany sales in the beginning inventory	30,000	40,000
Intercompany sales in the ending inventory	40,000	50,000
Gross profit rate in current year	40%	30%

On January 1, 20X3, Rick Company sold Plann Inc. a building for $100,000. The net book value was $80,000. The building is used as a sales office and has a 20-year depreciable life.

The corporate tax rate is 30%. The companies are taxed separately, since they do not meet the requirements for an affiliated group. (Income of the subsidiary is subject to an 80% exclusion for tax purposes.)

Instructions: Complete the following consolidated worksheet and income distribution schedules.

Rick Company and Subsidiary Plann Inc.
Worksheet for Consolidated Balance Sheet
For Year Ended December 31, 20X4

	Trial Balance		Eliminations and Adjustments		Consolidated Income Statement	NCI	Controlling Retained Earnings	Consolidated Balance Sheet
	Rick	Plann	Dr.	Cr.				
Inventory	200,000	80,000						
Other current assets	198,400	295,000						
Buildings (net)	500,000	320,000						
Investment in Plann	496,750							
Patents								
Common stock—Rick	(600,000)							
Retained earnings—Rick	(600,000)							
Common stock—Plann		(200,000)						
Retained earnings—Plann		(420,000)						
Sales	(900,000)	(600,000)						
Cost of goods sold	500,000	400,000						
Expenses	250,000	125,000						
Provision for income tax	47,205	22,500						
Subsidiary income	(36,750)							
Income taxes payable	(45,000)	(22,500)						
Deferred tax asset (liability)	(10,605)	(22,500)						
Total	0	0						
Consolidated net income								
To NCI								
To controlling interest								
Total NCI								
Controlling retained earnings								

Eliminations and Adjustments:

(CY₁) Eliminate Rick's entry to record its share of subsidiary income.

(EL) Eliminate 70% of the subsidiary equity balances.

(D)   Distribute the excess according to the determination and distribution of excess schedule.
(A)   Amortize the excess for prior and current years.
(BI) Remove the gross profit recorded by Plann for goods held in Rick's beginning inventory.
(EI) Remove the gross profit recorded by Plann for goods held in Rick's ending inventory.
(IS) Eliminate the current-year intercompany sales.
(FI) Adjust the retained earnings and asset balances for the fixed asset sale.
(F2) Adjust current-year depreciation for fixed asset sale.

(T1) Adjust the beginning retained earnings balances and create a deferred tax asset (DTL)
      on prior period adjustments as follows:

DTA/DTL adjustments		Total	Parent	Sub.
To beginning retained earnings			_____	_____
Subsidiary transactions:			_____	_____
Beginning inventory	_____		_____	_____
Total	_____		_____	_____
First tax		_____	_____	_____
Second tax		_____	_____	_____
Parent transactions:				
Remaining fixed asset profit	_____		_____	_____
Amortization of excess	_____		_____	_____
Total	_____		_____	_____
First tax		_____	_____	_____
Total increase in retained earnings and DTA	_____	_____	_____	_____

(T2) Adjust current-year tax provision and adjust deferred tax asset (DTA) for the tax effects of current
      year income adjustments:

Subsidiary transactions:		Total	Parent	Sub.
Beginning inventory	_____		_____	_____
Ending inventory	_____		_____	_____
Total	_____		_____	_____
First tax		_____	_____	_____
Second tax		_____	_____	_____
Parent transactions:				
Fixed asset profit realized	_____		_____	_____
Amortization of excess	_____		_____	_____
Total	_____		_____	_____
First tax		_____	_____	_____
Increase (decrease) in DTA	_____	_____	_____	_____

Subsidiary Plann, Inc. Income Distribution:

Unrealized gain on ending inventory			Internally generated net income (before tax)		
			Realized gain beginning inventory		
			Total income before tax		
			Tax provision (30%)		
			Net income		
			NCI share (30%)		
			Controlling share (70%)		

Parent Rick Company Income Distribution

			Internally generated net income (before tax)		
Amortization of patent			Realized gain beginning inventory		
			Total income before tax		
			Tax provision (30%)		
			Net income		
			Controlling share of subsidiary income (net of first tax)		
			Second tax on share of subsidiary income		
			Total controlling interest		

PART 7

On January 1, 20X5, Able Company purchased a 30% interest in the Baker Company common stock for $350,000. On that date, Baker's stockholders' equity was $800,000. Any excess of cost over book value was attributed to equipment, which was understated $50,000 and had a 5-year life. Any remaining excess is attributed to goodwill.

Baker sells merchandise to all customers to yield a 25% gross profit. Intercompany sales to Able and ending inventories of intercompany goods were as follows:

	Dec. 31, 20X5	Dec. 31, 20X6
Baker sales to Able	$150,000	$200,000
Baker goods in Able's December 31 inventory	50,000	60,000

On July 1, 20X5, Able sold a machine with a 5-year life to Baker for $100,000. The cost of the machine to Able was $75,000. The machine is depreciated on a straight-line basis.

Both companies pay a 30% corporate tax rate. The income earned on the investment in Baker is subject to an 80% dividend exclusion. It is to be assumed that all Baker income will eventually be paid out in dividends.

Information about the income and dividends of Baker is as follows:

	20X5	20X6
Net income (after tax recorded only by Baker)	$90,000	$60,000
Dividends paid	10,000	10,000

Instructions:

1. Prepare a determination and distribution schedule that includes the annual amortization of excess amounts.

2. Complete the following information table and income distribution schedules:

	20X5	20X6
Investment account balance, January 1		
Share of adjusted income—from IDS schedule (prior to amortization adjustment)		
Amortization adjustment		
Dividend received		
Investment account balance, December 31		
Able Company deferred profit		
Balance, January 1		
Adjustment		
Balance, December 31		

Income Distribution Schedule: 20X5

Income Distribution Schedule: 20X6

3. Complete the following schedule of deferred tax asset (liability)—Investment in Baker:

	20X5	20X6
Balance, January 1		
Subsidiary income, 20% taxed at 30%		
Less: tax paid on dividends		
Deferred profit on machine sale		
Balance, December 31		

Chapter 7   Special Issues in Accounting for an Investment in a Subsidiary

OUTLINE FOR REVIEW

Continuing the analysis of consolidation procedures, specialized investment situations and the related consolidations procedures must be addressed.

I.   When the parent acquires stock from a newly organized subsidiary, the subsidiary receives the funds directly from the parent.
   A.   If the parent acquires all the stock or acquires a controlling interest and pays the same price as was received from outsiders, the determination and distribution of excess schedule will have no excess of cost or book value.
   B.   If the parent acquires its investment for a price different from that paid by other investors, the price paid by the parent will vary from its ownership interest in the subsidiary equity and will result in an excess of cost or book value.

II.   Control over a subsidiary may be achieved as a result of a series of purchases of subsidiary stock. Each block acquired must have a separate determination and distribution of excess schedule. Excess also must be distributed and amortized separately.
   A.   If control is achieved with the original purchase, consolidation procedures are being used from the time of original acquisition; consequently, no major changes in worksheet methods are required when a second block is acquired.
      1.   If the investment is being carried using the equity method, the current year's income entries must be eliminated for each block.
      2.   If the investment is being carried using the cost method, each block of stock purchased must be converted to the simple equity method as of the beginning of the year. The adjustment is based on the change in subsidiary retained earnings between the date of acquisition of the block and the beginning of the current year.
   B.   If the control over a subsidiary is achieved subsequent to the initial purchase of the investment, the procedures used depend on the accounting method used to carry the investment. The original investment must be subjected retroactively to the consolidation process.
      1.   If the original interest is accounted for under the sophisticated equity method, the original excess of cost or book value has been amortized as an adjustment to investment income. Once the parent achieves control, it is not necessary to amortize retroactively the original excess. Only the excess remaining at the time of the second purchase is amortized on the consolidated worksheet.
      2.   If the original interest is accounted for under the cost method, convert the investment account to the equity method as of the date control is achieved. The conversion entry may be made directly on the parent's books or on the worksheet if the parent uses the cost method. The original excess of cost or book value must be amortized for current and past periods on the worksheet.

III.   When the parent sells all or a portion of the investment in common stock, the accounting procedure used varies with the method used to record the investment and the amount of the investment sold.
   A.   The sale of the entire parent interest terminates the need for consolidation.
      1.   The results of subsidiary operations prior to the sale date often are not consolidated but are shown as a separate line item in the parent's statements.
      2.   In calculating the gain or loss on the sale of a subsidiary investment, the investment account must be adjusted for the parent's share of income and for amortization of excesses.
         a.   If the simple equity method is used, the investment account should be adjusted by the amount of prior years' amortizations.
         b.   If the cost method is used, the investment account should be increased for the prior year's share of subsidiary income, net of amortization of excesses.
         c.   Current year's income should be recorded using the sophisticated equity method.
   B.   When a portion of the subsidiary's investment account is sold, procedures depend on whether effective control is retained.

    1.   When control is lost, consolidation procedures will be discontinued. The entire investment is adjusted as in "A"; however, the gain or loss on sale is limited to the interest sold. The interest remaining is recorded using the sophisticated equity method if the interest is 20% or more; otherwise, the cost method is used.

    2.   When control is maintained, only the interest sold needs to be adjusted using the methods in "A." The portion retained does not need to be adjusted, since it is still subject to consolidation procedures. The resulting adjustment goes to parent paid-in capital in excess of par and does not impact the income statement.

  C. At the time of the sale, the parent should adjust the portion of the investment account sold for any unrealized, subsidiary-generated intercompany profits or losses.

IV.   If the subsidiary has preferred stock outstanding, the preferred shareholders may have a claim against retained earnings. Preferred claims arise from dividends in arrears on cumulative preferred stock and from participation privileges.

  A. The determination and distribution of excess schedule prepared as of the date of the parent's investment in common stock must include only the portion of retained earnings allocable to common stock.

  B. Segregate the preferred shareholders' claims on retained earnings from the retained earnings available to common stockholders on the consolidated worksheet.

  C. Periodic equity adjustments for the parent's investment in common stock are made only for the common shareholders' claim on income.

V.   When the parent also has an investment in subsidiary preferred stock, the parent's purchase is viewed as a retirement of preferred stock.

  A. Eliminate the entry recording the parent's income allocable to preferred stock for the current period.

  B. Eliminate the investment in preferred stock against the preferred stock equity accounts. The amount paid for the preferred stock is compared to the book value of the shares to determine the increase or decrease in equity on retirement. The increase on retirement is credited to the controlling paid-in capital. (A decrease is offset against previous paid-in capital from retirements or from deducted controlling retained earnings.)

  C. The income distribution schedule of the subsidiary will reduce the internally generated net income available on common stock for the preferred shareholders' current claim on earnings.

    1.   The total NCI in income is the sum of the NCI share of income available to common shareholders plus the NCI share of the preferred current claim on income.

    2.   The controlling interest will reflect the share of income attributable to preferred and common stock.

VI.   Balance-sheet-only worksheets require that all adjustments be made to balance sheet accounts.

  A. Under equity methods, eliminations are made as of the end of the year. Under the cost method, the equity conversion is made as of year end.

  B. Under the simple equity method, all amortizations of excess are made to retained earnings.

  C. Only those intercompany profits and losses still unrealized at year end need to be adjusted for.

PART 1

Instructions: Use a check mark to indicate whether each of the following statements is true or false.

	True	False
1. In the case of a newly organized corporation, there will be no excess when the price per share paid by the parent is equal to the price paid by the NCI.	_____	_____
2. The excess of cost or book value on each block of stock, in a piecemeal acquisition, must be distributed and amortized separately.	_____	_____
3. Company P purchased a 70% interest in Company S on January 1, 20X1, and a 20% interest in the same company on July 1, 20X2. The controlling interest in subsidiary net income for 20X2 is 90% of Company S's reported net income.	_____	_____
4. When a parent owns 40% of a subsidiary, APB Opinion No. 18 requires that the excess of original cost over book value be amortized as an adjustment to investment income in subsequent years.	_____	_____

5. When control is achieved upon the second purchase of subsidiary stock, previous amortizations of excess under the sophisticated equity method must continue to be booked.   _____ _____

6. Upon a sale of a parent's investment in common stock when the parent loses control, the entire investment, if maintained under the simple equity method, must be adjusted for prior years' amortizations of excess.   _____ _____

7. When the parent sells a portion of the investment in common stock but retains control, the investment maintained under the simple equity method must be adjusted for prior years' amortizations of excess for only the portion of the investment sold.   _____ _____

8. The resulting gain or loss on a sale of a parent's entire interest in a subsidiary usually is treated as an income statement gain or loss.   _____ _____

9. The investment in subsidiary preferred stock may remain on the consolidated statements and need not be eliminated.   _____ _____

10. The percentage of preferred stock held by the parent is included in determining if the parent has the effective operating control required to consolidate.   _____ _____

11. Prior to the elimination of the parent's investment in subsidiary preferred stock, it is necessary to determine the portion of retained earnings applicable to preferred stock.   _____ _____

12. If the parent does not hold any of the subsidiary's cumulative preferred stock, the parent's determination and distribution of excess schedule need not show a distinction between the preferred and common stock claims on retained earnings.   _____ _____

13. In calculating the conversion-to-equity adjustment for an investment in common stock maintained under the cost method, the equity adjustment must take into account dividends in arrears on cumulative preferred stock.   _____ _____

14. The elimination of the parent's interest in subsidiary preferred stock creates a gain or loss that flows to the consolidated income statement.   _____ _____

PART 2

Instructions: Circle the letter that identifies the best response to each question. (Items 4 and 5 are AICPA adapted.)

1. In a prior period, the Palo Company purchased a 10% interest in the Saro Company at a price in excess of book value. In the current period, Palo purchased another 60% interest in Saro at a price in excess of book value. All prices in excess of book value are attributed to goodwill. The amount of goodwill to be included on the consolidated balance sheet is based on:
    a. Comparing the price for the 60% interest to 60% of Saro book value on the date of the second purchase.
    b. Comparing the price paid for the sum of the two interests to 70% of Saro book value on the date of the second purchase.
    c. Comparing the price of each interest to 10% and 60% of the Saro book values that existed on the date each purchase was made.
    d. Comparing the sum of the equity-adjusted cost of the 10% interest and the price paid for the 60% interest to the Saro book value on the date of the second purchase.

2. A parent owned a 90% interest in a subsidiary. Sufficient shares were sold by the parent so that the parent ownership interest was lowered to 60%. Which of the following statements is true?
    a. The interest sold must be equity adjusted including amortizations of excess.
    b. The gain (loss) is considered a gain (loss) on a discontinued operation.
    c. Consolidation procedures will not continue to be applied.
    d. No gain or loss is recorded.

3. Preferred stock of a subsidiary owned by a parent is treated as follows on the consolidated statements:
    a. It is listed as an investment.
    b. It is shown as treasury stock.
    c. It is treated as having been retired with an adjustment to paid-in capital.
    d. It is treated as retired with a gain or loss reflected in the income statement.

4. On September 1, 20X0, Phillips Inc. issued common stock in exchange for 20% of Sago Inc.'s outstanding common stock. On July 1, 20X2, Phillips issued common stock for an additional 75% of Sago's outstanding common stock. Sago continues in existence as Phillips' subsidiary. How much of Sago's 20X2 net income should be reported as accruing to Phillips?
    a. 20% of Sago's net income to June 30 and all of Sago's net income from July 1 to December 31
    b. 20% of Sago's net income to June 30 and 95% of Sago's net income from July 1 to December 31
    c. 95% of Sago's net income
    d. All of Sago's net income

5. Moss Corp. owns 20% of Dubro Corp.'s preferred stock and 80% of its common stock. Dubro's stock outstanding at December 31, 20X3, is as follows:

10% cumulative preferred stock	$100,000
Common stock	700,000

Dubro reported net income of $60,000 for the year ended December 31, 20X3. What amount should Moss record as equity in earnings of Dubro for the year ended December 31, 20X3?
    a. $42,000   b. $48,000   c. $48,400   d. $50,000

PART 3

Instructions: Describe the procedures that are necessary for consolidation in the following circumstances.

1. The parent acquires stock directly from the subsidiary and
    a. The parent acquires all of the stock.

    _____

    _____

    _____

    _____

    b. The parent acquires only a portion of the stock; the remaining stock is sold to an outside party for a price different from that paid by the parent.

    _____

    _____

    _____

    _____

2. The parent achieves control with the initial purchase and buys another block of stock.

    _____

    _____

    _____

3.   The parent does not achieve control with the initial purchase but makes a subsequent purchase that gives effective control to the parent.

4.   The subsidiary has preferred stock outstanding.

PART 4

Port Corporation acquired 10% of Dune Company's outstanding common stock on January 1, 20X2, when Dune had the following equity balances:

Common stock	$200,000
Retained earnings	250,000

Port paid $60,000 for the investment. Book values approximate market values. The resulting excess is assigned to a building and is to be amortized over 20 years.

On June 30, 20X5, Port acquired another 50% of Dune for $450,000, when Dune had the following equity balances:

Common stock	$200,000
Retained earnings, Jan. 1, 20X5	500,000

Dune's earnings for the period January 1–June 30 were $70,000. Equipment is undervalued by $50,000 and has a 5-year remaining life on the date of the second purchase. Any remaining excess is considered goodwill.

Instructions:

1. Complete the following determination and distribution of excess schedules:

10% Purchase

Price paid		
Less interest acquired:		
Common stock		
Retained earnings		
Total stockholders' equity		
Interest acquired	10%	
Excess of cost over book value		

50% Purchase

Price paid		
Less interest acquired:		
Common stock		
Retained earnings		
Income of Dune, Jan. 1 to June 30		
Total stockholders' equity		
Interest acquired	50%	
Excess of cost over book value		

2. Supply the simple equity conversion journal entry to update the original 10% investment to the simple equity method. (Conversion need not include income for current year, which may be recorded at year end.)

3.   Complete the following partial consolidated worksheet and the income distribution schedules:

Port Corporation and Subsidiary Dune Company
Partial Consolidated Worksheet
For Year Ended December 31, 20X5

| | Trial Balance | | Eliminations and Adjustments | | Minority Interest |
	Port	Dune	Dr.	Cr.	
Investment in Dune	657,200				
Building and equipment	600,000	250,000			
Accumulated depreciation	(300,000)	(125,000)			
Goodwill					
Common stock—Port	(800,000)				
Retained earnings—Port	(900,000)				
Common stock—Dune		(200,000)			
Retained earnings—Dune		(500,000)			
Sales	(600,000)	(557,000)			
Cost of goods sold	420,000	215,000			
Expenses	120,000	80,000			
Subsidiary income	(122,200)				
Purchased income					
Consolidated net income					
To NCI					
To controlling interest					

Eliminations and Adjustments:
(CY$_1$) Eliminate the current-year equity adjustment for subsidiary income.
(EL$_1$) Eliminate subsidiary equity from the January 20X2 purchase.
(D$_1$)   Distribute excess as determined in the January 20X2 determination and distribution of excess schedule.
(A$_1$)   Amortize January 20X2 excess for prior and current years.
(EL$_2$) Eliminate subsidiary equity balances for the June 20X5 purchase.
(D$_2$)   Distribute excess as determined in the June 20X5 determination and distribution of excess schedule.
      (1)   Equipment
      (2)   Goodwill
(A$_2$) Amortize the June 20X5 excess for one-half of the current year.

Subsidiary Dune Company Income Distribution

Building amortization	Internally generated income	
	Adjusted income	
	NCI share	40%
	NCI	

Parent Port Corporation Income Distribution

Less amortizations:	Internally generated net income
Building—Block 1	
Equipment—Block 2	
	Adjusted net income
	Share of first 1/2 year Dune income
	Share of second 1/2 year Dune income
	Controlling interest

PART 5

On January 1, 20X1, Pepper Company purchased 80% of the outstanding stock of Salt Company. The following determination and distribution of excess schedule was prepared:

Price paid		$875,000
Less interest acquired:		
Common stock	$350,000	
Retained earnings	613,750	
Total stockholders' equity	$963,750	
Interest acquired	80%	771,000
Excess of cost over book value		$104,000
Attributable to plant assets:		
80% x $30,000 (10-year amortization,		
$2,400 per year)		24,000
Patent (10-year amortization, $8,000 per year)		$ 80,000

Salt's reported income for the years 20X1, 20X2, and 20X3 was $112,500, $150,000, and $175,000, respectively. No dividends have been paid. Pepper accounts for the investment using the cost method.

Instructions: For each of the following cases, record the proper adjusting entry for the investment account and record the sale of the investment. All sales were made January 1, 20X4.

1. Pepper sells all of its investment in Salt for $1,250,000.

2. Pepper sells 60% of Salt's outstanding shares (75% of its interest) for $910,000.

3. Pepper sells 20% of Salt's outstanding shares (25% of its interest) for $300,000.

PART 6

On January 1, 20X4, Carry Corporation acquired a 60% interest in Kelley Corporation for $300,000. The following determination and distribution of excess schedule was prepared on the purchase date:

Price paid		$300,000
Less interest acquired:		
Common stock	$300,000	
Retained earnings	175,000	
Total common stockholders' equity	$475,000	
Interest acquired	60%	285,000
Goodwill		$ 15,000

On January 1, 20X7, Carry Corporation acquired 30% of Kelley's $100,000 cumulative preferred stock. Dividends were two years in arrears. The preferred stock was issued on January 1, 20X5, and bears a stated dividend rate of 6%. Carry Corporation paid $35,000 for the preferred stock.

Instructions:

1. Calculate the increase or decrease in equity on retirement of the preferred stock.

Price paid		
Less preferred interest acquired:		
Preferred stock		
Dividends in arrears		
Total preferred stockholders' equity		
Interest acquired	30%	
Increase (decrease) on retirement		

2.   Complete the following partial consolidated worksheet:

Carry Corporation and Subsidiary Kelley Corporation
Partial Consolidated Worksheet
For Year Ended December 31, 20X7

	Trial Balance		Eliminations and Adjustments	
	Carry	Kelley	Dr.	Cr.
Investment in Kelley common stock	300,000			
Investment in Kelley preferred stock	35,000			
Common stock—Carry	(800,000)			
Retained earnings—Carry	(1,500,000)			
Preferred stock—Kelley		(100,000)		
R. E. allocated to pref. stock				
Common stock—Kelley		(300,000)		
Retained earnings—Kelley		(612,000)		
Dividend income—common				
Dividend income—preferred	(1,800)			
Dividends declared—common				
Dividends declared—preferred		6,000		

Eliminations and Adjustments:
(P)   Segregate preferred shareholders' claim on retained earnings for dividends in arrears.
(CYP) Eliminate intercompany dividends on preferred stock.
(CV)   Convert investment in Kelley common stock to the equity method.
(EL)   Eliminate subsidiary common stock balances against investment in Kelley common stock.
(D)   Distribute excess according to the determination and distribution of excess schedule.
(ELP) Eliminate investment in Kelley preferred stock.

PART 7 (APPENDIX)

Following is a worksheet for a consolidated balance sheet only as of December 31, 20X6. Complete the worksheet using this information:

- Pam's 90% investment in Sy was purchased for $1,250,000 in cash on January 1, 20X6, and is accounted for by the cost method. On January 2, 20X6, Sy's retained earnings balance was $600,000, and its common stock balance was $200,000.

- The excess of cost over book value of Pam's investment in Sy was identified appropriately as attributable to the building and is being amortized over 20 years.

- Sy borrowed $100,000 from Pam on June 30, 20X6, with the 10% note maturing on June 30, 20X7. Correct accruals have been recorded by both companies.

- During 20X6, Pam sold merchandise to Sy at a total invoice price of $300,000, which included a profit of $60,000. At December 31, 20X6, Sy had not paid Pam for $90,000 of this merchandise, and 5% of the total merchandise purchased from Pam still remains in Sy's inventory.

- On July 1, 20X6, Sy sold Pam equipment for $50,000. Pam's cost was $60,000 and accumulated depreciation on the day of sale was $35,000. The remaining useful life was agreed to be 5 years.

Instructions: Complete the worksheet as necessary to produce the consolidated balance sheet of Pam Corporation and its subsidiary as of December 31, 20X6. Include the determination and distribution of excess schedule. Key all adjustments.

Pam Corporation and Subsidiary Sy Corporation
Worksheet for Consolidated Balance Sheet
For Year Ended December 31, 20X6

	Trial Balance		Eliminations and Adjustments		NCI	Consolidated Balance Sheet
	Pam	Sy	Dr.	Cr.		
Cash	65,000	25,000				
Accounts and other receivables	360,000	120,000				
Merchandise inventory	920,000	670,000				
Property, plant, and equipment (net)	1,000,000	400,000				
Investment in Sy Corporation	1,250,000					
Accounts payable and other current liabilities	(130,000)	(315,000)				
Common stock—Pam	(500,000)					
Retained earnings—Pam	(2,965,000)					
Common stock—Sy		(200,000)				
Retained earnings—Sy		(700,000)				
Total	0	0				
NCI						

Chapter 8   Subsidiary Equity Transactions: Indirect and Mutual Holdings

OUTLINE FOR REVIEW

Additional complications involving the recording and elimination of the parent's investment account are addressed.

I.   When the subsidiary declares and issues a stock dividend, the parent's ownership interest in the subsidiary remains unchanged.

    A.   Parent uses the simple or sophisticated equity method.

        1.   Parent records the receipt of the stock dividend as a memo entry acknowledging the number of shares received.

        2.   Parent records the equity income just as it did prior to the stock dividend.

    B.   Parent uses the cost method. To measure the parent's share of undistributed income for the conversion-to-equity adjustment, determine the parent's portion of the change in total subsidiary stockholders' equity.

II.   Certain transactions of the subsidiary affect the parent's investment, whether or not the parent is involved directly in the transaction.

    A.   When the subsidiary issues additional shares to the noncontrolling interest, the controlling interest ownership percentage is reduced. Such a transaction does not give rise to an income statement gain or loss.

        1.   An increase in the parent's investment account is recorded as a credit to the paid-in capital in excess account. A decrease in the investment account reduces paid-in capital in excess. Any amount not absorbable by paid-in capital in excess reduces retained earnings.

        2.   If the parent is using the equity method, it will adjust its investment for the change in the controlling interest at the time of the sale. The change is measured by the difference between the controlling interest subsequent to the stock sale and the controlling interest prior to the stock sale.

        3.   If the parent is using the cost method, the cost-to-equity conversion must account for the change in the controlling interest as a result of the subsidiary stock sale and the change in retained earnings for subsidiary income earned since the acquisition. Separate calculations must be made for the periods prior and subsequent to the sale. In each case, the applicable ownership percentage is used.

    B.   The parent may purchase some of the additional shares issued by the subsidiary.

        1.   If the parent acquires enough shares to exactly maintain its ownership interest, no additional equity adjustments are necessary. Increase the investment account for the price paid for the shares.

        2.   If the parent acquires new stock in excess of its presale ownership interest, the excess portion is treated as a new block of stock.

            a.   Prepare a determination and distribution of excess schedule for the purchase in excess of the prior ownership interest.

            b.   Future eliminations will be based on the new, increased ownership interest.

        3.   If the parent does not purchase enough stock to maintain its ownership interest, it must make an equity adjustment for the change in ownership interest.

            a.   The equity adjustment is measured by the change between the controlling interest in subsidiary shareholder equity subsequent to the sale and the prior interest, increased for the purchase cost of the new shares. The adjustment is to paid-in capital in excess unless there is a decrease that exceeds the available paid-in capital in excess. In this case, the retained earnings account is debited.

            b.   Future eliminations will be based on the new, lower ownership interest.

    C.   A subsidiary's purchase of its own stock is treated as if the parent purchased another block of stock. A determination and distribution of excess schedule is needed, and the investment is eliminated on the worksheet. The stock purchased should be recorded as treasury stock at cost to aid future worksheet eliminations.

    D.   The purchase and resale of stock by the subsidiary should be accounted for as two separate events using the above procedures. Where, however, the purchase and sale of treasury shares occur within the fiscal period, the parent ownership interest multiplied by the net change in equity may be accounted for as a debit or credit to the parent's paid-in capital in excess account.

III.   When a parent owns a controlling interest in a subsidiary, and the subsidiary purchases a controlling interest in another company, the parent company has an indirect holding in the subsidiary's acquisition.

     A.   When investments are accounted for using the equity method, equity adjustments to the investment account first must be made at the lowest level of holdings.

     B.   When investments are accounted for using the cost method, the equity conversion entries must first be made at the lowest level of holdings.

     C.   Eliminations on the consolidated worksheet are made from the highest to the lowest level of investment. This first determines the parent's interest in the retained earnings of the direct investment. This allows the NCI in the direct investment to be adjusted when the level-two investment is eliminated.

     D.   The income distribution schedules proceed from the lowest to the highest level of investment. This step-up procedure is necessary to ensure that the lower level income is "folded into" the income distribution schedule of the next highest level.

IV.   When the parent company acquires an interest in a subsidiary that already owns a controlling interest in another company, the parent is, in effect, purchasing a consolidated entity.

     A.   The determination and distribution of excess schedule must be based on the subsidiary's consolidated balance sheet.

         1.   The parent's ownership equity interest is based on its direct subsidiary's controlling retained earnings. The subsidiary's retained earnings must be adjusted for its share of income of its subsidiary, less amortizations of excess.

         2.   Adjustment to the valuation of a level-one asset is made for the direct ownership percentage of the change in valuations.

         3.   Adjustments to the valuation of a level-two asset are based only on the parent's share of its subsidiary's share of the under- and overvaluation.

         4.   Goodwill is based on the consolidated asset values.

     B.   Elimination and income distribution schedule procedures are the same as those described in "III."

V.   Mutual holdings exist when a subsidiary owns any of the outstanding shares of its parent. From a consolidated viewpoint, these shares have been taken off the market and must be eliminated. The shares do not receive any portion of consolidated income.

     A.   The treasury stock approach to consolidation is used when the subsidiary uses consideration other than its own shares to acquire the parent company shares.

         1.   The equity account adjustments, as a result of the treasury stock transactions, fall entirely on the parent.

         2.   The subsidiary makes no equity adjustments to its investment in the parent—it remains at cost.

         3.   On the consolidated worksheet, reclassify the subsidiary's investment in parent as treasury stock.

     B.   The stock swap method is used when the subsidiary issues its shares as consideration for the parent company shares.

         1.   The parent shares are translated into the equivalent number of subsidiary shares. The added subsidiary shares are treated as an acquisition of newly issued subsidiary shares.

         2.   The effect of the added purchase of shares is a new block of subsidiary shares with a new excess of cost or book value.

         3.   The investment in the parent is transferred to the investment in subsidiary account.

         4.   The current-year equity adjustments are eliminated on both investment blocks.

         5.   The combined investment amount is eliminated against the subsidiary equity and the excess is distributed.

PART 1

Instructions: Use a check mark to indicate whether each of the following statements is true or false.

                                                            True   False

1.   When the parent receives a stock dividend, it acknowledges the receipt by increasing the value of the investment by the fair market value of the shares issued.   _____   _____

2.   The equity conversion for an investment maintained at cost must include an increase to the parent's retained earnings for the parent's share of the amount of retained earnings transferred to the subsidiary's paid-in capital in excess as a result of a stock dividend.   _____   _____

3. When shares from an additional subsidiary stock issue are sold only to the NCI shareholders for a price greater than the book value per share, the dollar amount of the controlling interest increases. _____ _____

4. When the controlling interest changes as a result of a subsidiary stock sale, the gain or loss on the transaction may be recognized in the parent's income statement. _____ _____

5. Additional equity adjustments are not needed when the parent purchases a portion of the additional subsidiary stock issue. _____ _____

6. When a subsidiary purchases its own shares from noncontrolling shareholders and retires its shares, the parent will need to make an equity adjustment. _____ _____

7. When making conversion entries for indirect holdings maintained at cost, converting the lowest level investment first will allow for a proper accounting for retained earnings at the higher levels. _____ _____

8. When a level-two holding exists at the time of the level-one acquisition, the determination and distribution of excess schedule will include a portion of the under- or overvaluation of the level two assets. _____ _____

9. Under the treasury stock method of accounting for a mutual holding, the subsidiary is viewed as having a right to a portion of the parent's income. _____ _____

10. Using the parent's share of the total change in the subsidiary equity for determining the equity conversion amount subsequent to a stock dividend works well if there have been no sales or retirements of subsidiary shares affecting the subsidiary equity. _____ _____

11. When a parent purchases additional subsidiary shares in excess of that which would maintain its ownership percentage, a determination and distribution of excess schedule is prepared for all the shares acquired. _____ _____

PART 2

Instructions: Circle the letter that identifies the best response to each question. (Items 4–6 are AICPA adapted.)

1. Parent Company owns an 80% interest in Subsidiary Company. The subsidiary declares a 10% stock dividend. The result is:
    a. Parent Company has income equal to the market value of the shares received.
    b. Parent Company adjusts the carrying value of its investment and adjusts its paid-in capital.
    c. Parent Company's investment account is not affected.
    d. Parent Company records a decrease in its investment.

2. Parent Company owns an 80% interest in the Subsidiary Company. The subsidiary issues additional shares, none of which are purchased by the parent. The shares were sold at a price in excess of their book value. What is the impact on the parent company?
    a. Increase in investment, increase in paid-in capital in excess
    b. Increase in investment, income statement gain
    c. Decrease in investment, since percentage ownership decreased
    d. No effect

3. Baker owns an 80% interest in Cable Company. Able purchases a 70% interest in Baker. The price paid for the interest in Baker is in excess of the book value. Cable has a machine that has a book value $10,000 less than market value. In the consolidation process, the machine should be adjusted:
    a. $10,000   b. $5,600   c. $8,000   d. $0

4. Pride Inc. owns 80% of Simba Inc.'s outstanding common stock. Simba, in turn, owns 10% of Pride's outstanding common stock. What percentage of the common stock cash dividends declared by the individual companies should be reported as dividends declared in the consolidated financial statements?

	Dividends Declared by Pride	Dividends Declared by Simba
a.	90%	0%
b.	90%	20%
c.	100%	0%
d.	100%	20%

5. Sun Inc. is a wholly owned subsidiary of Patton Inc. On June 1, 20X3, Patton declared and paid $1 per share cash dividend to stockholders of record on May 15, 20X3. On May 1, 20X3, Sun bought 10,000 shares of Patton's common stock for $700,000 on the open market, when the book value per share was $30. What amount of gain should Patton report from this transaction in its consolidated income statement for the year ended December 31, 20X3?
    a. $0   b. $390,000   c. $400,000   d. $410,000

6. Mr. and Mrs. Gasson own 100% of the common stock of Able Corp. and 90% of the common stock of Baker Corp. Able previously paid $4,000 for the remaining 10% interest in Baker. The condensed December 31, 20X7, balance sheets of Able and Baker are as follows:

	Able	Baker
Assets	$600,000	$60,000
Liabilities	$200,000	$30,000
Common stock	100,000	20,000
Retained earnings	300,000	10,000
	$600,000	$60,000

In a combined balance sheet of the two corporations at December 31, 20X7, what amount should be reported as total stockholders' equity?
    a. $430,000   b. $426,000   c. $403,000   d. $400,000

PART 3

On January 2, 20X3, Patton Company acquired an 80% interest in the outstanding stock of Kern Company. At that time, the following determination and distribution of excess schedule was prepared:

Price paid		$350,000
Less interest acquired:		
Common stock ($25 par)	$125,000	
Retained earnings	300,000	
Total stockholders' equity	$425,000	
Interest acquired	80%	340,000
Goodwill		$ 10,000

On January 3, 20X5, Kern declared and distributed a 5% stock dividend. On that date, Kern common stock had a market value of $30 per share. Prior to the declaration of the stock dividend, Kern had the following equity balances:

Common stock ($25 par)	$125,000
Retained earnings	500,000
Total stockholders' equity	$625,000

During 20X5, Kern's earnings were $50,000.

Instructions:

1. Prepare a schedule showing the composition of Kern shareholders' equity subsequent to the stock dividend distribution.

2. Assuming that Patton uses the cost method, prepare the equity conversion entry needed to convert the investment to its January 1, 20X6, simple equity balance on the 20X6 worksheet.

Computations:

PART 4

On January 1, 20X7, Jeff purchased 80% of the outstanding stock of Jacklin. The following determination and distribution of excess schedule was prepared:

Price paid		$700,000
Less interest acquired:		
Common stock ($5 par)	$300,000	
Retained earnings	400,000	
Total stockholders' equity	$700,000	
Interest acquired	80%	560,000
Goodwill		$140,000

In 20X8, Jacklin issued 4,000 shares of previously unissued stock. Prior to the issuance of the additional shares, Jacklin's equity balances were:

Common stock ($5 par)	$300,000
Retained earnings	450,000
Total stockholders' equity	$750,000

All shares are sold to the noncontrolling interest.

Instructions:

1. Use the following table to determine the change in ownership interest for a sale of shares at each of the indicated prices:

	Case 1	Case 2	Case 3
Sales price per share	$5	$12.50	$15
Jacklin equity prior to sale	$750,000	$750,000	$750,000
Add to common stock ($5 par)			
Add to paid-in capital in excess of par			
Jacklin equity subsequent to sale			
Controlling interest subsequent to sale			
Prior controlling interest (80% x $750,000)	600,000	600,000	600,000
Net change in controlling interest			

2. Assume that Jacklin sold the 4,000 additional shares for $15 per share. Without regard to part (a) of this problem, determine the change in ownership interest for the following three cases, assuming that Jeff purchases the number of additional shares indicated. Use the format shown here and prepare a determination and distribution of excess schedule if necessary. Provide the journal entries for all three cases.
    (1) Jeff purchases 3,200 of the additional shares.
    (2) Jeff purchases 4,000 of the additional shares.
    (3) Jeff purchases 2,000 of the additional shares.

	(1) Maintain Interest	(2) Increase Interest	(3) Decrease Interest
Shares purchased	3,200	4,000	2,000
Total shares after purchase	51,200	52,000	50,000
Subsidiary equity after sale	$810,000	$810,000	$810,000
Ownership percent	_____	_____	_____
Ownership amount	_____	_____	_____
Subsidiary equity prior to sale	$750,000	$750,000	$750,000
Ownership percent	80%	80%	80%
Ownership amount	$600,000	$600,000	$600,000
Change in interest resulting from purchase	_____	_____	_____
Price paid ($15 per share)	_____	_____	_____
Excess of price over change in interest	_____	_____	_____

Entries: 1.

2.

3.

PART 5

On January 1, 20X3, Pine Corporation acquired 60% of Isle Corporation for $306,000. At that time, the following determination and distribution of excess schedule was prepared:

Price paid		$306,000
Less interest acquired:		
Common stock ($10 par)	$100,000	
Paid-in capital	60,000	
Retained earnings	300,000	
Total stockholders' equity	$460,000	
Interest acquired	60%	276,000
Goodwill		$ 30,000

On January 1, 20X5, Isle purchased 2,000 shares of its outstanding stock for $64 per share. Prior to the stock purchase, Isle had the following stockholders' equity:

Common stock ($10 par)	$100,000
Paid-in capital	60,000
Retained earnings	450,000
Total stockholders' equity	$610,000

The excess of the price paid over book value represents goodwill.

Instructions:

1. Record Isle's entry to purchase 2,000 shares at $64 per share.

2. Prepare the worksheet eliminations that would be made on the December 31, 20X5, trial balance working paper. Assume that Pine's investment in Isle is carried at cost.

Determination and Distribution of Excess Schedule for Treasury Stock

Price paid	$
Interest acquired	_____
Goodwill	$_____

60% interest eliminations:

Treasury stock eliminations:

PART 6

On January 1, 20X1, Sub-Par Incorporated purchased a 60% interest in Sub Company for $110,000. The purchase price represented a $10,000 excess of cost over book value, which was attributed to goodwill. The investment is maintained under the simple equity method.

On January 1, 20X3, Par Company purchased a 70% interest in Sub-Par Incorporated for $325,000. The equities of Sub-Par Incorporated and Sub Company on January 1, 20X3, prior to the purchase are as follows:

Stockholders' Equity	Sub-Par	Sub
Common stock ($5 par)	$150,000	—
Common stock ($10 par)	—	$100,000
Paid-in capital in excess of par	90,000	20,000
Retained earnings	165,000	80,000
Total stockholders' equity	$405,000	$200,000

An analysis of balance sheet values indicates that:

(a) Sub Company has land that has a market value of $10,000 in excess of cost.
(b) Sub-Par Incorporated has equipment that has a market value of $15,000 in excess of book value. Goodwill remaining from the purchase of Sub Company is not overstated.

(c)   All other assets and liabilities have market values similar to book values.

(d)   Sub-Par's retained earnings include simple equity income adjustments.

Instructions:

1.   Prepare a determination and distribution of excess schedule for the January 1, 20X3, purchase of the 70% interest in Sub-Par Incorporated by Par Company.

2.   On January 1, 20X4, Sub Company sold a machine with a cost to construct of $20,000 to Par Company for $30,000. The machine has a 5-year life. Prepare the worksheet adjusting entry needed as a result of the machine sale for a trial balance worksheet prepared as of December 31, 20X5.

PART 7

On December 31, 20X2, Ott Corporation acquired 75% of the outstanding stock of Basket Company. At that time, the following determination and distribution of excess schedule was prepared:

Price paid		$490,000
Less interest acquired:		
Common stock ($5 par)	$500,000	
Retained earnings	100,000	
Total stockholders' equity	$600,000	
Interest acquired	75%	450,000
Equipment (10-year life)		$ 40,000

On January 1, 20X5, Basket purchased a 15% interest in Ott for $187,500. The price paid for the investment reflects the underlying value in Ott equity.

During 20X5, Basket sold $60,000 of merchandise to Ott at cost plus 50%. $18,000 of the inventory is still on hand on December 31, 20X5.

Instructions: Complete the following partial worksheet and income distribution schedules, using the treasury stock method and assuming that both companies use the simple equity method.

Subsidiary Basket Income Distribution

	Internally generated net income
	Adjusted income
	NCI share
	NCI

Parent Ott Income Distribution

	Internally generated net income
	Total controlling interest

Ott Corporation and Subsidiary Basket Company
Partial Consolidated Worksheet—Treasury Stock Method
For Year Ended December 31, 20X5

	Trial Balance		Eliminations and Adjustments		NCI	Controlling Retained Earnings	Consolidated Balance Sheet
	Ott	Basket	Dr.	Cr.			
Current assets	738,750	545,833					
Investment in Basket (75%)	590,000						
Investment in Ott (15%)		187,500					
Equipment (net)							
Common stock—Ott	(750,000)						
Retained earnings—Ott	(500,000)						
Common stock—Basket		(500,000)					
Retained earnings—Basket		(208,333)					
Sales	(250,000)	(175,000)					
Cost of goods sold	160,000	100,000					
Expenses	30,000	50,000					
Subsidiary income	(18,750)						
Treasury stock							
	0	0					
Consolidated net income							
To NCI							
To controlling interest							
Total NCI							
Retained earnings, controlling interest, Dec. 31, 20X5							

Eliminations and Adjustments:
(CY₁) Eliminate the entry to record Ott's share of Basket subsidiary income.
(EL) Eliminate 75% of Basket equity balances against the investment in Basket.
(D)   Distribute the excess according to the determination and distribution of excess schedule.
(A)   Depreciate equipment for the current and prior years.
(TS) Reclassify investment in Ott to treasury stock.
(IS) Eliminate intercompany sales.
(EI) Eliminate ending inventory profit.

Special Appendix 1 Leveraged Buyouts

OUTLINE FOR REVIEW

A leveraged buyout is a unique purchase of an existing firm by a newly formed corporation created specifically to take over the exiting firm.

I.   The shares acquired from members of the former controlling group who are also members of the new controlling group are valued at their equity-adjusted cost to these owners. See the appendix coverage of Fair Value Block for exceptions that require the shares to be recorded at market value.

II.   If at least 80% of the consideration given to the former owners who are not part of the new control group is cash, all the shares acquired from this group are recorded at fair value.

III.   If the 80% test is not met, only those shares acquired for cash are recorded at fair value; the remaining shares are recorded at their existing book value.

PART 1

Pry Company was organized in December of 20X1. Two thousand shares of $1 par common stock were sold to the organizers for $30 each. The target company was Nail Inc., which had the following balance sheet on January 1, 20X2:

Current assets	$ 80,000	Long-term debt	$150,000
Equipment (net)	120,000	Common stock ($1 par)	10,000
Building (net)	150,000	Paid-in excess	90,000
		Retained earnings	100,000
	$350,000		$350,000

Pry Company borrowed $240,000 and used the funds plus cash on hand to buy 8,000 Nail shares at $35 each from shareholders who are not a part of the new control group. Two thousand Pry shares were exchanged for 2,000 Nail shares. Fifteen hundred of the shares belonged to continuing former shareholders who are now part of the new control group. Five hundred shares were from continuing former shareholders who are not part of the new control group. The simple-equity-adjusted cost of all former shareholders is $30.

All assets have a fair value equal to book value. Any excess cost is attributable to goodwill.

Instructions:

1. Calculate the total value to be assigned to the net assets of Nail Inc.

2. Prepare the determination and distribution of excess schedules.

Determination and Distribution of Excess Schedule
for 8,500 Shares at Fair Value

Price paid	_____
Equity	_____
Goodwill	_____

Determination and Distribution of Excess Schedule
for 1,500 Shares at Equity-Adjusted Cost

Price paid   _____
Equity   _____
Goodwill   _____

3.   Prepare the entry to record the formation of Pry Company.

4.   Prepare the entry to record the debt assumed by Pry Company.

5.   Prepare the entry to record the acquisition of Pry's interest in Nail Inc.

Special Appendix 2
Analysis of FASB Exposure Drafts for Business Combinations by Impact on Chapters 1–8

OUTLINE FOR REVIEW

Chapter 1

Following is a comparison of procedures as they exist and as they may result from contemplated FASB changes:

Existing Procedures	Possible New Procedures
Price includes direct acquisition costs.	Direct acquisition costs are expensed.
Contingent goodwill can be recorded at a later date when the contingency is resolved.	The contingent consideration is to be estimated and recorded as a liability at the time of purchase. Any adjustment impacts income of future periods.
Assignment of price paid: <ul><li>Price in excess of fair value of net assets results in goodwill.</li><li>Price greater than net priority assets but less than fair value of total net assets results in allocation of excess of price over net priority accounts to be allocated to nonpriority assets.</li><li>Price below net priority assets results in extraordinary gain.</li></ul>	Assignment of price paid: <ul><li>Price in excess of fair value of net assets results in goodwill (no change).</li><li>Price less than fair value of net assets results in ordinary gain.</li><li>There is no identification of accounts as priority or nonpriority.</li></ul>

Chapters 2 and 3

The "possible new procedures" from Chapter 1 are applied to the entire company acquired. The NCI is increased to fair value.

When the price paid exceeds the parent's percentage of the fair value of the subsidiary net assets:
- All accounts are adjusted to 100% of fair value regardless of the parent ownership percentage. The NCI is adjusted for its percentage of the adjustment.
- The goodwill applicable to the NCI is assumed to be proportional to that recorded for the controlling interest. That presumption can be overcome by evidence that indicates that the goodwill applicable to the NCI is less, in which case a lower amount of goodwill can be recorded for the NCI.

When the price paid is less than the parent's percentage of the fair value of the subsidiary net assets:
- All accounts are adjusted to 100% of fair value regardless of the parent ownership percentage. The NCI is adjusted for its percentage of the adjustment.
- A gain is recorded for the excess of the parent's percentage of net subsidiary net assets at fair value over the price paid. The NCI does not share in the gain.

Since assets subject to depreciation or amortization are adjusted to 100% of fair value, the NCI will share in the amortization of excesses.

Chapters 4–6

There are no significant changes to the content of these chapters except as they result from the changes to Chapters 2 and 3.

Chapter 7

The new procedures for block acquisitions would be:
- Control with the second block—The prior interest is adjusted to fair value and added to the block purchased to form a single price for the combined interest.
- Control with the first block—The later purchase is treated as a retirement of a portion of the NCI. A price less than the value of the NCI is a credit to paid-in excess of the controlling interest. A price greater than the value of the NCI is a debit to existing paid-in excess from retirements to the extent it exists. Any remaining amount is a debit to controlling retained earnings.

The sale of an interest by the parent company changes as follows:
- If a portion of the investment is maintained, but control is lost, the remaining interest is adjusted to fair value. The gain/loss on the sale includes both the shares sold and retained.
- If a portion of the shares are sold and control is retained, the transaction is treated as a retirement of the NCI shares. When the price paid is less than the value of the NCI, there is a credit to paid-in excess from retirement. If the price is greater, the debit would be to existing paid-in excess from retirement to the extent possible. Any remaining debit is to controlling retained earnings.

Chapter 8

The parent's ownership interest is calculated before and after the sale of additional subsidiary shares. The ownership interest is based on the value of the subsidiary established on the date control was achieved.
- If the parent buys some of the newly issued shares, the comparison is between the parent's ownership interest before the sale, plus the price paid for new shares, to the parent ownership interest after the sale.
- If there is an increase in the parent's position, the credit is to paid-in excess. If there is a decrease, the debit is to controlling retained earnings.

PART 1

Shopcom Inc. had the following balance sheet on January 1, 20X1:

Assets		Liabilities and Equity	
Accounts receivable	$ 50,000	Accounts payable	$ 40,000
Inventory	100,000	Bonds payable	100,000
Equipment (net)	200,000	Common stock, $1 par	10,000
Building (net)	400,000	Paid-in capital in excess of par	290,000
		Retained earnings	310,000
Total	$ 750,000	Total	$ 750,000

Fair values are as follows:

Accounts receivable	$ 50,000
Inventory	120,000
Equipment	300,000
Building	500,000
Patent	200,000
Accounts payable	40,000
Bonds payable	102,000

Instructions:

1. Assume the parent purchases the net assets of Shopcom Inc. for $750,000. Compare the journal entry for the purchase under existing versus proposed rules. Support your entry with appropriate zone or value analysis.

    Zone Analysis

Existing Rules	Dr.	Cr.	Proposed Rules	Dr.	Cr.

2. Assume the parent purchases the net assets of Shopcom Inc. for $ 20,000. Compare the journal entry for the purchase under existing versus proposed rules. Support your entry with appropriate zone or value analysis.

    Zone Analysis

Existing Rules	Dr.	Cr.	Proposed Rules	Dr.	Cr.

PART 2

Pearl purchased an 80% interest in the Sapphire Company on January 1, 20X4. On that date, Sapphire had the following balance sheet:

Assets		Liabilities and Equity	
Current assets	$190,000	Current liabilities	$100,000
Land	100,000		
Buildings	300,000		
Accumulated depreciation	(60,000)	Common stock—par	100,000
Equipment	300,000	Paid-in, excess of par	200,000
Accumulated depreciation	(30,000)	Retained earnings	400,000
	$800,000	Total	$800,000

Market values, which differed from book values on the purchase date, are:

Land	$120,000
Buildings	380,000 , 20-year remaining life, straight line
Equipment	300,000 , 10-year remaining life, straight line

Any remaining excess was attributed to goodwill.

Instructions:

1. Assuming that the parent pays $900,000 for its 80% interest, prepare a D&D schedule for the purchase, which includes revaluation of the NCI.

Value Analysis Schedule	Parent Price (80%)	NCI Value (20%)	Implied Company Value
1. Company fair value	$900,000		
2. Fair value of net assets excluding goodwill			
3. Goodwill—Fair value of company exceeds fair value of net assets excluding goodwill.			
4. Gain—Parent price is less the parent share of fair value of net assets excluding goodwill.			

Determination and Distribution of Excess Schedule	Implied Company Value	Parent Price	NCI Value	Worksheet Distribution
Fair value of subsidiary		$900,000		
Less book value interest acquired:				
Common stock, $1 par				
Paid-in excess of par				
Retained earnings				
Total equity				
Interest acquired				
Book value				
Excess of fair value over book value				
Adjustment of identifiable accounts:				
Land				
Buildings				
Equipment				
Goodwill				
Gain				
Total				

2. Assume the price paid is $580,000 for 80% interest.

Value Analysis Schedule	Parent Price (80%)	NCI Value (20%)	Implied Company Value
1. Company fair value	$580,000		
2. Fair value of net assets excluding goodwill			
3. Goodwill—Fair value of company exceeds fair value of net assets excluding goodwill.			
4. Gain—Parent price is less the parent share of fair value of net assets excluding goodwill.			

Determination and Distribution of Excess Schedule	Implied Company Value	Parent Price	NCI Value	Worksheet Distribution
Fair value of subsidiary		580,000		
Less book value interest acquired:				
Common stock, $1 par				
Paid-in excess of par				
Retained earnings				
Total equity				
Interest acquired				
Book value				
Excess of fair value over book value				
Adjustment of identifiable accounts:				
Land				
Buildings				
Equipment				
Goodwill				
Gain				
Total				

PART 3
(Revised Version of Chapter 3, Part 5)

On January 1, 20X5, Payrol Company purchased 80% of the outstanding common stock of Johnson Company for $1,500,000. The determination and distribution schedule prepared on the date of the purchase using current procedures was as follows:

Price paid for investment in Johnson		$1,500,000
Less interest acquired:		
Common stock, $1 par	$1,000,000	
Paid-in capital in excess	300,000	
Retained earnings	400,000	
Total stockholders' equity	$1,700,000	
Interest acquired	80%	1,360,000
Excess of cost over book (debit balance)		$ 140,000
Adjustments:		
Inventory (80% x $10,000)		8,000 Dr.
Equipment (80% x $50,000)		
(8-year amortization, $5,000 per year)		40,000 Dr.
Patents (80% x $100,000)		
(10-year amortization, $8,000 per year)		80,000 Dr.
Goodwill		$ 12,000 Dr.

During 20X5, all of the inventory was sold by Johnson Company.

Instructions:

1. Prepare a revised determination and distribution of excess schedule under the proposed rules.

Determination and Distribution of Excess Schedule				
	Implied Company Value	Parent Price	NCI Value	Worksheet Distribution
Fair value of subsidiary				
Less book value interest acquired:				
Common stock, $1 par	1,000,000			
Paid-in excess of par	300,000			
Retained earnings	400,000			
Total equity	1,700,000			
Interest acquired		80.00%	20.00%	
Book value		1,360,000	340,000	
Excess of fair value over book value				
Adjustment of identifiable accounts:				Amort. per year
Inventory				
Equipment				
Patent				
Goodwill				
Gain (not applicable)				
Total				

2. Complete the following consolidated worksheet for the year ending December 31, 20X7, and the income distribution schedules. Payrol Company uses the cost method to account for its investment in Johnson Company.

Eliminations and Adjustments:

CV   Convert from the cost to the equity method as of January 1, 20X7.

CY_2 Eliminate intercompany dividends.

EL   Eliminate subsidiary equities.

NCI   Adjust NCI to fair value

D   Distribute the excess cost.

Distribute adjustment to fair value as given by the determination and distribution schedule:

    (1)   Decrease retained earnings for inventory sold.

    (2)   Increase equipment.

    (3)   Increase patents.

    (4)   Increase goodwill.

A   Record amortizations resulting from the revaluations:

    (1)   No amortization necessary.

    (2)   Record annual increase in equipment depreciation for the current and past two years.

    (3)   Record annual increase in patent amortization for the current and past two years.

Payrol Company and Subsidiary Johnson Company
Worksheet for Consolidated Balance Sheet
For Year Ended December 31, 20X7

	Trial Balance		Eliminations and Adjustments		Consolidated Income Statement	NCI	Controlling Retained Earnings	Consolidated Balance Sheet
	Payrol	Johnson	Dr.	Cr.				
Cash	654,000	505,000						
Equipment (net)	1,290,000	940,000						
Patents	195,000	35,000						
Other assets	1,720,000	730,000						
Investment in Johnson Company	1,500,000							
Goodwill								
Accounts payable	(550,000)	(205,000)						
Common stock—Payrol ($5 par)	(2,000,000)							
Paid-in capital in excess—Payrol	(1,200,000)							
Retained earnings—Payrol 1/1/X7	(1,255,000)							
Common stock—Johnson ($1 par)		(1,000,000)						
Paid-in capital in excess—Johnson		(300,000)						
Retained earnings—Johnson 1/1/X7		(580,000)						
Sales	(1,100,000)	(425,000)						
Costs of goods sold	470,000	170,000						
Other expenses	250,000	100,000						
Dividend income	(24,000)							
Dividends declared	50,000	30,000						
Total	0	0						
Consolidated net income								
To NCI								
To controlling interest								
Controlling retained earnings, December 31, 20X7								

Subsidiary Johnson Company Income Distribution

Equipment depreciation Patent amortization	Internally generated net income
	Adjusted income NCI share
	NCI

Parent Payrol Company Income Distribution

	Internally generated net income 80% x Johnson Company adjusted income
	Controlling interest

Chapter 9   The International Accounting Environment

Outline for Review

Movement toward a global economy influences the development of accounting and the need for harmonization.

I. A global economy has become a reality for a number of countries and their business entities.
    A. As our global economy develops, it becomes apparent that goods and services, financial capital, and technology are being traded among a growing number of parties worldwide.
    B. It is only logical that financial information must also be exchanged on an international scale. Accounting must develop internationally in order to meet the needs of multinational companies, international capital markets, and international investors.
    C. An entity's involvement in international business can range from export or import activity to that of a multinational enterprise with a global approach to manufacturing, distribution, and sales.

II. The scope of international activity is quite varied and is influenced by a number of factors.
    A. The growth of the European Union has been a major factor in the formation of a single market, which is intended to serve the European community.
    B. The North American Free Trade Agreement (NAFTA) has reduced trade barriers between the United States, Canada, and Mexico.
    C. Securities of various companies are also being traded on an international basis.
    D. As international activity expands, there is an emerging need for international accounting standards that will provide information that can be used to make decisions on an international scale.

III. A separate area of international accounting has developed and is influenced by a variety of factors.
    A. There are several primary areas constituting the subject of international accounting, as follows:
        1. The identification and understanding of principles of financial accounting, managerial accounting, and taxation used in different nations, especially as to how they differ from nation to nation
        2. The identification of the various organizations and interests involved in the process of establishing international accounting and auditing principles and standards
        3. The special accounting valuation and recognition principles associated with accounting for transactions that are recorded in one nation's currency and settled in another nation's currency, referred to as foreign currency transactions
        4. The translation of financial statements that are measured in one nation's currency into another nation's currency
    B. There have been a variety of factors that have influenced the development of accounting as practiced in various nations.
        1. A major factor influencing the development of accounting principles has been the social and cultural values that differ between nations.
        2. The political and legal systems of a country have also been an influencing factor. For example, those countries that were colonized by another country tend to have developed accounting principles similar to those of the ruling nation.
        3. The type and pace of business activities and economic development of a country have also influenced accounting.
        4. The accounting standard-setting process and the respective views of the standard setters have certainly had an influence on how accounting has developed.
        5. The various forms of ownership and the development of capital markets influence the type of standards that are developed. As capital markets grow, accounting standards must also grow in order to meet the needs of users.
        6. Cooperative efforts between trading nations also influence the development of accounting standards. For example, NAFTA has placed a renewed interest in improving the comparability of accounting standards between the United States, Canada, and Mexico.

C. Several classification systems have been proposed as a means of analyzing the accounting standards of various nations. A classification system allows one to identify similarities and differences between various national accounting standards. One classification system uses cultural differences as the common denominator upon which to separate accounting standards.
1. Anglo-Saxon accounting: This category is identified with the United Kingdom, the United States, and countries that have been influenced by British colonization. The category is characterized by private standard setting, less conservative principles, less constrained by tax laws, and more financial disclosure.
2. Germanic accounting: This category is heavily influenced by the legal system, which is based on Roman law, and has a more conservative approach. Differences between accounting income and tax income are uncommon.
3. Nordic accounting: This category lies somewhere between Anglo-Saxon and Germanic accounting. The use of replacement-value accounting has been common.
4. Latin accounting: This category is heavily influenced by commercial laws and tax laws. Measurement principles tend to be very conservative, and the accounting profession in this category tends to be less developed than in other nations.
5. Asian accounting: This category has been influenced by several of the other categories due to the colonial history of the area. The government and tax laws have been a major influence. In the past, accounting had been more conservative and less open to disclosure. However, the development of Asian markets has resulted in more public disclosure.
D. Various accounting principles of several nations are presented in the textbook in order to illustrate some of the differences and similarities in principles.

IV. There are many factors that explain why similar transactions may receive different accounting treatments, depending on which nation's accounting standards are being followed. Differences in accounting treatment have a significant impact on the measurement and presentation of accounting information. Because of the importance and growth of international business activity, there are a number of parties who are interested in making accounting information more comparable through the harmonization of accounting principles.
A. The harmonization of accounting standards may take several approaches and is a combination of evolutionary and standard-setting processes.
1. One approach to harmonization involves developing bilateral agreements between two countries.
2. Another approach involves establishing standards on a regional basis, such as those developed by the European Union.
3. An additional approach involves an international standard-setting process that establishes standards that will be adopted by all countries.
B. The International Accounting Standards Board was created in 2001 and like its predecessor, the International Accounting Standards Committee, is a major force in the international accounting standard-setting process.
1. The trustees of the International Accounting Standards Committee (IASC) Foundation are the ultimate governing body and appoint the members of the International Accounting Standards Board (IASB), the Standards Interpretations Committee, and the Standards Advisory Board.
2. The IASB consists of 14 members and has responsibility for establishing a single set of international accounting standards now designated as International Financial Reporting Standards (IFRS). The International Accounting Standards (IAS) issued by the IASC have also been adopted by the IASB.
3. The IASB has received support from the Financial Accounting Standards Board (FASB). FASB has formally committed to the convergence of U.S. GAAP and international accounting standards.
a. Currently there are over 1,200 foreign companies registered with and reporting to the U.S. Securities and Exchange Commission. These companies may prepare their statements according to U.S. GAAP, IASB principles, or their own national principles. However, if these companies do not use U.S. GAAP, they must reconcile their basis of accounting to U.S. GAAP.
b. The convergence toward international accounting standards will continue in the United States as FASB moves forward with its convergence project.
C. The International Federation of Accountants (IFAC) is a private body that has over 150 members representing over 100 countries.
1. The IFAC is concerned primarily with aspects of the professional practice of accounting and represents accountants worldwide in all professional areas.
2. Rather than being involved in standard setting per se, the IFAC is focused on developing the profession and harmonizing its financial and auditing standards worldwide.

  D. The European Union (EU) is an alliance of nations that have come together to advance their common interests and consists of five major institutions, including the European Commission.
  1. The European Commission of the EU is the primary legislative body of the EU and has issued Directives on Company Law, which, in part, relate to accounting principles to be followed by member nations.
  2. With certain exceptions, all listed companies, including banks and insurance companies, within the EU are required to prepare their financial statements in accordance with IASs and IFRSs. EU members have the option as to whether such standards would be required of nonlisted companies.
V. There are a number of other international accounting issues of importance in addition to the harmonization of accounting standards.
  A. Transfer pricing is used to measure the value of goods and services conveyed between units of a multinational enterprise. The method of transfer pricing may serve a variety of purposes; for example, some relate to issues of taxation or the imposition of import/export tariffs or fees.
  B. The tax systems between nations also differ and must be understood by those parties involved in international business. For example, the value-added tax (VAT), which is common throughout Europe, is not employed in the United States.

PART 1

Instructions: Use a check mark to indicate whether each of the following statements is true or false.

	True	False
1. The Securities and Exchange Commission does not allow foreign registrants to submit statements that are presented on a basis other than U.S. GAAP.	_____	_____
2. Countries whose accounting principles do not differ significantly from tax laws and corporate commercial laws are probably more likely to have a standard-setting function that is independent of the government.	_____	_____
3. As the ownership base of an entity increases, its accounting principles would tend to increase in complexity and focus.	_____	_____
4. Anglo-Saxon accounting would be most descriptive of the accounting principles found in Sweden and Norway.	_____	_____
5. Both the North American Free Trade Agreement and the European Union are concerned with reducing trade barriers between trading nations.	_____	_____
6. The International Accounting Standards Board (IASB) would be more concerned with the establishment of international auditing standards than the International Federation of Accountants (IFAC).	_____	_____
7. The members of the European Union are free to allow their listed companies to follow national GAAP or principles developed by the IASB.	_____	_____
8. The value-added tax is often compared to the sales tax in the United States because the level of consumer on which the tax is assessed is similar.	_____	_____
9. If a multinational company were trying to shift profits to a foreign subsidiary due to the presence of a lower income tax structure, the company would establish high transfer prices if the domestic parent company imported goods from the foreign subsidiary.	_____	_____
10. International accounting only deals with issues that affect multinational enterprises.	_____	_____
11. The standards established by the IASB compete with the standards established by the IFAC.	_____	_____
12. The IASB's focus on the harmonization of accounting standards is centered around specific trading partners, which is similar to the efforts of the European Union.	_____	_____

PART 2

Instructions: Beside each of the following statements, write the letter that corresponds to the term that best characterizes the statement.

A. Exporting   F. Anglo-Saxon accounting

B. IFAC   G. Foreign currency transaction

C. IASC   H. European Union

D. Importing   I. International Financial Reporting Standards

E. Harmonization   J. U.S. GAAP

Term

1. The business activity engaged in by the parent of a foreign subsidiary that has instructed its subsidiary to establish lower transfer prices charged to the parent in order to reduce U.S. trade duties paid. _____

2. The category used to describe the accounting standards used in countries that were colonized by the United Kingdom. _____

3. A U.S. company purchasing raw materials from a French vendor with the amount due payable in euros. _____

4. Providing for comparable accounting standards among different nations. _____

5. The organization most interested in comparable accounting standards among specific trading nations. _____

6. An organization that has similar goals to the European Union, as they relate to accounting. _____

7. An organization that is concerned with the professional practice of accounting and is supported by more than 100 countries throughout the world. _____

8. The predecessor to the International Accounting Standards Board. _____

9. The statements issued by the International Accounting Standards Board and recognized along with International Accounting Standards issued by the IASC. _____

10. Foreign companies required to file statements with the U.S. Securities and Exchange Commission may be required to reconcile their statements to this. _____

Module   Derivatives and Related Accounting Issues

OUTLINE FOR REVIEW

Derivatives are used in a number of economic contexts, and accounting for them reflects various hedging strategies.

I.   Derivative instruments may be held as investments or as part of a strategy to reduce or hedge against exposure to risk associated with some other transaction.
   A.   Derivatives are defined by a number of characteristics.
      1.   A derivative instrument derives its value from *changes in* the *value* of a related asset or liability. The rates or prices that relate to the asset or liability underlying the derivative are referred to as *underlyings*.
      2.   The number of units (quantity) that is specified in a derivative instrument is referred to as the *notional amount* and is necessary in order to value a derivative. For example, an option to acquire stock at a given price can only be valued if the number of shares covered by the option is know.
      3.   Typically a derivative instrument requires little or no initial investments and frequently does not require the actual physical delivery of the asset that is associated with the underlying. Certain derivatives are embedded in another financial instrument.
   B.   Derivative instruments come in a variety of forms and vary in complexity. However, certain common forms of derivatives are encountered in a wide range of business settings.
      1.   A forward contract is an executory contract to buy or sell a specified amount of an asset at a specified fixed price with delivery at a specified future point in time.
         a.   The fixed price in the contract is known as the forward price or *forward rate.* The forward rate is different than the current rate, which is known as the *spot rate.*
         b.   The value of a forward contract is zero at inception of the contract. The value of a forward contract changes over time as measured by changes in the forward rate over time. The total change in the value of a forward contract is measured as the difference between the initial forward rate and the spot rate at the *forward date.* The value of the forward contract can increase or decrease over time resulting in a gain or loss and therefore is described as having a *symmetric return profile.*
         c.   Because the forward rate is a future value, the current value of a forward contract at a point in time is represented by the present value of the forward rate. At the contract's expiration date, the forward rate is equal to the spot rate because there is no more forward or future time remaining on the contract.
      2.   A futures contract is exactly like a forward contract in that it, too, provides for the receipt or payment of a specified amount of an asset at a specified price with delivery at a specified future point in time. However, a futures contract has several distinguishing characteristics.
         a.   Futures contracts are traded on organized exchanges and are standardized in nature rather than being customized contracts as is the case with a forward contract.
         b.   A futures contract requires an initial investment referred to as a *margin account.* A minimum balance in this account must be maintained and a margin call may be required in order to achieve the required minimum balance.
         c.   Future contracts are marked-to-market each day, and the price represents a present value, unlike the price of a forward contract that represents a future or forward value.
         d.   The party that writes a contract is said to be short, and the party that owns the contract is said to be long.
      3.   An option represents the right, rather than the obligation, to either buy or sell some quantity of an underlying at a specified price known as the *strike* or exercise *price.*
         a.   An option to buy a quantity is known as a *call option* and an option to sell a quantity is known as a *put option.*
         b.   The relationship between the strike price and the current price of the underlying defines whether the option does or does not have value (in-the-money and out-of-the-money respectively).

        c.   Noting that an option is a right versus an obligation, if an option remains out-of-the-money, the holder is not required to exercise the option. Therefore, an option is said to have an *asymmetric return profile.*

        d.   The current value of an option consists of the intrinsic value and/or the time value, which is a function of the spot prices and forward periods. The difference between the strike price and the spot price measures the *intrinsic value* of the option. Changes in the length of the remaining forward period will affect the *time value* of the option. The time value of an option represents a discounting factor and a volatility factor.

        e.   If an option can be exercised any time during a specified period it is referred to as an American option. A European option is only exercisable at the maturity date/expiration date of the option.

    4.   A swap is a customized type of forward contract represented by a contractual obligation that requires the exchange of cash flows between two parties. They are not traded on regulated exchanges.

        a.   The cash flows often take the form of swapping currencies such as swapping dollars for euros.

        b.   The cash flows being swapped could also represent the swap of interest payments. For example, a borrower with a loan requiring variable rate interest payments may swap those payments for making fixed rate interest payments. The borrower will make a fixed rate payment to a counterparty and receive a variable rate payment in exchange. The variable payment received will then be used to satisfy the payment due on the variable rate loan.

C.   Derivatives instruments may be acquired purely for investment purposes or as a hedging instrument. If an entity expects the value of its assets or liabilities to change in value over time, it would be desirable to avoid adverse changes in value. A way to offset, totally or partially, such adverse changes is to use a derivative as part of a hedging strategy.

D.   The concept behind a hedging strategy is that changes in the value of an asset or liability will be offset by changes in the value of the derivative hedging instrument. Hedges are generally designated as either a fair value hedge or a cash flow hedge.

II.   Fair value hedges hedge against a change in the fair value of a recognized asset or liability or hedge an unrecognized firm commitment. An unrecognized firm commitment is a binding agreement between two parties that specifies all significant terms related to the prospective transaction.

A.   Because the prices or rates of recognized assets or liabilities or unrecognized firm commitments are fixed, subsequent changes in prices or rates affect the value of the asset, liability, or commitment.

B.   If both increases and decreases in the value of an existing asset or liability are currently recognized per generally accepted accounting principles (for example, accounting for investments classified as a trading portfolio), the hedge of such items is not given special accounting treatment. However, if that is not the case, special accounting treatment is given fair value hedges.

C.   In order for a fair value hedge to receive special accounting treatment, a number of criteria must be satisfied.

    1.   The hedging relationship must have formal documentation of the hedging relationship and the entity's risk management objective and strategy. This criterion must be satisfied at inception of the hedging relationship.

    2.   The hedging relationship must be assessed both at inception and on an ongoing basis to determine if it is highly effective in offsetting the identified risks. Effectiveness may be assessed through critical term analysis or statistical analysis. The portion of a derivative instrument's value representing the time value may be excluded from the assessment of hedge effectiveness.

D.   Assuming the necessary criteria are satisfied, a fair value hedge can receive special accounting treatment characterized by a number of features.

    1.   The change in the value of the derivative hedging instrument will be recognized currently in earnings along with the change in the value of the hedged item.

    2.   The change in the value of the hedged item will be recognized by adjusting the carrying basis of the hedged item.

    3.   If the cumulative change in the value of the derivative instrument does not exactly offset the cumulative change in the value of the hedged item, the difference is recognized currently in earnings.

    4.   The special accounting treatment for a fair value hedge continues unless certain conditions occur. For example, if the hedging instrument is sold or the instrument is no longer highly effective, the special accounting treatment will stop.

E.   The logic behind hedging an existing asset or liability is obvious in that if the value of assets decreases or the value of liabilities increases, it would be desirable to offset the negative impact on equity with an increase in equity traceable to a fair value hedge. Obviously, one does not know in advance whether or not such adverse changes in value will occur; therefore, as a matter of policy, some entities automatically hedge selected assets and liabilities.

F. The logic behind hedging an unrecognized firm commitment may be less obvious. Because a commitment is firm, one is obligated to pay or receive a fixed rate or price (for example, a firm commitment to buy inventory at $2 per unit). If the rate or price of the subject of the commitment changes over time, the value of the commitment may also change. For example, the price of inventory that is the subject of a firm commitment subsequently decreases to $1.90 per unit signaling a possible writedown in the inventory when acquired. If a firm commitment loses value, a hedge could offset that decrease in value. For example, if an option to sell inventory were acquired, decreases in the per unit price of inventory would cause the value of the put option to increase. The suggested decrease in the value of the commitment and ultimately the value of the inventory acquired could be offset by the increase in the value of the option.

III. Cash flow hedges are generally associated with a hedge of a forecasted transaction or a recognized asset or liability with variable future cash flows. A forecasted transaction is one that is expected to occur in the future at a market price that will be in existence at the time of the transaction as compared to a price that has been previously determined (as in the case of a firm commitment).

A. Because fixed prices or rates are not present in a forecasted transaction of an asset or liability with variable future cash flows, there is risk that future cash flows may vary due to changes in prices or rates. A cash flow hedge is designed to hedge against this risk.

B. In order for a cash flow hedge to receive special accounting treatment, a number of criteria must be satisfied including those dealing with documentation and assessment of hedge effectiveness.

C. Assuming the necessary criteria are satisfied, a cash flow hedge can receive special accounting treatment characterized by a number of features.

1. The gain or loss on the hedging instrument will be reported in other comprehensive income (OCI) rather than being currently recognized in earnings. However, the ineffective portion of the hedge will be currently recognized in earnings.

2. Since the forecasted transaction or the future variable cash flows associated with a recognized asset or liability have not yet occurred, there is no accounting for those cash flows until they occur.

3. Once the forecasted cash flows or future variable cash flows actually occur, the resulting transaction signals the end of reporting changes in the derivative instrument as a component of OCI. In the period in which the actual transaction affects earnings, some or all of the OCI gain or loss will be reclassified as a component of earnings. For example, when a forecasted purchase of inventory occurs, the OCI item will be reclassified when that inventory is sold and affects earnings as a component of cost of sales.

IV. Entities that hold or issue derivative instruments are required to disclose the purpose for holding or issuing such instruments, the context needed to understand the objectives, and strategies for achieving the objectives. General disclosures are required for those instruments that are designated as hedges, and more detailed disclosures are required for both fair value and cash flow hedges.

PART 1

Instructions: Use a check mark to indicate whether each of the following statements is true or false.

		True	False
1.	In order to properly value a derivative instrument it is necessary to know the notional amount.	_____	_____
2.	A derivative instrument involving a futures contract to buy corn requires that the commodity actually be delivered.	_____	_____
3.	A forward contract to sell a foreign currency has increased in value if the forward rate is less than the current spot rate.	_____	_____
4.	The present value of a forward contract can only be determined if the forward rate is discounted to the present.	_____	_____
5.	A futures contract differs from a forward contract in that the former typically requires a margin account and is typically a standardized rather than customized contract.	_____	_____
6.	The value of an option can be allocated to two component parts, the time value and the intrinsic value.	_____	_____
7.	A put option and a call option refer to the right to buy and sell a quantity, respectively.	_____	_____
8.	If a put option at an exercise price of $12 per unit when the market value per unit is $13 has a value of $0.50 per option, then there is no time value associated with the option.	_____	_____
9.	An option related to a commodity with a lot of price volatility would tend to increase the time value of the option.	_____	_____
10.	If a borrower had debt financing requiring the payment of a fixed rate of interest, an interest rate swap would be prudent if it was assumed that variable interest rates were to increase over fixed interest rates.	_____	_____
11.	If a creditor with a loan bearing a variable rate of interest were to swap variable rates for fixed rates, their interest net cash flow would be the differential between the respective rates.	_____	_____
12.	If an entity were to acquire a derivative instrument purely for investment purposes, the investment would be marked-to-market with changes in value being recognized currently in earnings.	_____	_____

PART 2

Instructions: Use a check mark to indicate whether each of the following statements is true or false.

		True	False

1. Fair value hedges are hedges against the change in value of a recognized asset or liability or a forecasted transaction.

2. In order to qualify for special accounting treatment as a fair value hedge, the hedge must be highly effective.

3. The change in the value of a derivative instrument that is excluded from the assessment of effectiveness is recognized as a component of current period earnings.

4. If an option is used as a fair value hedge, its return profile is described as asymmetric whereas if it were used as a cash flow hedge its return profile would be described as symmetric.

5. Changes in the value of a fair value hedge are only sometimes recognized currently in earnings.

6. A cash flow hedge would be used with a forecasted transaction but not with a firm commitment.

7. Assume a firm commitment to sell 10,000 units of a commodity at a price of $2.10 per unit. If the current price per unit is $2.15, the commitment would have gained in value.

8. Given the above commitment, if a call option for a notional amount of 10,000 units were designated as a hedge on the firm commitment and deemed to be highly effective, changes in the value of the firm commitment would only be partially offset by the hedge.

9. A cash flow hedge is a hedge against the risk that future cash flows may vary due to changes in prices or rates.

10. An interest rate swap where variable interest payments are swapped for fixed interest payments would be an example of a cash flow hedge.

11. A cash flow hedge involving a forecasted purchase of raw materials could have the effect of protecting gross profit margins against declines due to increasing prices of raw materials.

12. The change in value of a cash flow hedge that is classified as a component of other comprehensive income will always be reclassified as a component of current period earnings when the underlying forecasted transaction occurs.

PART 3

The Monroe Corporation has a $500,000 note payable bearing interest at the rate of 6% with interest payments due quarterly. The note was dated 01/01/20X5 and matures in three years. In anticipation of declining variable interest rates, the company swaps fixed for variable rates beginning with the third quarter of 20X5. The reset variable rates were 5.6% and 5.2% at the beginning of the third and fourth quarters of 20X5, respectively.

Instructions: Determine the effect on the interest expense for the year 20X5 as a result of the swap.

PART 4

Jackson Industries has a firm commitment to buy 100,000 bushels of corn at $2.10 per bushel in 75 days. With 60 days prior to the sale date when corn is trading at $2.11 per bushel, the company acquires a forward contract to sell 100,000 bushels of corn in 60 days at a forward rate of $2.09 per bushel. After 30 days the spot rate is $2.10 per bushel and the 30-day forward rate is $2.08. When the commitment is settled, corn is selling for $2.07 per bushel.

Instructions: Assuming a discount rate of 6%, determine the gain or loss on the commitment and on the derivative instrument for the first 30 days of the forward contract and the last 30 days of the forward contract.

PART 5

On July 1, 20X5, the Merrill Milling Corporation forecasted that it would purchase 100,000 bushels of corn in 90 days. In order to protect itself against changes in the price of corn, on July 1, 20X5, the company acquired, at a cost of $700, a 90-day option to buy 100,000 bushels of corn at a strike price of $1.75 a bushel. Spot prices for a bushel of corn are as follows:

| 07/01/X5 | $1.74 | 08/31/X5 | $1.79 |
| 07/31/X5 | $1.77 | 09/30/X5 | $1.78 |

The option had a value at the end of July and August of $2,300 and $4,100, respectively. On 9/30/X5, the company purchased 100,000 bushels of corn at the spot rate. Sixty percent of the corn was milled and sold during the month of October 20X5.

Instructions: For each month during the period July through October calculate (a) the amount of the gain or loss to be reported as a component of other comprehensive income (OCI) and (b) the amount of hedge ineffectiveness to be reported in earnings. Assume that the time value of the option is excluded from assessment of hedge effectiveness.

Chapter 10   Foreign Currency Transactions

OUTLINE FOR REVIEW

Transactions denominated in a foreign currency must be properly recorded and reported by the domestic firm.

I.   When parties transact business, a decision must be made as to what currency should be used as a medium of exchange. Denominating a transaction in a currency other than an entity's reporting currency requires the establishment of exchange rates between currencies.

    A.   Several major international monetary systems have been established in the past that serve as a basis for setting rates of exchange between currencies.

        1.   Prior to 1944, the monetary system was the gold standard that provided a strict apolitical system based on gold.

        2.   In 1944, the International Monetary Fund (IMF) was created and a fixed-rate exchange system was adopted, which was abandoned in 1973.

        3.   At present, exchange rates are established in a floating system influenced by supply and demand and other factors.

    B.   An exchange rate is a measure of how much of one currency may be exchanged for another currency. Several terms are used to describe exchange rates.

        1.   A direct quote measures how much of the domestic currency must be exchanged to receive one unit of a foreign currency. Indirect quotes measure how many units of a foreign currency will be received for one unit of domestic currency.

        2.   A currency may either strengthen (gain) or weaken (lose) relative to another currency. A strengthening currency means that the direct quote amount decreases and the indirect quote amount increases. The opposite would be true for a weakening currency.

        3.   Buying and selling rates of exchange represent what a currency broker is willing to pay to acquire or to sell a currency, respectively.

        4.   A spot rate indicates the number of units of a currency that would be exchanged for one unit of another currency on a given date.

        5.   A forward rate establishes, at one point in time, the number of units of one currency to be exchanged for one unit of another currency at a specified future date. On a given date, different forward rates may exist for the same currency, depending on how far in the future an exchange is to take place.

            a.   The agreement to exchange currencies at a future date is called a forward contract.

            b.   A contract premium refers to when the forward rate is greater than the spot rate; a contract discount refers to when the foward rate is less than the spot rate.

II.   A foreign currency transaction is denominated in the currency required for settlement. A transaction is measured on the books of an entity in the currency in which those books are kept, regardless of the currency in which the transaction is denominated.

    A.   When a transaction is denominated in a foreign currency, fluctuations in the exchange rate will result in exchange gains and losses.

        1.   The amount of the exchange gain or loss is equal to the difference in exchange rates between the transaction date and the settlement date, multiplied by the foreign currency amount of the transaction.

        2.   Exchange gains or losses are generally required to be accounted for under the two-transaction method. This method accounts for the gains or losses separately from the basis of the initial transaction requiring settlement in a foreign currency.

        3.   If, at a reporting date, there are unsettled transactions denominated in a foreign currency, the receivable or payable balances related to those transactions must be adjusted to the amount required to settle them at that date, and an exchange gain or loss must be recognized for the difference between the spot rate on the date each transaction was recorded (or last adjusted) and the spot rate at the reporting date.

        4.   Exchange gains and losses of this type must be included in income in the period in which they occur.

    B.   To counteract, or hedge against, potential exchange gains or losses due to transactions denominated in a foreign currency, a company may choose to enter into a forward contract with a foreign currency broker to buy or sell the foreign currency to be paid or to be received when the transaction is settled.

1. The forward contract fixes the value of the obligation in terms of the domestic currency, using the forward rate for the specified amount of time until settlement as the contract rate.
2. If the forward rate exceeds the spot rate, the contract is at a premium. When the spot rate exceeds the forward rate, the contract is at a discount.
3. Subsequent to the transaction date, the gain (or loss) on the forward contract will offset the loss (or gain) on the transaction. The gain or loss on the forward contract is measured as the difference between the forward rate at inception of the contract and the spot rate at expiration of the contract.
4. Adjustments will be required at the end of the period if there is a forward contract to hedge a foreign currency transaction on the books. The forward contract receivable or payable (FC) must be adjusted for the difference between forward rates at the date of inception of the forward contract (or last adjustment date) and at the reporting date and the exchange gain or loss recorded.
5. Forward contracts may expire before or extend beyond the settlement date.
    a. Gains or losses on contracts expiring before the settlement date will partially offset losses or gains on the foreign currency transaction.
    b. Gains or losses on a contract that accrue after the settlement date do not offset losses or gains on the foreign currency transaction but are recognized as a component of current operating income.
    c. When the expiration date of the forward contract and the actual settlement date of the transaction do not coincide, it is often possible to roll the contract backward or forward.
6. Forward contracts may be for a lesser or greater number of foreign currency units than the foreign currency transaction.
    a. If for a lesser amount, the contract gain or loss is recognized as a partial hedge on the exposed position.
    b. If for a greater amount, the contract gain or loss traceable to that portion of the contract that exceeds the transaction amount is accounted for as a speculative hedge.
7. Although forward contracts are a common way to hedge a foreign currency transaction, a number of financial instruments may be used as a hedge. Many of these instruments are derivatives; that is, they derive their value from a related or underlying commodity or instrument. Derivatives have two distinguishing characteristics—one or more underlyings and one or more notional amounts.

C. A forward contract may also be used to hedge against the change in value of an identifiable foreign currency commitment due to exchange rate fluctuations between the commitment date and the date the transaction is recorded.
1. This type of hedge is referred to as a fair value hedge and must meet specific criteria in order to receive special accounting treatment.
2. If the criteria are met, the gain or loss on the fixed contract is recognized currently in earnings. The gain or loss on the contract prior to the transaction date is measured as the difference between the forward rate at inception of the contract (generally the commitment date) and the forward rate for the contract at the date of the transaction (i.e., the spot rate at the date of the transaction).
3. The gain or loss on the fixed contract recognized is offset by a corresponding loss or gain recognized on the financial instrument component of the firm commitment. The carrying amount of the hedged item is adjusted at the date of the transaction to the extent of the loss or gain recognized on the firm commitment.

D. Forward contracts may also be entered into for strictly speculative purposes.
1. The investor need not hold the contracts until maturity but may buy and sell the contracts, rather than the actual foreign currency, as they change in value.
2. A gain or loss on a speculative forward contract is based on the difference between the forward rates—for the appropriate length of time—at the date the forward contract is entered into (or last adjusted) and the date the contract is sold (or the period ends).
3. Exchange gains or losses due to speculation are included in current income.

E. A forecasted transaction may also be hedged through the use of a forward contract or other types of derivatives.
1. This type of hedge is referred to as a cash flow hedge and must meet specific criteria in order to receive special accounting treatment.
2. If the criteria are met, the gain or loss on the hedging instrument prior to the transaction or commitment date is not recognized in current earnings. Rather, the gain or loss is included in other comprehensive income. The amount included in other comprehensive income will subsequently be recognized in earnings in the same period in which the hedged transaction affects earnings.

F. In order for users to better understand how an entity employs derivatives as foreign currency hedges, the FASB requires various disclosures.

PART 1

Instructions: Use a check mark to indicate whether each of the following statements is true or false.

	True	False

1. If the spot rate for a currency is greater than the forward rate, the forward contract is said to be at a premium.   _____ _____

2. If the U.S. dollar weakens relative to a foreign currency, a receivable resulting from a sale that is denominated in foreign currency will increase in value.   _____ _____

3. An option that is "out of the money" has intrinsic value equal to the option premium.   _____ _____

4. Given a forward contract to buy foreign currency in excess of the amount of currency represented by an exposed liability position, the gain or loss on the excess hedge should be included in other comprehensive income.   _____ _____

5. The gain or loss on a hedge of a foreign currency commitment is not recognized in earnings but is deferred until the date at which the transaction is settled.   _____ _____

6. Assume that there is an exposed asset position that will be settled in the next year. The gain or loss on a forward contract used to hedge this position is measured by the difference between the forward rate at inception of the contract and the forward rate at the end of the current year.   _____ _____

7. The gain or loss on an option used to hedge a foreign currency forecasted transaction is recognized in the same manner as if it was used to hedge a foreign currency commitment.   _____ _____

8. The gain or loss on a hedge of a foreign currency forecasted transaction is recognized in current earnings when the forecasted transaction is settled.   _____ _____

9. If the interest yield on the U.S. dollar is greater than the yield on a foreign currency, the forward rate will be less than the spot rate.   _____ _____

10. Assuming that a commitment has been made to acquire inventory on account and settle the transaction in foreign currency, a hedge of the commitment will produce an adjustment to the resulting accounts payable.   _____ _____

11. Derivatives representing assets or liabilities should be presented on a balance sheet at their amortized cost.   _____ _____

12. Prior to the transaction date, the net effect on income of a firm commitment and a hedge on the commitment is zero.   _____ _____

13. The premium or discount on a forward contract that is used to hedge a foreign currency commitment is recognized over the time period prior to the transaction date.   _____ _____

PART 2

Instructions: For each of the following statements, write the letter that corresponds to the term that best characterizes the statement.

A. Other comprehensive income	F. Weakening dollar
B. Transaction loss	G. Contract premium
C. Strengthening dollar	H. Indirect quote
D. Floating system	I. Transaction gain
E. Fair value hedge	J. Cash flow hedge

Term

1. The exchange rate changes and the U.S. dollar can be exchanged for more units of a foreign currency.   _____

2. The forward exchange rate is greater than the spot rate.   _____

3. The rate of exchange between two currencies is not tied to a gold standard but rather is influenced by factors of supply and demand.   _____

4. The number of foreign currency units that can be received in exchange for one unit of domestic currency.   _____

5. A purchase of inventory is payable in foreign currency and is subsequently paid for after the U.S. dollar has weakened.   _____

6. The gain on a forward contract acquired as a hedge on a forecasted foreign currency transaction that occurs prior to the transaction date.   _____

7. The carrying value of the hedged item is adjusted at the time of the transaction by the amount of gain or loss recognized prior to the transaction date.   _____

8. A sale of inventory is receivable in foreign currency and is received after the U.S. dollar has strengthened.   _____

9. The movement of the U.S. dollar relative to foreign currencies that is preferred by exporters.   _____

10. When the hedged foreign currency transaction affects earnings, the gain or loss on the hedge prior to the transaction date is also recognized in earnings.   _____

PART 3

Portal Manufacturing Inc. purchased raw materials from a foreign vendor on March 1, 20X9, to be paid for on April 30, 20X9. The purchase price was 10,000 foreign currency (FC) units when the rate of exchange was 1 FC = $0.60. The spot rate when the transaction was settled was 1 FC = $0.66.

Instructions: For each of the following cases, determine the effect on the income as of April 30, 20X9, resulting from the previous transaction and hedges, if applicable.

Case A: The purchase of inventory was not hedged.

Case B: On March 1, 20X9, a forward contract to buy FC on April 30 was acquired to hedge the purchase transaction. The contract to buy 10,000 FC has a forward rate of $0.62.

Case C: On March 1, 20X9, a forward contract to buy FC on April 30 was acquired to hedge the purchase transaction. The contract to buy 15,000 FC has a forward rate of $0.62.

Case D: Thirty days prior to the transaction date, when the spot rate was 1 FC = $0.58, a forward contract to buy FC on April 30 was acquired. Assume that the contract qualifies as a fair value hedge on a purchase commitment. The contract to purchase 10,000 FC has a forward rate of $0.63. The forward rate for the contract at the end of April was $0.64.

PART 4

In late 20X8, your client engaged in the following hedging transactions:

Instructions: For each hedge, identify and calculate the effect on income for the year 20X8 of the hedge and related transaction.

Hedge A: On November 1, 20X8, the company forecasted a sale of inventory to a foreign customer. The anticipated amount of the sale was 100,000 foreign currency (FC) units. The inventory had a cost basis of $80,000. At that time the company acquired a forward contract to sell 100,000 FC on December 15, 20X8, at a forward rate of 1 FC = $1.045. On December 15, 20X8, the sale occurred when the spot rate was $1.042.

Hedge B: On December 1, 20X8, the company committed to buy inventory from a foreign vendor in early 20X9 for 200,000 FC, and it paid $3,000 for an option to buy FC in early 20X9 at the price of 1 FC = $1.047. At the end of year 20X8, the option had a fair market value of $3,800.

Hedge C: On December 1, 20X8, the company borrowed 384,000 FC from a foreign bank. The 90-day note is to be repaid in FC. Simple interest is at the rate of 1% per month and is to be paid in FC at the maturity date of the loan. On December 1, it also acquired a forward contract to buy 395,000 FC in 90 days at a forward rate of $1.0405. The forward rate on the contract at December 31 is $1.042. The spot rates on December 1 and December 31 are $1.041 and $1.043, respectively.

Hedge D: On December 20, 20X8, the company paid $2,000 for an option to sell 400,000 FC on February 28, 20X9. The strike price for the option is $1.0425, and the option has a value at year end (20X8) of $2,100.

PART 5

On October 1, 20X8, Jem Company delivered goods to a German company. The invoice amount of 300,000 foreign currencies (FC) is payable on January 31, 20X9, in FC. On November 1, 20X8, Jem purchased a 90-day forward contract to sell 300,000 FC on January 31, 20X9, at a forward rate of $0.535. Direct spot rates are as follows:

October 1, 20X8	$0.54
November 1, 20X8	$0.55
December 31, 20X8	$0.53
January 31, 20X9	$0.52

The rate on the forward contract as of December 31, 20X8, is $0.53.

Instructions: Assuming Jem's year end is December 31, prepare the journal entries necessary for Jem to account for all the transactions. Ignore present-value calculations.

PART 6

Cortez Electronics buys subassemblies from a foreign vendor. On June 1, 20X9, the company committed to acquire subassemblies costing 400,000 foreign currency (FC) units. The parts will be shipped, f.o.b. shipping point, on June 15, 20X9, with payment due on July 31, 20X9. Cortez is considering two alternative forms of hedging their exposed liability position. One alternative would involve acquiring a forward contract on June 1 to buy 400,000 FC for delivery on July 31, 20X9. The forward rate would be 1 FC = $0.62 and the spot rate on June 1 is 1 FC = $0.60. As an alternative, the company has an opportunity to lend $240,000 to another party with payment due in FC and interest at the rate of 8%. The loan would be dated June 1, 20X9, and would be due on July 31, 20X9.

Instructions: Determine under what conditions the company would favor one alternative over the other.

Chapter 11 Translation of Foreign Financial Statements

OUTLINE FOR REVIEW

Accounting for an investment in a foreign entity, including the translation of foreign currency financial statements, must follow certain procedures.

I. When an entity has a branch, subsidiary, or equity investee that records and reports in a foreign currency, the foreign currency financial statements must be translated into U.S. dollars before results can be combined, consolidated, or reported under the equity method.
    A. Financial statements reported in a foreign currency must be in conformity with U.S. generally accepted accounting principles (GAAP) before they are translated into dollars.
    B. The development of rational and acceptable methods to meet the objectives of translation has been difficult, and several methods have been developed in the past.

II. The FASB has issued several standards that address the translation of foreign currency financial statements.
    A. FASB Statement No. 1, which has been superseded, did not require a particular translation method but rather set forth certain disclosure requirements.
    B. FASB Statement No. 8 called for the use of the temporal method of translation, which is still applicable in some situations.
    C. FASB Statement No. 52 is the current standard applicable to the translation of foreign currency financial statements and is based on a functional currency approach.
        1. The functional currency of an entity normally is the currency of the primary economic environment in which the entity generates its cash flows.
        2. The identification of the functional currency is not subject to definitive criteria.
        3. Certain economic factors should be considered as potential indicators of the functional currency, such as cash flows, sales prices, sales markets, expenses, financing, and intercompany arrangements.
        4. The translation method prescribed by FASB Statement No. 52 should accomplish several objectives.
            a. The translation process should result in information that is compatible with the economic effects of rate changes on an entity's cash flows and equity.
            b. The translation process should result in financial statements that reflect the financial results and relationships of companies as measured in their functional currency and in conformity with U.S. GAAP.

III. Translation of financial statements from their functional currency into U.S. dollars as prescribed by FASB Statement No. 52 involves a specific methodology.
    A. Under the current rate (or functional method), the translation of specific accounts requires the use of certain exchange rates.
        1. All assets and liabilities are translated using the current exchange rate at the date of translation.
        2. All income statement items are translated at the rates in effect on the dates of the transactions; as a practical matter, an appropriately weighted average for the period can be applied to these items.
        3. Stockholders' equity accounts, other than retained earnings, are translated at historical exchange rates. If an acquisition is accounted for as a purchase, historical rates at the date of acquisition are used.
        4. Retained earnings are the net total of the translated beginning-of-the-period balance and the translated net income, plus or minus the effects of any other events affecting retained earnings (translated at the historical rate for each event). If an interest in a foreign subsidiary is acquired during the current year, the retained earnings balance at that date should be translated using the rate at the date of acquisition.
        5. Components of the statement of cash flows are translated at the rates in effect at the time of the cash flows. Operations are translated at the rates used for translation of the income statement amounts.
    B. Translation of a functional currency trial balance or balance sheet will result in a balancing item—the cumulative translation adjustment.
        1. The cumulative translation adjustment is included as a component of other comprehensive income. In the case of an equity investee, the appropriate percentage of the cumulative translation adjustment is included as a component of other comprehensive income.

2. The translation adjustment for a given period can be calculated directly as a net total of the following items (assuming that an average rate was used to translate all income statement items):
    a. Foreign currency net asset amount at the beginning of the period multiplied by the change in exchange rates during the period.
    b. Foreign currency net income multiplied by the difference between the average and the end-of-period exchange rates.
    c. Foreign currency amount of change in net assets due to capital transactions occurring during the period multiplied by the difference in exchange rates between the date of the transaction and the end of the period.
3. In computing the translation adjustment for the period, an element that results in an increase in the value of the net assets—an increase in net assets combined with an increase in the value of the foreign currency—results in a credit effect on the translation adjustment.
4. The cumulative translation adjustment remains as a component of other comprehensive income until there is a partial or complete sale or complete (or substantially complete) liquidation of the investment in the foreign entity. At that time, the cumulative translation adjustment, in total or in part, will be included in the determination of net income as part of the gain or loss on sale.
5. The cumulative translation adjustment balance also includes exchange gains and losses on the following types of foreign currency transactions:
    a. Foreign currency transactions that are designated as, and effective as, economic hedges of a net investment in a foreign entity from the designation date forward.
    b. Intercompany foreign currency transactions that are of the nature of a long-term investment in a foreign entity that is to be consolidated, combined, or accounted for under the equity method.

IV. Once a foreign investee's financial statements have been translated into U.S. dollars, the entity must be either consolidated or accounted for by the cost or equity method.
A. If a foreign entity is to be consolidated with the parent, certain eliminations and adjustments must be made.
    1. Intercompany balances, except for intercompany profits and losses, should be translated at rates used for other accounts.
    2. Intercompany profits and losses should be translated at rates existing at the date of the transaction or, as a practical matter, at weighted average rates.
    3. The initial difference between cost and book values of the equity acquired should be calculated in foreign currency and then translated using the rate existing at the date of the acquisition.
B. The investment in the foreign entity may be accounted for under the cost method.
    1. If the cost of the investment is incurred in foreign currency, the exchange rate at the date of acquisition should be used.
    2. Investment income is translated at the exchange rate existing when dividends are declared.
C. The investment in the foreign entity may be accounted for under the sophisticated equity method.
    1. The investor's interest in the investee's translated income must be adjusted for any amortization of excess of cost over book value at the date of acquisition using weighted average exchange rates.
    2. The investor must also recognize its share of the cumulative translation adjustment.

V. When an entity does not maintain its records in the functional currency and/or the functional currency is that of a highly inflationary economy, the financial statements must first be remeasured into the functional currency.
A. An entity may measure its financial results in a currency other than its functional currency (e.g., a French company may present its financial statements in euros, although its functional currency is pesos). Such statements must first be remeasured into the functional currency, with the intention of producing the same result as if the events had been originally recorded in the functional currency.
    1. If the functional currency is the U.S. dollar, no further translation is necessary after remeasurement.
    2. If the functional currency is another foreign currency, after remeasurement the statements must still be translated from the functional currency into U.S. dollars.
B. The remeasurement of financial statements into their functional currency employs the temporal method with the following characteristics:
    1. Assets and liabilities that are measured in terms of current values will be remeasured using the current end-of-period exchange rate.
    2. Assets and liabilities that are not measured in terms of current values will be remeasured using historical rates, the rate in effect on the date of occurrence of the transaction giving rise to the balance. Equity accounts, excluding retained earnings, will be remeasured at historical rates. Retained earnings is the remeasured beginning balance plus remeasured net income less dividends (remeasured at historical rates).

        3.   Most revenues and expenses will be remeasured using the weighted average rate for the period. Revenues and expenses representing the amortization of items translated at historical rates also will be translated at the historical rates.

        4.   The remeasurement adjustment (needed to balance) will be included in income.

   C. An entity whose functional currency is that of a country that is deemed to be highly inflationary (a cumulative 3-year inflation rate of 100% or more) must be remeasured directly into dollars using the temporal approach.

VI.   The translation and/or remeasurement of financial statements may necessitate tax allocation procedures and also requires certain specific disclosures.

   A. Tax allocation procedures will be necessary for certain types of gains or losses traceable to translation and/or remeasurement.

        1.   If gains or losses are included in income in a different period for tax purposes than for accounting purposes, interperiod tax allocation is necessary.

        2.   For those gains and losses that are included in stockholders' equity rather than in income, the related tax effects will be included in stockholders' equity as well, using intraperiod tax allocation.

   B. As set forth in FASB Statement No. 52, the financial statements or the accompanying notes should present an analysis of the changes in the cumulative translation adjustment, including as a minimum the following:

        1.   The beginning and ending cumulative translation adjustment balances

        2.   The aggregate adjustment for the period due to translation adjustments and gains and losses from certain hedges and intercompany balances

        3.   The amount of income taxes for the period allocated to the stockholders' equity component

        4.   The amounts transferred from the cumulative translation adjustment and included in net income for the period because of the sale or the substantially complete liquidation of an investment in a foreign entity

   C. Foreign currency transactions and hedging gains and losses included in the determination of net income should be disclosed in the financial statements or the accompanying notes.

   D. The effect of rate changes subsequent to the end of the period on unsettled balances arising from foreign currency transactions should be disclosed if significant.

SUMMARY
DISPOSITION OF TRANSLATION ADJUSTMENTS

Include in Net Income

1.   Gains and losses resulting from remeasurement of an entity's financial statements from its reporting currency into its functional currency

2.   Cumulative translation adjustment when the investment in the foreign entity is sold or substantially liquidated

3.   Gains and losses resulting from the remeasurement of statements when the functional currency is that of a country with a highly inflationary economy

Include in Other Comprehensive Income

1.   Translation adjustment resulting from translation of an entity's trial balance or financial statements from its functional currency to the parent's reporting currency

2.   Exchange gains or losses on transactions that are designated as, and are effective as, hedges of a net investment in a foreign entity

3.   Exchange gains or losses on intercompany foreign currency transactions that are of a long-term investment nature

PART 1

Instructions: Use a check mark to indicate whether each of the following statements is true or false.

	True	False

1. The methods promulgated by FASB Statement No. 52 for the translation of foreign currency financial statements from the functional currency into U.S. dollars are designed to show what the results would have been had all transactions of the foreign entity occurred in U.S. dollars rather than in the functional currency.

2. If Chile's 3-year cumulative inflation rate is 113%, the Chilean peso will not be acceptable as a functional currency, and Chilean peso financial statements will be remeasured as if the functional currency were the U.S. dollar.

3. A British division of an American company manufactures products primarily for sale in America, and the home office routinely withdraws operating profits from that division to finance its American operations. If the financial statements of the division are prepared in euros, the euro is the division's functional currency.

4. Along with allowing the use of different functional currencies to reflect the differences in economic operating environments of foreign entities, FASB Statement No. 52 permits the use of different accounting principles that are generally accepted in those environments.

5. Depreciable assets and common stock would both be translated from functional currency to U.S. dollars, using historical exchange rates.

6. When financial statements are first remeasured into the functional currency, then translated into the reporting currency, translation adjustment effects will be included in both net income and other comprehensive income.

7. Intercompany profits should be translated at the current rate at the end of the period.

8. There is no translation adjustment balance if a foreign entity's financial statements are translated on the date the investment in the foreign entity is made.

9. Foreign statements of an investee accounted for by the equity method should first be translated into U.S. dollars and then the equity method applied.

10. The declaration of a dividend by a foreign subsidiary, coupled with a decrease in exchange rates between the declaration date and year end, has a credit effect on the current period's translation adjustment.

11. If a parent company sells one-ninth of its 90% ownership interest in a foreign subsidiary, one-ninth of the cumulative translation adjustment balance is removed from other comprehensive income and is included in the determination of net income for the period of the sale.

12. Intercompany transactions are to be eliminated prior to translation of the foreign currency financial statements.

13. The tax effects of an exchange gain or loss on a transaction that is designated as, and is effective as, a hedge of the net investment in a foreign entity are to be included in net income.

14. If a parent company sells a 90% interest in a foreign subsidiary, the cumulative translation adjustment in other comprehensive income will be included in the determination of net income in the year of sale.

15. If a foreign entity uses the lower-of-cost-or-market method of valuing inventory, functional currency values for cost and market are used to apply the rule rather than similar amounts measured in the books-of-record currency.

16. If an excessive amount is paid for an investment in a foreign entity and it can be traced to a depreciable asset, additional depreciation expense will not affect the cumulative translation adjustment of the domestic entity.

PART 2

Shaid Corporation is a wholly owned subsidiary of Hawkes Inc. Shaid, a South American company, was organized on July 1, 20X5, when the general price level index in its country was 400. The price level index is 1,000 on December 31, 20X6. The general price level index in the United States, where Hawkes is incorporated, has gone from 110 to 121 during the same time period.

Shaid's accounting records contain the following information:

1. Inventory is accounted for using the LIFO inventory method on a periodic basis. The 20X6 beginning inventory is composed entirely of purchases made on July 1, 20X5. Inventory information for 20X6 is as follows:

Date	Account	Amount in Foreign Currency
January 1	Beginning inventory	30,000 FC
April 1	Purchases	18,000
June 1	Purchases	25,000
October 1	Purchases	40,000
November 1	Purchases	20,000
December 31	Ending inventory	52,000

2. Equipment was acquired and sold as detailed in the following schedule. There were no intercompany equipment transactions.

Date	Cost Acquired (Sold)
July 1, 20X5	120,000 FC
April 1, 20X6	50,000
October 1, 20X6	(16,000)

The selling price of the equipment was 13,200 FC. This equipment was acquired on July 1, 20X5.

3. Depreciation is computed using the straight-line method over an 8-year life. Salvage value is ignored. A half-year depreciation is taken in the years of acquisition and disposition.

4. The November 1 inventory purchase in part (a) was acquired from Hawkes Inc., with payment due in foreign currency in 90 days. On November 1, Hawkes purchased a 90-day forward contract to sell the 20,000 FC to a broker at a forward rate of 1 FC = $1.27.

5. Relevant exchange rates are as follows:

Date	Rate
July 1, 20X5	1 FC = $1.19
April 1, 20X6	1 FC = 1.23
June 1, 20X6	1 FC = 1.22
October 1, 20X6	1 FC = 1.25
November 1, 20X6	1 FC = 1.26
December 31, 20X6	1 FC = 1.28
20X6 average	1 FC = 1.24

Instructions: Calculate the translated value of the following accounts:

1. Cost of goods sold for 20X6

2. Gain or loss on the October 1, 20X6 equipment sale

3. Hawkes' liability to broker associated with the forward contract, as of December 31, 20X6

PART 3

Questions 1–8 are based on the following information:

Johnson Incorporated, a U.S. company, has a wholly owned foreign subsidiary with the following December 31, 20X3, trial balance in foreign currency:

	Debit	Credit
Current assets	1,000,000	
Building and equipment	5,800,000	
Land	1,500,000	
Cost of sales	4,000,000	
Selling, general, and administrative expenses	375,000	
Current liabilities		500,000
Mortgage payable		3,000,000
Common stock		800,000
Paid-in capital in excess of par		1,000,000
Retained earnings		1,800,000
Sales revenue		5,500,000
Accumulated depreciation		75,000
	12,675,000	12,675,000

When Johnson acquired the subsidiary, 1 FC was equal to $0.58. Other exchange rates are as follows:

Date	Rate
June 1, 20X2	1 FC = $0.62
January 1, 20X3	1 FC = 0.60
February 1, 20X3	1 FC = 0.61
Weighted average, 20X3	1 FC = 0.70
December 31, 20X3	1 FC = 0.75

Instructions: Circle the letter that identifies the best response to each question.

1. Assuming the foreign currency is the functional currency, the December 31, 20X3, translated value of current liabilities is
   a. $350,000   b. $500,000   c. $300,000   d. $375,000

2. Land costing 900,000 FC was acquired on June 1, 20X2, and 600,000 FC was acquired on February 1, 20X3. Assuming the functional currency is the dollar, the December 31, 20X3, translated value of land is
   a. $1,500,000   b. $1,125,000   c. $924,000   d. $870,000

3. Assuming the foreign currency is the functional currency, the December 31, 20X3, translated value of sales revenue is
   a. $4,125,000   b. $3,300,000   c. $5,500,000   d. $3,850,000

4. Assuming no additional common stock has been issued since acquisition of the subsidiary, the translated value of common stock
   a. Is the same regardless of whether the dollar or the foreign currency is the functional currency.
   b. Is always translated at the beginning-of-the-year exchange rate.
   c. Is translated at the current exchange rate.
   d. Is translated at the rate of exchange when the stock was originally issued rather than at the time the shares were acquired by the parent.

5. If the foreign currency was not the functional currency, accumulated depreciation would be remeasured into the functional currency through the use of the
   a. Current exchange rate.
   b. Exchange rate at the date the subsidiary was acquired if after the date the depreciable assets were acquired.
   c. Exchange rates existing when the depreciable assets were acquired.
   d. Weighted exchange rate.

6. Assume the foreign currency is not the functional currency and the mortgage was secured on February 1, 20X3, when 1 FC equaled 2 functional currency units. One functional currency unit equaled $1.45 on February 1, 20X3, and $1.50 on December 31, 20X3. The translated value of the mortgage payable on December 31, 20X3, is
    a. $6,000,000   b. $1,830,000   c. $9,000,000   d. $4,500,000

7. If the foreign currency were that of a highly inflationary economy
    a. The foreign currency would be considered the functional currency.
    b. Land would be remeasured at the current exchange rate.
    c. The mortgage payable would be remeasured at the historical exchange rate.
    d. Net income would not be affected by the remeasurement process.

8. If retained earnings reflected the declaration of a 200,000 FC dividend on February 1, 20X3, which was paid on June 1, 20X3, the translated value of the dividend would be
    a. $122,000   b. $140,000   c. $150,000   d. $120,000

PART 4

Instructions: Circle the letter that identifies the best response to each question.

1. The gain or loss on translation or remeasurement would affect income in which of the following instances?
    a. When translating from a functional currency to the dollar
    b. When 10% of the foreign subsidiary is disposed of
    c. When remeasuring the financial statements of a subsidiary in a highly inflationary economy
    d. When the parent company hedges its net investment in the foreign subsidiary

2. Which of the following elements would not enter into the direct computation of the current period's translation adjustment?
    a. The foreign currency amount of net income multiplied by the difference between the average and the year-end exchange rates.
    b. The foreign currency amount of proceeds from the issuance of capital stock multiplied by the difference in exchange rates between the issuance date and year end.
    c. The year-end foreign currency net asset total multiplied by the difference between the average and the year-end exchange rates.
    d. The beginning-of-the-period foreign currency stockholders' equity total multiplied by the change in exchange rates during the period.

3. A foreign entity had net assets of 2,000,000 FC at January 1, 20X3. The net loss for 20X3 was 10,000 FC, and common stock was issued for 50,000 FC on October 15, 20X3. The relevant exchange rates were as follows:

January 1, 20X3	1 FC = $0.69	December 31, 20X3	1 FC = $0.71
October 15, 20X3	1 FC = 0.72	20X3 average	1 FC = 0.70

    The 20X3 translation adjustment is
    a. $40,600 credit   b. $40,400 credit   c. $39,900 credit   d. $39,400 credit

4. A foreign subsidiary of a U.S. corporation maintains its books of record in currency A. However, financing, sales, and production are denominated in currency B. A loan taken out on September 1, 20X8, was recorded for 100,000, and inventory acquired on December 1, 20X8, was recorded for 50,000. Relevant exchange rates are as follows:

	A to B	B to $	A to $
September 1, 20X8	1 = 0.90	1 = 2.00	1 = 1.50
December 1, 20X8	1 = 1.10	1 = 2.10	1 = 1.60
December 31, 20X8	1 = 1.20	1 = 2.25	1 = 2.00
20X8 average	1 = 0.75	1 = 1.80	1 = 1.40

    The loan and inventory should be included in the December 31, 20X8, U.S. balance sheet as follows:
    a. $150,000 and $80,000, respectively   c. $200,000 and $105,000, respectively
    b. $200,000 and $100,000, respectively   d. $270,000 and $135,000, respectively

5. Which of the following exchange gains or losses or translation adjustments would not be included in the cumulative translation adjustment component of stockholders' equity?
   a. Translation adjustment arising from translation of foreign subsidiary's trial balance from the functional currency into dollars.
   b. Exchange gain or loss on intercompany long-term investment transaction between investor and equity investee.
   c. Exchange gain or loss on a forward contract held for speculative purposes.
   d. Exchange gain or loss on a transaction that serves to hedge the net investment in a foreign entity.

6. An American company owns a 100% interest in a French entity. The functional currency of the entity is FCA, but the statements are prepared in FCB. If the depreciable assets with a cost of 100,000 FCB (10-year useful life) were acquired on July 1, 20X8, what would be the translated U.S. dollar value of the assets at December 31, 20X9, given the following exchange rates?

	FCB to FCA	FCA to $
July 1, 20X8	0.67 FCA	$0.50
December 31, 20X8	0.69	0.53
20X8 average	0.66	0.52
December 31, 20X9	0.58	0.55
20X9 average	0.61	0.54

   a. $31,900   b. $33,500   c. $36,850   d. $33,550

7. Given the information in question 6, which of the following is the translated value of depreciation expense assuming straight-line depreciation?
   a. $3,685   b. $5,400   c. $3,564   d. $3,618

8. An investment was made on January 1, 20X9, to acquire a wholly owned subsidiary. The cumulative translation adjustment for the first year would have a debit balance in which of the following circumstances?
   a. Beginning stockholders' equity of 100,000 FC, dividend paid to parent of 50,000 FC, income of subsidiary of 20,000 FC, and the exchange rate remains at 1 FC = $1.00 throughout the year.
   b. Beginning stockholders' equity of 100,000 FC, and subsidiary loss of 20,000 FC. Exchange rates occur as follows: January 1, 20X9, $1.00; 20X9 average, $0.90; and December 31, 20X9, $0.80.
   c. Beginning stockholders' equity of 100,000 FC, dividends declared July 1, 20X9, of 50,000 FC, and subsidiary income of 50,000 FC. Exchange rates occur as follows: January 1, 20X9, $1.00; July 1, 20X9, $1.05; December 31, 20X9, $1.00; and 20X9 average, $0.95.
   d. Both (b) and (c).

9. Inventory with a historical cost of 100,000 FCA was acquired uniformly throughout the foreign entity's first year of business (20X8). The functional currency of the entity is FCB. The parent, a U.S. company, is translating the value into U.S. dollars for financial statement presentation and employs the lower-of-cost-or-market method for inventory valuation. Given the following exchange rates, at what value will the inventory be presented if the market value on December 31, 20X8, is 95,000 FCA?

	FCB to FCA	$ to FCB
January 1, 20X8	0.50 FCB	$0.90
December 31, 20X8	0.51	1.05
20X8 average	0.48	0.95

   a. $50,400   b. $50,873   c. $47,880   d. $45,600

PART 5

On January 1, 20X8, a U.S. company invested 4,000,000 FC in its acquisition of 100% of the voting stock of a foreign company. On November 1, 20X8, the foreign company issued 1,000,000 FC more of stock, which the U.S. company also acquired for par. Dividends of 500,000 FC were declared on July 1, 20X8, and July 1, 20X9. Net incomes for years ending December 31, 20X8, and December 31, 20X9, were 830,000 FC and 720,000 FC, respectively. Exchange rates for selected dates were as follows:

	FC to $		FC to $
January 1, 20X8	$1.00	July 1, 20X9	$1.00
July 1, 20X8	1.02	December 31, 20X9	0.97
November 1, 20X8	1.05	20X8 average	1.03
December 31, 20X8	0.99	20X9 average	0.98

Beginning stockholders' equity in 20X8 was:

Common stock	2,000,000	FC
Paid-in capital in excess of par	680,000	
Retained earnings	1,100,000	
	3,780.000	FC

Instructions: Given the above information, calculate the translation adjustment for 20X8 and 20X9 using the direct calculation method.

PART 6

Grandey Corporation acquired a 25% interest in a foreign entity on January 1, 20X9, for $2,900,000. The book value of the entity on that date was 20,800,000 foreign currency (FC) units, and any excess cost over book value is allocated to depreciable assets with a 10-year life and no salvage value. The straight-line method of depreciation is used. A dividend of 1,800,000 FC was declared on November 1, 20X9, and paid on December 1, 20X9. There were no intercompany transactions between the two entities during 20X9, and the foreign entity had the following condensed trial balance on December 31, 20X9.

Condensed Trial Balance (in FC)
December 31, 20X9

Assets	138,000,000	Liabilities	110,000,000
Expenses	59,000,000	Sales	68,000,000
		Stockholders' equity	19,000,000
Total debits	197,000,000	Total credits	197,000,000

The foreign entity's functional currency is FC; various spot exchange rates in 20X9 are as follows:

January 1	1 FC = $0.50
November 1	1 FC = 0.58
December 1	1 FC = 0.59
December 31	1 FC = 0.62
Average	1 FC = 0.54

Instructions: Determine the December 31, 20X9, balance in Grandey's investment in foreign entity account.

Chapter 12   Interim Reporting and Disclosures about Segments of an Enterprise

OUTLINE FOR REVIEW

Timeliness is an important factor affecting the relevance of accounting information. This chapter discusses interim reporting, which is designed to provide timely information. Special reporting problems for diversified business operations also are addressed in this chapter.

I.   Interim reporting provides financial information on a monthly or quarterly basis.
    A.   There are two approaches to reporting interim data.
        1.   The interim period may be viewed as an independent accounting period; therefore, the interim period net income is determined by employing the same principles and estimations that are used for annual reporting.
        2.   The interim period may be viewed as an integral part of the annual accounting period. Therefore, determination of interim financial data, such as deferrals, accruals, and estimations, should be based on estimates of annual revenue and expense relationships.
    B.   APB Opinion No. 28 establishes that the interim period should be viewed as an integral part of the annual period. Financial statements for each interim period should be based on the same accounting principles and practices used for the preparation of annual financial statements, with certain modifications.
        1.   Modifications are acceptable in the area of inventory costing for the determination of cost of goods sold.
            a.   The gross profit method or other estimation methods that are not acceptable for annual purposes may be used for interim purposes.
            b.   Significant differences between perpetual estimates of annual inventory and the annual physical inventory should be recorded in interim statements on a proportionate basis.
            c.   The interim cost of goods sold should include the replacement cost of liquidated inventory when the use of LIFO results in inventory liquidations that will be replaced by year end.
            d.   If the lower-of-cost-or-market rule is employed for interim purposes, subsequent recoveries of earlier interim period losses may be recognized as gains to the extent of the losses previously recognized within the same fiscal year. As an alternative, temporary market declines that can reasonably be expected to be recovered during the fiscal year need not be recognized for interim purposes.
            e.   When a standard cost system is used, material price variances and volume variances that are planned and expected to be absorbed by year end are deferred until year end.
        2.   Costs and expenses (other than product costs) should be expensed in the interim period in which they were incurred, unless they can be allocated among interim periods based on an estimate of benefit received or activity associated with other interim periods. Arbitrary assignment of costs should not be made.
        3.   A portion of estimated year-end adjustments should be allocated to each interim period on the basis of a revenue or cost relationship.
        4.   Adjustments related to prior interim periods are given special treatment in interim reports.
            a.   An adjustment or settlement of litigation or of income taxes should not affect current interim income if the following occur:
                (1)   The effect of the adjustment is material in relation to income from continuing operations of the current fiscal year.
                (2)   All or part of the adjustment can be specifically identified with and is directly related to business activities of specific prior interim periods of the current fiscal year.
                (3)   The amount of the adjustment could not be reasonably estimated prior to the current interim period but becomes reasonably estimable in the current interim period.
            b.   If an adjustment or settlement occurs in other than the first interim period of the current fiscal year and all or part of the item is an adjustment related to prior interim periods of the current fiscal year,
                (1)   The portion of the item directly related to activities of the current interim period is included in the determination of net income for that period.

    (2) Prior interim periods of the current fiscal year are restated to include the portion of the item directly related to business activities during each prior interim period.

    (3) The portion of the item directly related to business activities of the enterprise during prior annual fiscal periods is included in the determination of net income of the first interim period of the current fiscal year.

  c. Adjustments related to prior interim periods do not include normal recurring corrections and adjustments that result from the use of estimates.

C. Because an interim period is viewed as an integral part of a larger annual period, interim financial statements should reflect a proportionate amount of the estimated annual income taxes. Therefore, a basic objective of accounting for income taxes in interim periods is to estimate the annual effective tax rate and apply that rate to the interim pretax income.

  1. Estimates of the effective annual tax rate should be made or revised each interim period and should reflect tax-planning alternatives, permanent differences, and tax credits.

  2. Nonordinary items of income or loss (unusual or infrequently occurring items, extraordinary items, discontinued operations, and the cumulative effect of changes in accounting principles) are not included in the computation of the estimated annual effective tax rate, nor are these items prorated over the balance of the fiscal period. The tax effect on these items is determined incrementally.

  3. The interim tax expense is the difference between the year-to-date (YTD) tax expense or benefit and the amount of tax reported in previous interim periods. This difference represents the following:

    a. The tax on the current interim period's pretax income at the present estimated effective annual tax rate.

    b. Corrections of previous interim periods' tax expense or benefit resulting from a change in the estimated effective annual tax rate as compared to earlier estimated rates. Therefore, changes in the tax rates (a change in estimate) are accounted for currently rather than retroactively.

D. The tax benefit associated with YTD operating losses must be determined.

  1. If the YTD operating loss is able, more likely than not, to be offset against projected operating income for the remaining interim periods of the current year, a tax benefit traceable to the loss may be recognized.

  2. If an estimated annual operating loss exists, the potential tax benefit traceable to this loss is a function of the following factors:

    a. The extent to which the operating loss may be offset by current-year income of a nonoperating nature (e.g., extraordinary gain),

    b. The extent to which the operating loss may be offset by income of prior fiscal years included in the carryback period, and/or

    c. The extent to which the operating loss may be offset by future annual income that is, more likely than not, to be recognized in the carryforward period.

  3. If it is not likely that a YTD loss will be offset by subsequent interim period income, a tax benefit may still be recognized based on carryback provisions. The tax benefit of an estimated annual loss may be recognized if the loss can offset income earned in the prior two years. The loss must be carried back to the earliest of the two prior years and then proceeds to the next earliest year. The tax rate effective in the prior years represents the rate at which benefit should be recognized on the current loss.

  4. To the extent that losses are not absorbed by income in later interim periods and/or the prior two years of income, tax benefits may still be recognized currently. Losses not offset already may be carried forward against future annual income, which, more likely than not, will be recognized in the 20-year carryforward period.

  5. If estimated annual losses cannot be offset totally by the above options, no tax benefit is currently recognized on those losses not offset. However, these remaining losses may be offset by subsequent annual income. At the time of subsequent offset, the tax benefit associated with the loss may be recognized and should be classified the same as the item against which it was offset. For example, if the item offsets subsequent income from continuing operations, then the tax benefit on the loss should be classified as a component of continuing operations.

E. Discontinued operations, extraordinary items, and the cumulative effects of changes in accounting principles are examples of nonordinary interim items that are to be separately reported net of tax.

  1. The tax effect of nonordinary items is independently determined on an incremental basis. If one nonordinary item exists, the incremental income tax is the difference between

      a.   The income tax expense (benefit) traceable to the estimated annual pretax ordinary income (loss), and

      b.   The income tax expense (benefit) traceable to the total pretax income (loss) (estimated annual ordinary income plus the incremental nonordinary item).

  2. When several nonordinary items exist, the calculation of their individual tax impact becomes more complex. This complexity usually occurs because of differences in tax rates for nonordinary items, surtax charges, and tax credit limitations. If several nonordinary items exist, the incremental tax traceable to each nonordinary item or category is determined as follows:

      a.   The incremental income tax expense (benefit) traceable to all nonordinary categories is the difference between

         (1) The income tax expense (benefit) traceable to the estimated annual pretax ordinary income (loss), and

         (2) The income tax expense (benefit) traceable to the total pretax income (loss) (the estimated annual ordinary income (loss) and all nonordinary gains and losses).

      b.   The incremental income tax benefit traceable to all nonordinary loss categories is the difference between

         (1) The income tax expense (benefit) traceable to the total pretax income (loss) [a.(2)], and

         (2) The income tax expense (benefit) traceable to the total pretax income, excluding all nonordinary loss categories.

      c.   The income tax expense traceable to all nonordinary gain categories is the difference between

         (1) The incremental tax expense (benefit) traceable to all nonordinary items (a), and

         (2) The incremental tax benefit traceable to all nonordinary loss categories (b).

      d.   Next, the incremental tax benefit traceable to each individual nonordinary loss category is the difference between

         (1) The income tax expense (benefit) traceable to the total pretax income (loss), and

         (2) The income tax expense (benefit) traceable to total pretax income (loss), excluding the individual nonordinary loss category.

      e.   The total tax benefit traceable to all nonordinary loss categories (b) is then apportioned ratably to each individual loss category based on the incremental tax benefit of each individual loss category (d).

      f.   Next, the incremental tax expense traceable to each individual nonordinary gain category is the difference between

         (1) The income tax expense (benefit) traceable to the total pretax income (loss), and

         (2) The income tax expense (benefit) traceable to total pretax income (loss), excluding the individual nonordinary gain category.

      g.   The total tax expense traceable to all nonordinary gain categories (c) is then apportioned ratably to each individual gain category based on the incremental tax benefit of each individual gain category (f).

  3. The principles regarding the recognition of tax benefits associated with pretax losses are also applicable in determining the tax impact of nonordinary loss categories.

F. The restatement of prior interim data due to a current decision to discontinue an operation involves a reallocation of the previously reported tax.

  1. The original year-to-date and balance-of-the-year projections used to calculate the estimated effective tax rate are allocated between the continuing and discontinued operations.

  2. The original tax planning alternatives, permanent differences, and tax credits used to calculate the tax rate are allocated between the continuing and discontinued operations.

  3. The projected items being allocated in (1) and (2) are the originally reported amounts.

  4. The amounts now allocated to continuing operations are used to calculate a new effective tax rate traceable to continuing operations. The tax on the prior period(s) continuing operations is then recalculated.

  5. The new tax on the prior period(s) continuing operations is compared to the originally reported tax with the difference representing the prior period(s) tax traceable to the discontinued operation.

  6. Once prior interim periods have been restated, current and future interim periods must reflect the tax impact traceable to the discontinued operation. The principles relating to the calculation of the tax impact traceable to nonordinary items of income should be followed.

G. Generally, a change in accounting principle during an interim period is accounted for in accordance with APB Opinion No. 20.

1. Changes requiring retroactive restatement of previously issued financial statements will require the restatement of previously issued interim financial information. Restatement of taxes to reflect the estimated effective tax rate in accordance with the newly adopted accounting principle is also necessary.
2. The interim financial treatment for a change in accounting principle requiring a cumulative effect depends on when the change is adopted.
   a. When the change in principle is adopted in the first interim period of the fiscal year, the cumulative effect of the change is included in the determination of net income of the first interim period.
   b. When the change is adopted in other than the first interim period, for accounting purposes it is assumed that it took place in the first interim period. Financial statements for all interim periods in the current fiscal year should be restated to reflect the adoption of the new principle, and the cumulative effect of the change as of the beginning of the current fiscal year should be included in the restated net income of the first interim period.
3. The tax previously reported for the prechange interim periods should be restated to reflect the year-to-date amounts and annual estimates originally used for the prechange interim periods, modified only for the effect of the change in accounting principle on those year-to-date and estimated annual amounts.
4. The tax impact traceable to the pretax cumulative effect of the change is computed on an incremental basis. The principles relating to the calculation of the tax impact traceable to nonordinary items of income should be followed.

H. To maintain the timeliness of interim data, companies often report summarized interim data. In those instances, certain minimal disclosures are required.

II. Segmental reporting has become increasingly more useful as a result of the diversified nature of many business enterprises. FASB Statement No. 131, which is applicable to public enterprises, sets forth the disclosures that are to be provided regarding segmental information.

A. The definition of an operating segment emphasizes a "management approach," which focuses on how management organizes information for purposes of making operating decisions and assessing performance. Based on this approach, operating segments are defined as a component of an enterprise
   1. That engages in business activities from which it may earn revenues and incur expense.
   2. Whose operating results are regularly reviewed by the enterprise's chief operating decision maker to make decisions about resources to be allocated to the segment and to assess its performance.
   3. For which discrete financial information is available.

B. Certain segments may appear to be similar, and it is possible to combine two or more segments into a single segment if they are similar in each of the following areas:
   1. The nature of the product and services.
   2. The nature of the production process.
   3. The type or class of customer for their products and services.
   4. The methods used to distribute their products and services.
   5. The nature of the regulatory environment, if applicable.

C. Given a defined operating segment, segmental data need not be disclosed unless the segment qualifies as a reportable segment by satisfying at least one of the following criteria:
   1. The reported revenue (including intersegmental sales) of the segment is 10% or more of the combined total revenue, internal and external, of all reported operating segments.
   2. The absolute amount of its reported profit or loss is 10% or more of the greater—in absolute amount—of the:
      a. Combined profit of all operating segments that did not incur an operating loss, or
      b. Combined loss of all operating segments that did incur an operating loss.
   3. The operating segment's assets are 10% or more of the combined assets of all operating segments.

D. Segments which fail the above criteria will constitute a separate "all other" category for reporting purposes.
   1. Management may elect to report information about individual segments that fail the above criteria if management believes it to be material.
   2. It is possible for a segment to be classified as reportable in one period but not in another. In order to maintain comparability, there are criteria that allow for the inclusion of a segment even if it is not deemed to be reportable.

E. There are practical limitations concerning the number of reportable segments.
   1. As the number of reportable segments increases above 10, the volume of segmental data begins to diminish the utility of segmental reporting.

    2.   The reportable segments should, in the aggregate, represent a substantial portion of the total enterprise's activities. Therefore, external revenues for reportable segments must constitute at least 75% of the total consolidated revenue.

F. For all segments that have been deemed to be reportable, as well as the aggregate of all segments not deemed to be reportable, the following must be disclosed:

    1.   The factors used to identify reportable segments along with a discussion of how the segments are organized.

    2.   The nature of the segment's products and services.

    3.   Segmental profit or loss. The measurement of profit or loss is based on what information is reviewed by the chief operating decision maker of the enterprise and, therefore, follows a management approach. The focus is on measures of profit or loss for internal decision-making purposes rather than a strict definition of profit used for external reporting purposes.

    4.   Segmental assets, which are evaluated by the chief operating decision maker.

    5.   Disclosures that will assist the user in understanding how profits/losses and asset values are measured. (These additional disclosures are necessary due to the use of a management approach rather than a strict definition of what constitutes a segment's profits/losses and assets.)

    6.   A reconciliation of the total of all reportable segments' revenues, profits/losses, and assets to the respective consolidated amounts. (This reconciliation is necessary because not all consolidated amounts will be traceable to individual reportable segments.)

G. Condensed financial statements for interim periods must include certain information regarding reportable segments. Complete interim financial statements must include the more comprehensive disclosures regarding reportable segments that are found in annual financial statements.

H. If information regarding product/service groups and/or geographical areas is not provided as part of the segmental disclosures, certain information must be disclosed on an enterprise-wide, rather than segmental, basis. The disclosures would include:

    1.   Revenues from external customers for each product or service or each group of related products or services. Revenues are based on information used for general-purpose financial statements.

    2.   Revenues from external customers for the enterprise's country of domicile and all foreign countries in total. Revenues are based on information used for general-purpose financial statements. Information for separate countries or groups of countries should be disclosed, if material.

    3.   Long-lived assets located in the enterprise's country of domicile and all foreign countries in total. The measurement of assets is based on the information used for general-purpose financial statements. Information for separate countries or groups of countries should be disclosed if material.

I. If an enterprise has sales to any single customer that accounts for 10% or more of total enterprise revenues, the nature and amount of major sales and the identity of the segments making the sales should be disclosed. Each federal, state, local, and foreign government should be considered a single customer.

PART 1

Instructions: Use a check mark to indicate whether each of the following statements is true or false.

	True	False
1. Estimated annual year-end bonuses should be included in interim income on a proportionate basis.		
2. LIFO liquidations occurring during an interim period should be recorded at historical cost.		
3. Because interim periods are viewed as separate and distinct periods, research and development costs should be expensed in total in the period in which they are incurred.		
4. Permanent tax differences have no effect on the calculation of the estimated effective annual tax rate.		
5. If an earlier estimate of the effective tax rate is revised, the effect on prior interim periods is accounted for retroactively.		

6. The tax benefit associated with a year-to-date pretax operating loss can always be recognized if annual pretax income is projected.   _____ _____

7. A tax benefit on a projected pretax annual operating loss may be recognized, even if carrybacks are not available, due to the presence of likely future annual income in the carryforward period.   _____ _____

8. The tax impact on nonordinary items of income is determined incrementally based on the order in which such items appear in the income statement.   _____ _____

9. When a prior interim period is restated due to a decision to discontinue an operation, changes in estimated amounts of permanent differences and tax credits may enter into the calculation of a restated effective tax rate.   _____ _____

10. The calculation of a segment's operating profit or loss is required to include the same revenues and expenses that exist for external reporting purposes.   _____ _____

11. The determination of whether or not an operating segment is reportable is made without consideration of the level of intersegmental sales.   _____ _____

12. The management approach to defining segments focuses on the decision-making processes employed by the chief operating decision maker.   _____ _____

13. In the aggregate, reportable segments should represent at least 75% of the total consolidated revenue.   _____ _____

14. Even if operating segments are not defined around geographical areas, certain information must be presented on an enterprise-wide basis regarding operations in foreign geographical areas.   _____ _____

PART 2

Dreyfus Corporation has second-quarter revenues of $730,000. In addition, the following expense information is available:

1. During the quarter, 4,000 units of inventory were sold even though only 3,400 units were purchased at an average price of $150 each. The first-quarter ending inventory consisted of 2,000 units with a cost of $120 each. The company anticipates additional purchases will cost $170 each, and its inventory at year end will consist of 3,000 units. Cost of sales is determined by the LIFO inventory method.

2. An outside research organization was paid $120,000 during the quarter for new technology, which should benefit the company for three years.

3. The company allows employees to carry over vacation time that has not been previously used to future years. At year end, the company typically accrues a vacation liability, which averages about $80,000. Vacation time is assumed to be both earned and taken uniformly throughout the year.

4. The company has a statutory tax rate of 30% on the first $100,000 of pretax income and 32% on all additional amounts. Tax credits of $8,000 have been earned to date, although $15,000 of credits are anticipated for the entire year. The company had pretax income in the first quarter of $40,000 and an effective tax rate of 25%. The company is projecting third- and fourth-quarter pretax income to be $70,000.

Instructions: Calculate the second-quarter after-tax net income operations.

PART 3

Instructions: For each of the cases A through D, calculate the estimated effective annual tax rate on income from continuing operations.

	Case A	Case B	Case C	Case D
Year-to-date pretax income (loss)	$ 40,000	$ 40,000	$ 40,000	$ (40,000)
Projected pretax income (loss) for the balance of the year	60,000	(55,000)	(100,000)	(60,000)
Total estimated annual pretax income (loss)	100,000	(15,000)	(60,000)	(100,000)
Nontaxable (deductible) income (expense)				
included in accounting income	10,000	10,000	0	(10,000)
Statutory tax rate	30%	30%	30%	30%
Estimated annual tax credits	4,000	2,000	0	0
Pretax income (loss) in prior two years	40,000	40,000	40,000	40,000
Effective tax rate in prior two years	20%	20%	20%	20%
Pretax income (loss) considered more likely than not				
in the next 20 years	400,000	0	0	30,000

PART 4

Dober Inc. has year-to-date pretax income from continuing operations of $150,000 and is projecting pretax income of another $60,000 for the balance of the year. The current-quarter results also include the following nonordinary items:

	Pretax Income (Loss)
Item A	$(180,000)
Item B	20,000
Item C	30,000

The statutory tax rate is 15% on the first $50,000 of income, 25% on the next $25,000 of income, and 35% on income in excess of $75,000.

Instructions: Determine the tax impact traceable to each of the nonordinary items.

PART 5

Silkway Inc. is a manufacturer and distributor of various health and beauty aids. The following data are available for Silkway's segments:

Segment	Revenues Unaffiliated Customers	Revenues Intersegmental Sales	Total	Operating Profit (Loss)	Identifiable Assets
A	$ 300,000	—	$ 300,000	$ 20,000	$ 600,000
B	245,000	$ 50,000	295,000	(22,000)	200,000
C	820,000	40,000	860,000	175,000	750,000
D	410,000	20,000	430,000	60,000	500,000
E	115,000	—	115,000	(8,000)	150,000
Total	$1,890,000	$110,000	$2,000,000	$225,000	$2,200,000
Corporate level	90,000	—	90,000	20,000	300,000
Total	$1,980,000	$110,000	$2,090,000	$245,000	$2,500,000

Instructions: Complete the following to determine which of the segments are reportable:

1. Sales to unaffiliated customers   _____

   Intersegmental sales   _____

   Combined revenue   _____

   Segmental revenue required to satisfy revenue criterion: _____

2.

Segment	Operating Profit	Operating Loss
A		
B		
C		
D		
E		
Total		

Portion of absolute amount of the greater of operating profit or operating loss to satisfy operating profit/loss criterion:

_____

3. Segment's identifiable assets required to satisfy identifiable asset criterion:

_____

4. Summary:

Segment	Revenue ≥ oooooooooo ?	Operating Revenue ≥ oooooooooo ?	Identifiable Assets ≥ oooooooooo ?	Segment Reportable?
A				
B				
C				
D				
E				

Chapter 13　Partnerships: Characteristics, Formation, and Accounting for Activities

OUTLINE FOR REVIEW

In the majority of states, the Uniform Partnership Act governs the legal nature and functioning of the partnership. This chapter addresses the characteristics and basic principles of accounting applicable to this popular form of business organization.

I.　A partnership represents a voluntary association of individuals to carry out a business purpose. The partners are bound in a fiduciary relationship.

　　A.　An individual partner is viewed as a co-owner of partnership property. Specific assets contributed by a partner lose their identity, as to the source, and become the shared property of the partnership.

　　B.　The relationship of the partners is characterized as one of mutual agency. Acts of a general partner, acting within authority, bind both the partnership and the other partners.

　　C.　The general partnership is characterized by unlimited liability, in that all partners are liable, both jointly and severally, for acts that bind the partnership. This liability may extend to a partner's personal net worth.

　　D.　A limited partnership consists of one or more general partners and one or more limited partners who contribute capital but do not participate in the management of the firm. The limited partners' liability for partnership obligations is usually restricted to their interest in the partnership.

　　E.　Two other forms of organization, which offer some of the benefits of a partnership and also limit liability of the equity holders, are a limited liability company (LLC) and a limited liability partnership (LLP).

　　F.　The partnership characteristics are traceable to two equity theories: the proprietary theory and the entity theory.

　　　　1.　Partnership characteristics that are traceable to the proprietary theory include:

　　　　　　a.　Partners' salaries that are viewed as a distribution of income and are not deductible as ordinary business expenses.

　　　　　　b.　Unsatisfied partnership liabilities that are viewed as debts of the individual partners.

　　　　　　c.　The absence of the continuity of the partnership interest.

　　　　2.　Partnership characteristics that are traceable to the entity theory include:

　　　　　　a.　The ability of a partnership to enter into contracts in its own name.

　　　　　　b.　The partnership's right to property contributed by a partner; the contributing partner no longer retains a claim to the specific asset contributed.

II.　A partnership may come into existence without having to receive formal, legal, or state approval. However, forward thinking when organizing a partnership will benefit both the business and its partners.

　　A.　The articles of partnership serve as a document that sets forth the intent of the partners on a variety of matters including in part:

　　　　1.　Powers and duties of partners.

　　　　2.　Procedures governing the admission and withdrawal of partners.

　　　　3.　Procedures for the allocation of profits and losses.

　　　　4.　Allowable withdrawals of capital.

　　　　5.　Methods for determining a partner's equity in the partnership.

　　B.　The Uniform Partnership Act (UPA) also sets forth concepts and procedures governing a partnership. Often the UPA is applicable in the absence of a partnership agreement.

　　C.　Partnerships may account for their activities in conformity with generally accepted accounting principles (GAAP) or acceptable other comprehensive bases of accounting (OCBOA). OCBOA often provide partnerships with a basis of accounting that is better suited to their needs. Frequent OCBOA adopted by partnerships include the following:

　　　　1.　The cash (receipts and disbursements) basis of accounting and modifications of the basis, such as a modified accrual basis.

　　　　2.　The tax basis of accounting based on taxation principles that are used to file an income tax return.

　　D.　Dissolution of a partnership occurs when there is a change in the relation of the partners, caused by any partner ceasing to be associated in the carrying on of the business or by a new partner being admitted.

E. The partnership is not viewed as a separate taxable entity but rather as a conduit through which taxable items pass to the individual partners. Therefore, activities of the partnership must be evaluated from a tax standpoint based on their impact on individual partners.

III. The activities of a partnership consist of several phases, including contributions and distributions of capital and the allocation of operating profits and losses.

A. The activities of the partnership are accounted for using several special accounts, in addition to the normal asset, liability, revenue, and expense accounts.

1. A drawing account is established for each partner. This account, which is closed into the partner's capital account at year end, is debited for periodic withdrawals of partnership assets up to a specified amount. Each partner's initial investment in the partnership is recorded in a separate capital account.

2. The capital account is adjusted for:

a. Subsequent investments of capital.

b. Withdrawals in excess of an amount specified in the partnership agreement.

c. The closing of the net balance from the partner's drawing account.

d. The partner's share of partnership profits and losses as specified in the partnership agreement.

B. The postclosing balances in the capital accounts of the various partners represent each partner's interest in the net assets of the partnership at a point in time.

1. A partner's interest in the partnership capital is different from a partner's interest in profits and losses of the partnership.

2. If assets contributed to the partnership by a partner are truly loans versus investments of capital, they should be accounted for as loans. This distinction becomes especially important from a legal standpoint.

C. The manner in which profits and losses are to be divided among partners should be specifically stated in the articles of partnership. If the agreement does not provide for a specific division of profits and losses, they are to be divided equally among partners. The division of partnership income should be based on an analysis of the correlation between the capital and service (labor) committed to the firm by the individual partners and the income subsequently generated.

1. The profits and losses may be divided according to a predetermined ratio that incorporates both the capital and service contributions of the partners.

2. A portion of the profits and losses may be divided on the basis of the capital investments of the partners. The partnership agreement should specify the rate of interest that partners should earn on their invested capital. The agreement should also indicate whether the partners' drawing accounts should be closed to capital before computing interest. The interest may be calculated on beginning or ending capital or perhaps on the basis of a weighted average capital.

3. A portion of net income may be allocated to the partners as a salary or bonus to recognize the partners' labor or service to the firm as a primary force in the generation of revenue. Generally, a partner's drawing is not viewed as salary but as a withdrawal of assets, which reduces the partner's capital.

4. If the partnership income is not sufficient in amount to satisfy all of the provisions of the profit and loss agreement, two alternatives may be employed.

a. Completely satisfy all provisions of the profit and loss agreement and use the profit and loss ratios to absorb any deficiency or additional loss caused by such action.

b. Satisfy each of the provisions to whatever extent is possible. For example, the allocation of salaries would be satisfied to whatever extent possible before the allocation of interest is begun.

APPENDIX: OUTLINE FOR REVIEW

I. A partnership is not a separate taxable entity. Rather, it is a conduit through which taxable items pass to individual partners.

A. Because partnership profits and losses affect individual partners' tax returns, elements of revenue and expense at the partnership level flow through to the individual partners. Certain elements must maintain their specific identity because they are subject to special rules and limitations.

B. The tax basis of a partner's interest must be separately determined. This basis is generally different from a partner's interest in capital. Assets contributed by a partner to a partnership retain the same tax basis that the partner had prior to the contribution. The initial tax basis of a partner's interest is the sum of the:

1. Tax basis of the individual assets contributed to the partnership, and the
2. Tax basis of other partners' liabilities assumed by the partner, less the
3. Tax basis of the individual partner's liabilities assumed by other partners.

C. The initial tax basis of a partner subsequently changes due to the ongoing activities of the partnership.
   1. A partner's tax basis is increased by the following:
      a. Additional contributions of individual assets.
      b. The partner's share (based on profit and loss ratios) of increases in partnership liabilities resulting from assuming partners' personal liabilities and direct liabilities of the partnership.
      c. The partner's share of partnership taxable income.
      d. The partner's share of separately identified items of income not included in taxable income (loss).
   2. A partner's tax basis will be decreased by the following:
      a. Distributions of partnership assets.
      b. The portion of the partner's additional personal liabilities assumed by other partners.
      c. The partner's share of decreases in the liabilities of the partnership.
      d. The partner's share of partnership tax losses.
      e. The partner's share of separately identified items of loss not included in taxable income (loss).
   3. A partner's tax basis may not be decreased below zero. If operating losses would decrease the basis below zero, they are carried forward by the partners and used to offset subsequent increases in basis.

D. The partnership form of organization provides a means of avoiding double taxation. Double taxation refers to the taxation of corporate income when the income is earned by the corporation and a second taxation of the income when it is distributed as a dividend to shareholders. Double taxation may also be avoided by retaining versus distributing earnings or electing to be taxed as a Subchapter S corporation.

PART 1

Instructions: Circle the letter that identifies the best response to each question.

1. Which of the following is not a characteristic of a partnership?
   a. Salaries are not considered a component of net income.
   b. In a limited partnership there must be at least one general partner.
   c. Annual drawings may exceed the amount of annual salaries.
   d. Income tax rates are comparable to those of corporations.

2. Which of the following is not an advantage of a partnership over a corporation?
   a. Relative ease of formation.
   b. Avoidance of double taxation.
   c. Unlimited liability of individual owners.
   d. Theoretical ability to attract more capital.

3. Which of the following is not a difference between the financial statements of a partnership and those of a corporation?
   a. Partnerships do not have income tax expense.
   b. Partnerships do not include owners' salaries as an expense.
   c. Partnerships include interest on loans from owners as an expense.
   d. Partnerships do not have deferred income tax liabilities.

4. Which of the following is not characteristic of the proprietary theory as it relates to partnerships?
   a. Assets contributed by partners are recorded at their fair market value for accounting purposes.
   b. Partners' salaries are considered a distribution of income.
   c. Partnerships are not separate taxable entities.
   d. Changes in the ownership structure result in dissolution of the partnership.

5. Which of the following is not appropriate when a partnership loss is being allocated to the partners?
   a. Bonuses based on net income after the bonus are not used.
   b. Bonuses based on net income before the bonus are not used.
   c. Interest in invested capital is always allocated to the partners.
   d. The profit/loss percentages are used to recoup any previous allocations.

6. Which of the following best describes how a partner's withdrawals may affect the allocation of partnership profits?
   a. Withdrawals have no effect on the allocation of profits.
   b. Withdrawals are considered to be the same as salaries.
   c. They reduce invested capital and could affect the amount of interest on capital used as a component of a profit-sharing agreement.
   d. They could reduce the amount of net income upon which a bonus is based.

7. Which of the following best describes the relationship between drawing and capital accounts?
   a. The drawing account may never exceed the balance in the capital account.
   b. Both the drawing and capital accounts are nominal (temporary) accounts.
   c. The capital account will ultimately reflect the activity of the drawing account.
   d. Only the drawing account is used to reflect excessive withdrawals during the period.

PART 2

Hanyard, Robertson, Turman, and Kelly own a publishing company that they operate as a partnership. The partnership agreement includes the following:

1. Hanyard receives a salary of $20,000 and a bonus of 3% of income after all bonuses.
2. Robertson receives a salary of $10,000 and a bonus of 2% of income after all bonuses.
3. All partners are to receive 10% interest on their average capital balances.

   The average capital balances are as follows:

Hanyard	$50,000
Robertson	45,000
Turman	20,000
Kelly	47,000

4. Any remaining profits are to be divided equally among the partners.

Instructions:
1. Determine how a profit of $105,000 would be allocated among the partners.
2. Determine how a loss of $40,000 would be allocated among the partners.
3. Determine how a profit of $40,000 would be allocated among the partners assuming the following priority system: Income should be allocated by first giving priority to interest on invested capital, then bonuses, then salary, and then according to the profit/loss percentages.

PART 3

Instructions: Circle the letter that identifies the best response to each question based on the following situation.

Andersen, Blum, and Norwood are partners who have agreed to allocate profits as follows:
1. Salaries will be allocated to Blum and Norwood in the amounts of $45,000 and $60,000, respectively.
2. Blum will be allocated a bonus.
3. Interest of 10% per year will be allocated on weighted-average capital balances.
4. Weighted-average capital balances are $200,000, $100,000, and $30,000 for partners Andersen, Blum, and Norwood, respectively.

1. Assuming that partnership net income is $176,000 and that Blum's bonus is 10% of net income after the bonus, Blum's share of the net income is
   a. $71,000   b. $83,733   c. $78,333   d. $83,400

2. Assuming that partnership net income is $160,000 and that Blum's bonus is 10% of net income after salaries and interest, Blum's bonus is
   a. $16,000   b. $20,000   c. $2,200   d. $2,500

3. Assuming that partnership net income is $164,000, Blum's bonus is 10% of net income, and the partners' profit/loss percentages are 30%, 50%, and 20% for Andersen, Blum, and Norwood, respectively, Andersen's share of income is
     a. $76,200   b. $22,880   c. $23,200   d. $20,000

4. Assume that the partnership net income is $66,000 and that Blum's bonus is 10% of net income after the bonus. Using profit and loss ratios to absorb any deficiency, Norwood's share of the income would be
     a. $35,000   b. $15,000   c. $36,800   d. $37,000

5. Assume the same facts as in question 4, except that each provision of the profit and loss agreement is to be satisfied to whatever extent possible. Assuming that the components of the agreement are described in order of priority, Norwood's share of the income is
     a. $37,714   b. $28,286   c. $21,000   d. $47,000

PART 4

Instructions: Circle the letter that identifies the best response to each question based on the following situation.

Holmes and Meyers formed a partnership in 20X8 by each contributing $30,000. In addition, Meyers contributed equipment with a fair market value of $40,000 and a tax basis to Meyers of $32,000. Meyers' equipment loan with a balance of $24,000 was assumed by the partnership. During the year 20X8, the following additional events occurred:

> Holmes and Meyers each contributed an additional $10,000.
> Holmes withdrew $12,000 for personal reasons.
> Meyers made a $15,000 loan to the partnership payable on demand.

Net income for the year was $82,000 of which $36,000 was allocated to Holmes. The allocation of net income is partially based on salaries of $20,000 and $30,000 being allocated to Holmes and Meyers, respectively.

1. The preclosing 20X8 balance of Holmes' drawing account is
     a. $32,000   b. $12,000   c. $22,000   d. $24,000

2. The postclosing 20X8 balance of Meyers' capital account is
     a. $126,000   b. $117,000   c. $102,000   d. $106,000

3. Upon formation of the partnership, Meyers' tax basis in the partnership is
     a. $46,000   b. $62,000   c. $70,000   d. $50,000

4. If the partnership were to have borrowed $30,000 from a bank during 20X8, the effect on Meyers' tax basis and capital balance, respectively, would have been to increase them by
     a. $30,000 and $30,000   c. $15,000 and $0
     b. $30,000 and $0   d. $15,000 and $15,000

5. The adjustment of a partner's tax basis for loans assumed by the partnership is influenced by a partner's
     a.   Percentage interest in capital.   c.   Drawing account balance.
     b.   Profit/loss percentage.   d.   Personal tax basis in assets contributed.

6. Holmes' tax basis in the partnership at the end of 20X8 is
     a. $83,500   b. $95,500   c. $71,500   d. $64,000

Chapter 14   Partnerships: Ownership Changes and Liquidations

OUTLINE FOR REVIEW

The dissolution of a partnership occurs when the partnership's ownership changes as a result of the admission or withdrawal of a partner. Liquidation is the termination of partnership operations.

I.   Accounting for changes in the ownership of a partnership is heavily influenced by the legal concept of dissolution. When there is a change in the ownership structure, the original partnership is dissolved and a new partnership is created.

A.   Changes in ownership involve exchanges of consideration that reflect the current value of the partnership interest. Such changes may indicate that:

1.   The existing assets of the original partnership should be revalued.

2.   Previously unrecorded intangible assets, such as goodwill, exist that are traceable to the original partnership.

3.   Intangible assets, such as goodwill, exist that are traceable to a new partner.

B.   The admission of a new partner should be distinguished from an assignment of a partnership interest.

1.   An assignment of a partnership interest does not dissolve the partnership. The assignee is not allowed to participate in the management and does not have the right to review the transactions and records of the partnership.

2.   The admission of a new partner requires the approval of the existing partners. The new partner normally experiences the same general risks and rights of ownership as do the other existing partners. The new partner is liable for all the obligations of the partnership arising before admission, except that those liabilities may be satisfied only from partnership property.

C.   One method of gaining admission to an existing partnership is to contribute assets directly to the partnership entity. The amount of the contribution reflects the current value of the partnership; however, the book value of the original partnership's net assets may not approximate the fair market value.

1.   The incoming partner may acquire an interest in the partnership for a price in excess of the indicated book value of the original partnership's net assets. This suggests the existence of unrecorded appreciation on existing net assets and/or previously unrecorded intangible assets.

2.   The incoming partner may acquire an interest in the partnership for a price less than that indicated by the book value of the original partnership. This suggests the existence of unrecorded depreciation on existing net assets and/or a contribution of goodwill by the incoming partner.

D.   When an incoming partner's contribution is different from that indicated by the book value of the original existing partnership, the admission of a new partner is recorded by either the bonus method or the goodwill method. The use of either method does not preclude the recognition of previously unrecorded appreciation or depreciation on existing assets as otherwise permitted by GAAP.

1.   The bonus method adheres to the historical cost concept of accounting. It is objective in the sense that the total capital of the new partnership is established at an amount based on the actual consideration received from the new partner. The bonus method indirectly acknowledges goodwill by giving a bonus to the old or new partners.

a.   The application of the bonus method results in the following conditions:

(1) The total capital of the new partnership will be equal to the book value of the existing partners' capital plus the recorded value of the incoming partner's investment.

(2) Upon admission, the incoming partner's capital is determined by multiplying the total capital of the new partnership by the acquired percentage interest in capital.

b.   When the new partner's interest in capital is less than the amount of capital invested, the excess investment is credited to the original partners' capital accounts according to their profit and loss ratios.

c.   When the new partner's interest in capital is greater than the amount of capital invested, the amount of the deficiency is charged against the capital accounts of the original partners according to their profit and loss ratios.

2. The goodwill method results in the recognition of an asset implied by a transaction rather than recognizing an asset actually purchased. Goodwill is determined as follows:
   a. Determine the entity's fair market value, as evidenced by the new partner's investment, divided by the percentage interest in the new partnership.
   b. If the fair market value of the entity is greater than the book value of the new partnership, implied goodwill is traceable to the old partners and is allocated to the old partners according to their profit ratios.
   c. If the fair market value of the entity is less than the book value of the new partnership, implied goodwill is traceable to the new partner. The amount of goodwill is the difference between the amount paid by the new partner and the amount that should have been paid by the new partner to acquire an interest in the book value of the partnership.
   d. The initial capital balance of the new partner is equal to the new partner's interest in the total capital of the new partnership, which includes the implied goodwill.
3. Although the bonus or goodwill methods are mutually exclusive choices, the use of either of these methods may be accompanied by the revaluation of existing assets.
4. The use of the goodwill method could produce inequitable results if:
   a. The new partner's interest in profits does not equal the new partner's initial interest in capital.
   b. The former partners do not share in profits and losses in the same relationship to each other as they did before the admission of the new partner.

E. A new partner may acquire an interest in the partnership by purchasing the interest from the individual partners rather than from the partnership entity. The acquisition price is paid directly to the partner. The partnership will record the redistribution of capital between the old and new partners and does not record the transfer of any assets.
1. If the consideration paid by the incoming partner is not used to impute the fair market value of the entity, the capital accounts of the original partners are reduced for the portion sold and the incoming partner's capital account is credited for the amount of the interest purchased.
2. If the consideration paid by the incoming partner is used to impute the fair market value of the entity, the asset and capital accounts of the original partners are first adjusted to reflect the fair market value of the entity. After the adjustments are made, the capital accounts of the selling partner(s) is reduced for the portion sold and the incoming partner's capital account is credited.

F. When a partner withdraws, the fair market value of the partnership should be determined and the partnership income to the date of withdrawal should be measured. The equity of the retiring partner may not be equal to the capital balance as a result of the existence of accounting errors, unrecorded differences between the fair market value and the recorded book value of the assets, and/or unrecorded assets such as goodwill.
1. When a withdrawing partner sells his or her interest to the existing partners or a new partner, the result is a mere redistribution of the withdrawing partner's equity to the purchasing partner(s).
2. When a withdrawing partner sells his or her interest to the partnership, either the bonus method or the goodwill method is applied.
   a. When the bonus method is used, the difference between the payment to the withdrawing partner and that partner's capital balance is allocated to the capital accounts of the remaining partners according to their profit and loss ratios.
   b. When the goodwill method is used, the amount of the payment to the withdrawing partner in excess of that partner's capital balance represents the goodwill attributable to only the withdrawing partner's interest. The implied total goodwill of the partnership is equal to the withdrawing partner's goodwill divided by that partner's percentage interest in profit and loss.
      (1) The partnership may recognize goodwill only on the goodwill it actually purchased from the retiring partner. This involves debiting goodwill and crediting only the retiring partner's capital account for the amount of goodwill purchased. Then, the retiring partner's capital account is eliminated with a credit to cash or other assets that were paid to the partner.
      (2) The partnership may decide to recognize the total goodwill implied by the transaction with the retiring partner. This involves debiting goodwill and crediting each partner's capital account for its share of the total goodwill according to its profit and loss ratio.
   c. If the goodwill method is used and the payment to the withdrawing partner is less than that partner's capital balance, this suggests that existing assets are overvalued and should be written down. The write-down may be recognized either as only that portion traceable to the withdrawing partner or the total amount traceable to the entire partnership.

II.   The process of liquidation consists of the conversion of partnership assets into a distributable form and the distribution of these assets to creditors and owners.

    A. A liquidation distribution should recognize the legal rights of partnership creditors and the individual partners. All liquidation expenses and gains or losses from the conversion of partnership assets must be allocated to the individual partners. If there is a premature or incorrect distribution to the partners, which later may not be recovered to satisfy creditors, the authorizing partnership fiduciary may be held liable. The sequence of payments should be observed as follows:

        1. Amounts owed to creditors other than partners.

        2. Amounts owed to partners for loans to the partnership.

        3. Amounts owed to partners for capital.

        4. Amounts owed to partners as profits not currently closed to partners' capital accounts.

    B. The right-of-offset doctrine has the effect of combining amounts owed to partners for loans to the partnership with their capital balances. This reduces the risk of premature distributions to partners.

    C. Partners should contribute assets to the partnership to cover a debit balance in their respective capital accounts. If this is not possible, the debit balance should be viewed as a realized loss and allocated to the remaining partners according to their proportionate profit and loss ratios. A partner who absorbs another partner's debit balance has a legal claim against the deficient partner.

    D. The marshaling-of-assets doctrine is applied when the partnership and/or one or more of the partners is insolvent.

        1. Partnership assets are first available for the payment of partnership obligations. Any excess assets are available to satisfy the individual partner's personal debts only to the extent of the partner's capital balance.

        2. Personal assets of a partner are applied against personal debts; they are ranked in order of priority as follows:

            a. Amounts owed to personal creditors.

            b. Amounts owed to partnership creditors.

            c. Amounts owed to partners by way of their contribution.

        3. Under common law or federal bankruptcy law, the marshaling-of-assets doctrine is applied differently than above. In those instances amounts owed to partners by way of contribution are on an equal basis (pari passu) with personal creditors of the partner.

III.   A lump-sum liquidation requires that all assets be realized before a distribution is made to partners.

    A. A schedule of the balances and transactions that affect cash, noncash assets to be converted, liabilities, and capital balances of the partners is maintained.

    B. The assets are liquidated, and gains and losses from their realization are allocated to the partners' capital accounts according to their profit and loss ratios.

    C. Partnership liabilities are satisfied from partnership assets.

    D. A partner who is personally solvent but has a debit capital balance should reduce the debit capital balance to the extent possible.

    E. The remaining debit capital balances are treated as realized losses and allocated to the remaining partners according to their proportionate profit and loss ratios.

    F. The remaining assets are distributed to the partners with credit capital balances.

IV.   Payments in a liquidation may be made in installments to creditors and partners during the liquidation process. Installment payments may be made to partners only after anticipating all liabilities, possible losses, and liquidation expenses. An installment liquidation assumes that all noncash assets are worthless and that the loss is allocated to the partners according to their profit and loss ratios.

    A. A schedule of the balances and transactions that affect cash, noncash assets to be converted, liabilities, and capital balances of the partners is maintained.

    B. As the assets are liquidated, cash is increased for the selling price, the noncash assets are reduced by the book value of the disposed assets, and the gain or loss is allocated to the partners according to their profit and loss ratios.

    C. Before a distribution to the partners is made, the available cash must be reduced for the payment of liabilities.

    D. A schedule of safe payments is prepared prior to each distribution to the partners.

        1. The capital and loan balances of each partner—before the distribution—are combined.

        2. The estimated liquidation expenses, allocated to the partners according to their profit and loss ratios, are subtracted.

        3. The amount of the maximum loss possible, which assumes that all noncash assets are worthless, is subtracted. Losses are allocated to the partners according to their profit and loss ratios.

     4.   Partners' debit capital balances are allocated to the remaining partners.

     5.   The resulting capital balances are the amount of safe payments that are entered in the installment liquidation statement.

  E. A predistribution plan provides an easier means of determining distributions to partners. The predistribution plan provides the user with information regarding the order and amount of all future distributions. The predistribution plan also combines the partners' loan and capital balances; anticipates all possible liabilities, losses on realization, and liquidation expenses; and recognizes that the partner with the greatest ability to absorb anticipated losses is the first to receive safe payments.

     1.   The maximum loss each partner can absorb before a debit balance is created in the capital account is determined by dividing each partner's capital balance by that partner's profit/loss percentage.

     2.   The partners are ranked in descending order according to the amount of their maximum loss absorbable.

     3.   The amount of the safe payment that may be paid to the first-ranked partner, before achieving equality between the maximum losses absorbable of the first- and second-ranked partner, is determined.

     4.   The amount that may be paid to those partners having equivalent maximum losses absorbable, so that their new maximum losses absorbable would be equal to that of the next-highest-ranked partner, is determined.

     5.   When all partners have equal maximum losses absorbable, distributions are allocated according to the partners' profit ratios.

PART 1

Instructions: Use a check mark to indicate whether each of the following statements is true or false.

	True	False
1. A new incoming partner's contribution may suggest either the presence of previously unrecorded goodwill or the appreciation of existing assets but not both.		
2. Use of the bonus method and use of the goodwill method are mutually exclusive choices.		
3. Under the bonus method, the new incoming partner's initial capital balance is equal to that partner's percentage interest in capital times the book value of the old partnership.		
4. The goodwill method recognizes increases in asset values that have not been realized or purchased.		
5. If a withdrawing partner receives consideration that is less than his/her capital balance, goodwill would not be recognized.		
6. If only purchased goodwill could be recognized, then only transactions involving the withdrawal, versus the admission, of a partner would be applicable.		
7. Unsatisfied personal creditors of a partner can attach to the net assets of the partnership without regard to the partner's capital balance.		
8. Amounts due to partners by way of loans to the partnership are usually combined with capital balances in order to avoid premature distributions during a liquidation.		
9. Unsatisfied partnership creditors cannot attach to the net personal assets of a partner unless the partner has a debit capital balance.		
10. Before distributing assets to partners as part of an installment liquidation, it is assumed that all noncash assets are worthless.		
11. The amounts to be distributed to partners, as determined by a schedule of safe payments, are generally different from the amounts suggested in a predistribution plan.		
12. Legally speaking, amounts incurred as liquidation expenses must be paid before a distribution can be made to the partners.		

PART 2

Gabriel and Hall are partners and had capital balances at the end of year 20X5 of $190,000 and $100,000, respectively. Gabriel and Hall have profit/loss percentages of 40% and 60%, respectively.

Instructions: Answer questions 1 to 5 based on the following situation. (Each each question is independent.)

1. Assume that Rogers purchased from Gabriel one-half of Gabriel's interest in the partnership for $135,000. Determine Gabriel's capital balance after this transaction.

2. Assume that Rogers purchased from the partnership a 30% interest in the business for $150,000. Determine Gabriel's capital balance after this transaction using the bonus method.

3. Assume that net tangible assets of the partnership are overstated by $40,000 and that Rogers wants to acquire from the partnership a one-third interest. Determine the price to be paid by Rogers using the bonus method.

4. Assume that tangible assets of the partnership are overstated by $50,000 and that Rogers acquires a one-third interest from the partnership for a cash contribution of $150,000. Determine Gabriel's capital balance after this transaction using the goodwill method.

5. Assume that Rogers acquires a one-third interest in the partnership for a cash contribution of $150,000 and that recorded tangible assets are undervalued by $50,000. Determine Rogers' capital balance after this transaction using the goodwill method.

PART 3

Instructions: Circle the letter that identifies the best response to each question based on the described situation. Unless otherwise stated, the questions are independent.

Norris and Vander have capital balances of $20,000 and $50,000, respectively. They have agreed to admit Wright as a partner with a 30% interest in capital. Prior to Wright's admission, the partners allocated profits 40% and 60%, respectively, for Norris and Vander. The new partnership will allocate profits equally among the partners.

1. If the bonus method is employed and Wright invests $32,000 in the partnership, Wright's initial capital balance will be
    a. $32,000   b. $30,600   c. $34,000   d. $30,000

2. If the bonus method is employed and Wright invests $36,000 in the partnership, Norris' new capital balance will be
    a. $21,400   b. $22,100   c. $21,680   d. $35,333

3. Given the facts of question 2, assume that existing assets are undervalued by $10,000. Norris' new capital balance will be
    a. $24,480   b. $26,480   c. $24,600   d. $24,400

4. If Wright acquired a 30% interest in the partnership by paying $36,000 to Vander in exchange for a portion of Vander's interest in the partnership, Wright's initial capital balance would be
    a. $31,800   b. $35,333   c. $36,000   d. $21,000

5. If the goodwill method is employed and Wright invests $36,000 in the partnership, Vander's new capital balance will be
    a. $55,600   b. $58,400   c. $53,000   d. $57,000

6. Given the facts of question 5, assume that existing assets are undervalued by $10,000. Vander's new capital balance will be
    a. $58,400   b. $63,000   c. $64,400   d. $58,000

7. If the goodwill method is employed and Wright invests $24,000, how much implied goodwill is traceable to Wright?
    a. $0   b. $6,000   c. $2,000   d. $4,200

8. Given the facts of question 7, assume that existing assets are undervalued by $7,000. How much implied goodwill is traceable to Wright?
    a. $0   b. $13,000   c. $9,000   d. $6,300

PART 4

Instructions: Answer questions 1 to 5 based on the following situation.

A partnership consist of partners A, B, and C whose profit/loss percentages are 40%, 40%, and 20%, respectively. Their personal assets and liabilities are as follows:

	Partner		
	A	B	C
Assets	130,000	230,000	60,000
Liabilities	62,000	210,000	56,000

The net assets are before any further contribution to or from the partnership. The partners have agreed that net personal assets should be used to eliminate any actual (versus possible) deficit balances in their capital accounts. (Unless otherwise stated, the questions are independent.)

1. Assume that the following partnership balances exist: cash, $94,000; noncash assets, $124,000; liabilities, $73,000; capital—A, $70,000; capital—B, $72,000; and capital—C, $3,000. How much of the available cash will be distributed to partner A?

2. Assume that the following partnership balances exist: cash, $74,000; noncash assets, $144,000; liabilities, $73,000; capital—A, $70,000; capital—B, $72,000; and capital—C, $3,000. After these balances were determined, the partnership sold assets with a book value of $70,000 for $50,000. After considering the marshaling of assets and the sale of assets, what would partner C's capital balance be?

3. Assume that the following partnership balances exist: cash, $20,000; equipment, $144,000; outside liabilities, $0; capital—A, $70,000; capital—B, $72,000; and capital—C, $3,000. Furthermore, the following loan balances exist: loan receivable—partner B, $16,000; loan payable—partner B, $20,000; and loan payable—partner C, $15,000. How much of the available cash would be received by each of the partners?

4. Assume that the following partnership balances exist: cash, $40,000; liabilities, $100,000; capital—A, $30,000 deficit; capital—B, $25,000 deficit; and capital—C, $5,000 deficit. Furthermore, the marshaling-of-assets doctrine is followed. What are the partners' capital balances after payment of the liabilities?

5. Assume that the following partnership balances exist: cash, $40,000; noncash assets, $120,000; liabilities, $0; capital—A, $80,000; capital—B, $70,000; and capital—C, $10,000. If partner A receives a noncash asset with a book value of $10,000 and a fair market value of $20,000, how much of the available cash should partner A receive?

PART 5

Martini, Manhatton, and Moskel have voted to dissolve the MMM partnership. The liquidation will take place over a prolonged period of time. The partnership's account balances on December 31, 20X2, are shown in the installment liquidation statement.

Martini, Manhatton, and Moskel share in the profits and losses in the ratio 4:4:2.

Sales of assets were as follows:

Date	Book Value	Selling Price
January 5	$75,000	$55,000
January 20	40,000	25,000
May 6	50,000	60,000
May 21	75,000	79,000

Liquidation expenses are estimated to be $15,000. Installment distributions of unrestricted cash are made on January 15, February 28, May 15, and June 1.

Total liquidation expenses of $20,000 are paid on May 10.

Instructions: Complete the following supplementary schedule for the calculation of safe payments and the installment liquidation statement.

Schedule of Safe Payments

	Martini	Manhatton	Moskel	Total
Profit/loss percentage	40%	40%	20%	100%

January 15 distribution:

	Martini	Manhatton	Moskel	Total
Combined capital and loan balances before distribution	$52,000	$102,000	$26,000	$180,000
Estimated liquidation expenses				
Balances				
Maximum loss possible				
Balances				
Allocation of debit balances				
Safe payments				

February 28 distribution:

	Martini	Manhatton	Moskel	Total
Combined capital and loan balances before distribution				
Estimated liquidation expenses				
Balances				
Maximum loss possible				
Balances				
Allocation of debit balances				
Safe payments				

May 15 distribution:

	Martini	Manhatton	Moskel	Total
Combined capital and loan balances before distribution				
Maximum loss possible				
Safe payments				

Installment Liquidation Statement

	Cash	Noncash Assets	Liabilities	Loans from Martini	Martini	Manhatton	Moskel
Beginning balances	$20,000	$240,000	$60,000	$10,000	$50,000	$110,000	$30,000
Jan. 5, sale of assets							
Balances							
Payment of liabilities							
Jan. 15, distribution							
Balances							
Jan. 20, sale of assets							
Balances							
Feb. 28, distribution							
Balances							
May 6, sale of assets							
May 10, payment of liquidation expenses							
Balances							
May 15, distribution							
Balances							
May 21, sale of assets							
Balances							
June 1, final distribution							
Balances							

Chapter 15 Governmental Accounting: The General Fund and the Account Groups

OUTLINE FOR REVIEW

The fundamental purpose of governmental as well as commercial accounting is to provide financial information useful in evaluating the activity and financial position of an entity and to assist in planning future actions and making resource allocation decisions.

I. Differences in operating environments between business enterprises and governments cause different measurement focuses to be applied to their financial reporting.
   A. Governments have a service motive whereas business enterprises have a profit motive. Governments raise and use resources to produce goods and services consumed by those who have a legal right to receive them. Business enterprises raise and use resources to produce goods and services sold to buyers who can pay the purchase price (revenue to the seller).
   B. The measurement focus of governmental funds is flows of financial resources, which measure interperiod equity, or the extent to which financial resources obtained during a period are sufficient to finance expenditures made during the period. Such financial reporting helps a government be publicly accountable to its citizenry and provides useful information to financial report users on working capital needs of the government.
   C. The measurement focus of business-type activities is flows of economic resources, which match revenues earned (inflows of economic resources) against expenses incurred (outflows of economic resources) to determine net income for a period. Such financial reporting helps financial report users assess whether an entity's capital has been maintained.
II. State and local government financial reports should possess the characteristics of understandability, reliability, relevance, timeliness, consistency, and comparability.
III. Each major activity of a government is accounted for in its own self-balancing set of accounts called funds. There are three types of funds:
   A. Governmental funds account for activities that provide citizens with services financed primarily by taxes and intergovernmental grants.
   B. Proprietary funds account for business-type activities that derive their revenue from charges to users for goods and services.
   C. Fiduciary funds account for resources for which the governmental unit acts as a trustee or agent.
IV. Long-term assets acquired with governmental fund resources and long-term debt that provides governmental fund resources are accounted for in account groups. There are two types of account groups:
   A. General fixed assets account group is a self-balancing set of accounts that includes a listing of the general fixed assets, including infrastructure assets, of a government as debits and the funding source of the general fixed assets as credits.
   B. General long-term debt account group is a self-balancing set of accounts that reports unpaid long-term debt as credits and the amounts available and yet to be provided for the payment of the debt as debits.
V. Five governmental funds may be used by governments:
   A. The general fund accounts for resources that have no specific restrictions and that are available for operational expenditures not accounted for in another fund.
   B. Special revenue funds account for financial resources raised from specific revenue sources and expended for specific operational purposes.
   C. Capital projects funds account for financial resources raised and used to acquire major capital facilities for the general government. Many capital-improvement special assessment projects are also accounted for in capital projects funds.
   D. Debt service funds account for financial resources raised and used to pay general long-term debt principal and interest.
   E. Permanent funds account for resources that are legally restricted so that only their earnings, not the principal, may be used to finance operations.

VI.   Recognition of financial transactions of a government is on a modified accrual basis.
   A.   *Revenues* are increases in a governmental fund's financial resources from transactions with external parties that do not have to be repaid. Revenues may be from non-exchange transactions, such as taxes, fines, fees, licenses or permits, or donations. Revenues may also be from exchange transactions, such as user fees or investment income and gains.
   B.   Other financing sources are inflows of financial resources to governmental funds. These arise from issuance of general long-term debt, recording the present value of capital lease obligations, proceeds from the sale of capital assets, and from interfund operating transfers-in.
   C.   Most expenditures are decreases in financial resources as a result of transactions to acquire goods and services from external parties. Some expenditures, however, result from consumption of previously purchased financial resources, such as inventories and prepaid items.
   D.   Other financing uses are outflows of financial resources from governmental funds. The greatest use of this account classification is for operating transfers-out to other governmental funds.

VII.   Budgetary accounting is used by managers to achieve control over the raising and spending of resources through governmental funds.
   A.   Neither control of financial activity nor assessment of the results of operations is measurable in terms of net income in governmental funds.
   B.   Control of financial activity is accomplished by recording the annual operating budget and later comparing projected with actual results.
   C.   The entry to record the budget is:

Estimated revenues	XXX	
Estimated other financing sources	XXX	
Appropriations		XXX
Estimated other financing uses		XXX
Budgetary fund balance—unreserved*		XXX

   *This account may be debited or credited, depending on the amounts of the other items.
   D.   Almost all accounts in governmental accounting are control accounts. Details of their composition are maintained in subsidiary records.

VIII.   Accounting in the general fund:
   A.   Actual inflows of resources in the general fund are recorded as:
      1.   Revenues, with revenues defined as in VI.A., or
      2.   Other financing sources, with other financing sources defined as in VI.B.
   B.   Actual outflows of resources from the general fund are recorded as:
      1.   Expenditures, with expenditures defined as in VI.C., or
      2.   Other financing uses, with other financing uses as defined in VI.D.
   C.   To prevent overexpenditure, the general fund uses an encumbrance system.
      1.   Under this system, the estimated cost of a commitment is recorded with the following entry:

Encumbrances	XXX	
Fund balance—reserved for encumbrances		XXX

      (This entry is reversed when the actual expenditures are recorded.)
      2.   Encumbrances outstanding at year end are temporarily closed with the following entry:

Fund balance—unreserved, undesignated	XXX	
Encumbrances		XXX

      3.   At the start of the new year, the outstanding encumbrances are reinstated with the following entry:

Encumbrances	XXX	
Fund balance—unreserved, undesignated		XXX

      Also, the amount of the outstanding encumbrances is included in the budgetary entry for appropriations.
      4.   Short-term debt to cover operating needs in anticipation of tax revenues is accounted for in the fund as a current liability.
      5.   Investments of a government are reported at fair value. The change in fair value is reported as "net increase (decrease) in fair value of investments" and is included as revenue on the statement of revenues, expenditures, and changes in fund balances.
      6.   At the end of the period, revenue and other financing sources are closed against expenditures and other financing uses with the net to the Fund balance—unreserved undesignated.

IX.   Special and extraordinary items are reported separately in the financial statements.
   A.   Extraordinary items are both unusual in nature and frequent in occurrence.

       B.   Special items arise from significant transactions or other events that are (1) within the control of management, and (2) either unusual in nature or infrequent in occurrence.

X.   All fixed assets, except for those of a proprietary or fiduciary fund, are accounted for in the general fixed assets account group. This account group may be thought of as an inventory of general fixed assets and their source of funding.

       A.   The recommended fixed asset categories are:
1. Land
2. Buildings
3. Improvements other than buildings
4. Infrastructure fixed assets, including sidewalks, streets, curbs, and bridges
5. Machinery and equipment
6. Construction in progress

       B.   The basis of an asset is its cost. When the asset is donated, the basis is the appraised market value at time of donation.

       C.   Leasing of equipment has become common practice among governments. If a lease qualifies as a capital lease, then the asset is recorded in the account group. The general fund will debit expenditures and credit other financing sources.

       D.   Depreciation expense is not reported in governmental funds statements since depreciation neither provides nor uses financial resources. Governments must, however, report depreciation in the government-wide statements.

       E.   The schedule of capital assets shows the total amount of each category of capital assets along with accumulated depreciation.

XI.   Long-term debt is accounted for in the general long-term debt account group, which furnishes a record of the unmatured principal of general long-term capital obligations of the governmental unit.

       A.   Interest is not accounted for in this account group. Payments of both principal and interest are handled by the debt service fund.

       B.   The schedule of long-term liabilities shows the amount available in the debt service fund for term bonds, serial bonds, and other general long-term debt (unfunded pension obligations, claims and judgments, lease obligations, unfunded compensated absences), as well as the amounts that are still to be provided for their retirement.

PART 1

Instructions: Use a check mark to indicate whether each of the following statements is true or false.

	True	False
1. For an auditor's opinion of governmental financial statements to be unqualified, the statements must be presented in conformity with GAAP.	_____	_____
2. The three broad categories of funds in governmental accounting are governmental funds, proprietary funds, and fiduciary funds.	_____	_____
3. Proprietary funds account for sales of goods or services for which a fee is charged.	_____	_____
4. A credit balance in the Fund balance—Unreserved, Undesignated account of a general fund represents the excess of inflows over outflows of financial resources available for expenditure.	_____	_____
5. The general fund includes current assets, current liabilities, fixed assets, and general long-term debt.	_____	_____
6. The measurement focus for governmental funds is flows of economic resources.	_____	_____
7. Each transaction affecting a governmental fund requires an entry in only one fund or account group.	_____	_____

8. Depreciation is required to be reported in the government-wide statements, but not in the account groups. _____ _____

9. The liability resulting from the issue of serial bonds is accounted for in the general fund. _____ _____

10. Long-term debt that will be paid from governmental funds may be operating debt or capital. _____ _____

PART 2

Instructions: A list of transactions that occurred in the city of Irin's general fund follows. Beside each transaction write the letter(s) that classifies each transaction:

A . Revenue   E. Other financing uses
B. Other financing sources   F. Borrowing transaction within the fund
C. Expenditures   G. Designation of the fund balance
D. Encumbrances   H. None of the above

Classification

1. Property taxes are levied for the current year. _____

2. Using "tax anticipation" notes, $100,000 is borrowed, which will be repaid when property taxes are collected. _____

3. Income is transferred to the general fund from a municipal trust fund. _____

4. The city is notified of the receipt of a state "road improvement grant." _____

5. Interest is recorded on the collection of delinquent taxes. _____

6. A used fixed asset is sold. _____

7. Salaries are paid. _____

8. An order is placed for supplies. _____

9. The invoice for supplies that were received in the prior fiscal year is paid. _____

10. Supplies are consumed. The physical inventory is recorded. _____

11. A new fixed asset is purchased. _____

12. Funds are transferred to the debt service fund. _____

13. A portion of the fund balance is voted to be "set aside" for the purchase of a new fire truck. _____

14. A bond is sold to finance the purchase of new road repair equipment. _____

15. Equipment was acquired with a capital lease. _____

16. Investments increase in value. _____

PART 3

Instructions: Record the journal entries for each of the transactions listed for the city of Watertower Park. The trial balance for the city on January 1, 20X7, is given next.

	Debit	Credit
Cash	$10,000	
Delinquent taxes receivable	32,000	
Allowance for uncollectible delinquent taxes		$15,000
Tax liens receivable	6,000	
Allowance for uncollectible tax liens		2,000

Supplies inventory	8,000	
Vouchers payable		13,000
Fund balance—reserved for encumbrances		7,000
Fund balance—reserved for inventory		8,000
Fund balance—unreserved, undesignated		11,000
Totals	$56,000	$56,000

The transactions to be recorded (without explanations) are:

1. A budget is adopted that includes estimated revenues of $375,000, expenditures of $300,000, and other financing uses of $60,000.

2. Encumbrances of the prior year were included in the budget estimates. The prior year encumbrances are reinstated on the books.

3. Current property taxes are levied at $350,000 with a 2% allowance for uncollectible property taxes.

4. Delinquent property taxes of $20,000 are collected plus $1,200 in interest. The allowance for uncollectible delinquent taxes is adjusted.

5. Property to which tax liens apply is sold for $3,500, and the account is closed.

6. Current property taxes are collected in the amount of $340,000.

7. Remaining current property taxes are considered delinquent; previously delinquent property taxes are converted to tax liens.

8. The city is notified that it has been awarded a state grant in the amount of $45,000.

9. Orders are placed for equipment at an estimated cost of $23,000.

10. Vouchers are recorded in the amount of $290,000. Included in this amount are $7,000 of items encumbered last year, items estimated to cost $20,000 that were encumbered this year, and inventory purchases of $15,000.

11. Vouchers of $290,000 are paid.

12. The physical inventory taken at year end is $6,000. The inventory and appropriate reserved fund balance are adjusted.

13. $59,000 is transferred to the debt service fund.

PART 4

The following preclosing trial balance of a general fund has been prepared:

Village of Victory
General Fund Trial Balance
December 31, 20X8

Cash	$ 55,000	
Taxes receivable—delinquent	30,000	
Allowance for uncollectible delinquent taxes		$ 15,000
Tax liens receivable	10,000	
Allowance for uncollectible tax liens		5,000
Marketable equity securities	120,000	
Vouchers payable		25,000
Fund balance—reserved for encumbrances		12,000
Fund balance—unreserved, undesignated, January 1, 20X2		140,000
Budgetary fund balance—unreserved		50,000
Estimated revenues	525,000	
Revenues		500,000
Appropriations		475,000
Expenditures	470,000	
Encumbrances	12,000	
	$1,222,000	$1,222,000

Instructions:

1. Guided by the explanations provided, prepare the necessary entries.
   (a) To reverse entry recording budget:

(b) To close nominal accounts:

2. Complete the following budgetary comparison schedule.

Village of Victory
General Fund
Budgetary Comparison Schedule—General Fund
For Fiscal Year Ended December 31, 20X8

	Budget	Actual Results	Variances—Favorable (Unfavorable)
Revenues	_____	_____	_____
Expenditures	_____	_____	_____
Excess of revenues over expenditures	_____	_____	_____
Fund balances, January 1, 20X8	_____	_____	_____
Fund balances, December 31, 20X8	_____	_____	_____0

3. Prepare the balance sheet as of December 31, 20X8.

Village of Victory
General Fund Balance Sheet
December 31, 20X8

Assets   Liabilities and Fund Equity

PART 5

Instructions: Following is a list of transactions that are to be recorded in the general fund of Carleton City. The transactions may also require entries in the general fixed assets account group or in the general long-term debt account group. For each transaction, indicate the fund or group required and provide the entry (or entries).

1. The city orders two new fire trucks at an estimated cost of $150,000.

   Fund or group:
   Entry:

2. The fire trucks arrive. The invoice price is $154,000. The city pays $54,000 cash and finances the balance with a 4-year note payable to the manufacturer.

   Fund or group:
   Entries:

   Fund or group:
   Entry:

   Fund or group:
   Entry:

3. One of the city's old fire trucks with an original cost of $50,000 is sold for $15,000.

   Fund or group:
   Entry:

   Fund or group:
   Entry:

4. The city entered into a capital lease agreement for an ambulance. The present value of the lease payment is $50,000 (equal to the fair market value of the ambulance).

   Fund or group:
   Entry:

   Fund or group:
   Entry:

   Fund or group:
   Entry:

5. The city makes a direct payment of $35,000 to retire bonds at face value.

   Fund or group:
   Entry:

   Fund or group:
   Entry:

Chapter 16   Governmental Accounting: Other Governmental Funds, Proprietary Funds, and Fiduciary Funds

OUTLINE FOR REVIEW

In governmental accounting, special funds, proprietary funds, and fiduciary funds are used to record events and exhibit results for a specific area of responsibility. When these funds are used, some transactions are recorded in more than one fund.

I.   Special revenue funds are used to account for revenues received that are to be devoted to a specified current operating purpose or to the acquisition of relatively minor fixed assets. The revenues received are unrelated to the value of services rendered.

   A.   The accounting must be designed to permit close scrutiny of activities. The project must not be permitted to expand beyond its original authorization. This control is achieved by following the same accounting procedures used by the general fund.

   B.   For a governmental unit having more than one special revenue fund, a combining balance sheet and a combining statement of revenues, expenditures, and changes in fund balances are prepared.

   C.   Pass-through grants and on-behalf payments where the government operates a program—for example, food stamps— are accounted for in special revenue funds.

   D.   Public-purpose trust funds where both principal and interest may be spent are also accounted for in special revenue funds.

II. Capital projects funds account for the construction or acquisition of major fixed assets, excluding fixed assets of proprietary funds.

   A.   When projects are expected to take several years, budgetary control is advisable.

      1.   The operating budget is prepared on an annual basis.

      2.   Resources for the project contributed by the general fund or from sources that must be repaid, such as bonds, are accounted for in other financing sources.

      3.   Resources for the project contributed by outsiders who do not have to be repaid are accounted for in revenues. These would include federal or state grants and interest earned on temporary investments.

   B.   The entries to record the budget, to record encumbrances and their reversal upon receipt of invoices, and to close accounts at year end are the same as similar entries for the general fund.

   C.   Although a project may not be completed at year end, annual closing entries are recorded for control purposes. In the closing process, the credit to expenditures provides the amount to be capitalized in the general fixed assets account group.

   D.   When a governmental unit has more than one capital project, combining financial statements are prepared with separate columns for each project and their totals.

III. Debt service funds are used to account for cash accumulation to cover payment of both principal and interest on general long-term obligations.

   A.   Budgetary entries are seldom used, since expenditures for principal and interest are known.

   B.   Resources to cover expenditures may come from several sources:

      1.   A portion of a property tax levy may be authorized to be recorded directly in a debt service fund. The entries are similar to those made in the general fund to record taxes. The net amount collectible is credited to revenues.

      2.   The bond premium from the sale of general long-term bonds may be transferred to the debt service fund. Other financial sources is credited.

      3.   Other transfers from funds that have already recorded the receipt of resources as revenues received by a debt service fund are credited to other financing sources.

      4.   Special assessments levied and demanded to pay for debt on projects billed to particular groups of property owners.

   C.   Prior to the redemption of a bond, no liability for unmatured debt is recorded in a debt service fund since the unmatured debt is recorded in the general long-term debt account group. When a serial bond matures or when payment of interest is due, expenditures is debited. Matured bonds payable and matured interest payable are credited. The latter two accounts are debited as payment is made.

      D.   Assets transferred to a debt service fund must be used to redeem bonds or to pay interest. Any excess of assets over liabilities is reserved for debt service. At year end, the accounts are closed to fund balance—reserved for debt service.

      E.   Debt refunding and in-substance defeasance of debt are handled by the debt service fund. If existing debt is refunded or all criteria for in-substance defeasance of debt are met, the refunding bonds are included in the account group and the old debt is removed.

      F.   Combining statements are prepared if the government has more than one debt service fund.

IV.   Permanent funds account for public-purpose trust funds for which the earnings are expendable for a specific government purpose, but the principal amount must be left intact. Permanent funds are often called endowments.

V.   Proprietary funds account for events in which goods or services are provided for a fee. Proprietary funds focus on the total cost of services and the amount of cost recovered by revenues. Accounting for proprietary funds is similar to that for a private organization, including the measurement of net income. Expenses are recognized and fixed assets and long-term liabilities are accounted for within the proprietary fund. There are two types of proprietary funds: enterprise funds and internal service funds.

      A.   Enterprise funds account for goods or services provided by a governmental unit to the general public. The user is charged for the goods or services based on consumption. Enterprise funds continue indefinitely and are partially or totally self-supporting.

           1.   At the inception of an enterprise fund, capital must be provided either by the issuance of long-term debt or by a transfer from some other source. If the capital is transferred from another fund, such as a municipality's general fund, the amount received is credited to interfund transfers and closed at year end to net assets.

              a.   All earnings must benefit a government activity or program.

              b.   Examples include cemetery trust, park trust, and library trust fund.

           2.   Accounting for revenues is handled with two control accounts.

              a.   Operating revenues records charges for services.

              b.   Nonoperating revenues records revenues from grants received, interest and rental income, and other miscellaneous financial revenues.

           3.   Accounting for expenses is also handled through two control accounts.

              a.   Operating expenses records expenses directly related to goods or services produced, including depreciation expense.

              b.   Nonoperating expenses records financial expenses.

           4.   Journal entries for revenues and expenses, including adjustments, are much the same as in private enterprise accounting. One unusual feature of accounting for enterprise funds is the use of restricted assets and current liabilities to be paid with restricted assets.

              a.   Restricted assets are current assets upon which some limitation has been imposed that makes them available only for designated purposes.

              b.   Restricted current assets and the related current liabilities payable from those assets must be recorded in specially designated accounts to permit segregation.

           5.   Landfills are often accounted for in enterprise funds. Expense and liability for closure and post-closure care of landfills are accrued over the useful life of the landfill based on the percentage of the landfill capacity used to date.

      B.   Internal service funds are used when a governmental unit provides services to other departments of the same governmental unit or to another governmental unit. As with enterprise funds, internal service funds record their fixed assets and long-term liabilities.

           1.   Resources of internal service funds result from:

              a.   Billings to other departments within the governmental unit.

               b.   Billings to outside governmental units.

           2.   The accounting procedures resemble those for a commercial enterprise. Internal service funds must recover their costs, including depreciation, or be subsidized. Therefore, charges to other departments for services are based on full costs.

           3.   When risk and insurance activities are accounted for in an internal service fund, the charge to other departments can be based on actuarial estimates, including a charge for future catastrophic losses.

VI.   Fiduciary funds account for resources for which a governmental unit is acting as a trustee or agent for an individual, group, or corporation. This category of funds includes private-purpose trust funds, investment trust funds, pension trust funds, and agency funds.

A. Accounting for assets held by a governmental unit that functions as a trustee depends on the document that created the fund. The trust fund may be either expendable or nonexpendable.
1. If both the earnings and the principal may be expended, the fund is an expendable trust fund.
2. If the earnings but not the principal may be expended, the fund is a nonexpendable trust fund, or endowment fund. To segregate the principal and earnings, two endowment funds may be established: one to record principal items and another to record earnings and expenditures.
3. Financial statements for the trust funds consist of a statement of fiduciary net assets and a statement of changes in fiduciary net assets.
B. Investment trust funds are used to account for assets, liabilities, and net assets of external participants in an investment pool managed by the government for other governments and not-for-profit organizations. The primary focus in accounting for these funds is proper recording of invested gains and losses.
C. Pension trust funds use an accrual basis of accounting for public employees' retirement system funds.
1. All assets of a pension trust fund belong to the employees and are reflected in either the liabilities or pension net asset balances.
2. Additions are the result of contributions, investment earnings, and realized and unrealized gains.
3. Deductions result from payments to retired employees or from refunds to employees no longer employed who withdraw their contributions. Investment fees and realized and unrealized losses also are listed as deductions.
4. Pension trust fund financial statements consist of a statement of plan net assets and a statement of changes in plan net assets.
5. Extensive note disclosures are also required.
D. An agency fund is required when money collected or withheld must be forwarded to another destination, and the government has no discretion over the money. A liability is created for assets that have not yet been forwarded to the proper party. There is no fund balance account.

PART 1

Instructions: Use a check mark to indicate whether each of the following statements is true or false.

		True	False
1.	Premiums received upon the sale of general obligation bonds usually are transferred to the general long-term debt account group.		
2.	Enterprise and internal service funds are accounted for in a manner similar to that of a commercial company.		
3.	When a capital project is financed entirely by a general obligation bond issue, the credit entry in the capital projects fund for the proceeds from the sale of the bond is to the account other financing sources.		
4.	A private-purpose fund is established when assets are held for external parties or for an external purpose.		
5.	A trust fund may be either expendable or nonexpendable.		
6.	The internal service fund is a proprietary fund.		
7.	Encumbrances would normally be used in accounting for an enterprise fund.		
8.	Agency funds are fiduciary funds that do not have fund balances.		
9.	A capital projects fund of a municipality is an example of a proprietary fund.		
10.	Room taxes collected from hotels and motels by a city government that are used for a program to promote economic development within the city would be accounted for in an internal service fund.		

PART 2

Instructions: Circle the letter that identifies the best response to each question.

1. In the final year of a capital project that took several years to complete, the total cost of the project would be shown in the capital projects fund as the balance in which of the following accounts?
   a. Expenditures
   b. Construction in progress
   c. Fund balance—reserved for encumbrances
   d. No account

2. A bond issue is floated to provide resources for a major capital improvement whose cost is to be met by special assessments against the property owners who will benefit. Generally, the amount of the bond proceeds is approximately equal to
   a. The estimated total cost of the project.
   b. The amount of the deferred special assessments.
   c. The total of all special assessments on the project.
   d. The amount debited to expenditures over the life of the project.

3. A governmental unit assumes responsibility in case of default for the bond debt related to a special assessment capital project for a general fixed asset. In this case, the bond liability is reflected in the
   a. General long-term debt account group.
   b. Capital projects funds.
   c. Debt service funds.
   d. General fund.

4. Measurement focus for enterprise funds is on
   a. The flow of financial resources.
   b. The assets entrusted.
   c. Net income and capital maintenance.
   d. The unreserved fund balance.

5. A successful computer center operated as an internal service fund made a payment of cash for services provided to the general fund. The account to be debited in the internal service fund to record the payment is
   a. Other financing uses.
   b. Expenditures.
   c. Financial expense.
   d. Retained earnings—unreserved.

6. A government-owned electric utility has a debit balance account called customers' deposits refundable. It is an illustration of a(n)
   a. Appropriated asset.
   b. Restricted asset.
   c. Reserved asset.
   d. Funded asset.

7. A solid-waste landfill at December 31, 20X9, has a capacity of 1,000,000 cubic yards. Usage prior to 20X9 was 500,000 cubic yards. Usage in 20X9 totaled 40,000 cubic yards. Estimated total life of the landfill is 20 years. Closure costs incurred to date total $300,000. Estimated future costs of closure and post-closure care are $1,700,000. Prior to 20X9, $973,000 of expenses for closure and post-closure care was recognized prior to 20X9. What 20X9 closure and post-closure care expenses should be reported in the solid-waste landfill enterprise fund?
   a. $1,080,000   b. $ 107,000   c. $ 300,000   d. $1,700,000 (AICPA adapted)

8. Part of the proceeds from general obligation bonds was used to pay for the cost of a city hall. The remainder of the proceeds was transferred to help repay the debt. The complete recording of these events would involve the
   a. General fund and general long-term debt account group only.
   b. General fund, general long-term debt account group, and debt service fund only.
   c. Trust fund, debt service fund, and general fixed assets account group only.
   d. General long-term debt account group, general fixed assets account group, debt service fund, and capital projects fund only.

PART 3

1. The city of Southbridge plans to build a storage facility for its out-of-season heavy equipment at an estimated cost of $1,300,000. The project will begin in 20X7 and will be completed in 20X8.

Instructions: Record the journal entries for the following events in its capital projects fund and in other funds or account groups, as indicated.

   a. It is estimated that $575,000 of costs will be incurred in the first year of the project. Southbridge will issue $1,000,000 of 7% general obligation term bonds. The federal government has awarded the project a $300,000 grant to be received during the first year. The grant is not expenditure-driven.

   b. The $1,000,000 bond issue is sold on an interest payment date for $990,000.

      General long-term debt account group:

   c. The federal grant of $300,000 is received.

   d. An invoice for architectural services for $45,000 is received and paid. The item had not been encumbered.

   e. Southbridge signed a contract for $1,250,000 to cover the major cost of the project.

   f. Orders were placed for additional building supplies at an estimated cost of $30,000, and the encumbrance is recorded.

   g. An invoice for $35,000 is received for supplies ordered in question f. Perpetual inventory for building supplies is used. No previous inventory existed.

   h. A partial billing for $375,000 is received from the contractor, which is equal to the amount encumbered for it.

i. At year end, $12,000 of supplies remain in inventory.

j. Closing entries for the capital projects fund are prepared by first reversing the budgetary entries and then closing the nominal accounts. Progress to date is recorded in the general fixed assets account group.

General fixed assets account group:

2. The $1,000,000 7% general obligation term bonds were issued on January 1, 20X8. Interest payments are due each December 31. Resources to pay interest and to provide for principal repayment are transferred from the general fund.

Instructions: Record the following events in the fund or account group indicated.

a. On December 30, 20X8, $320,000 from the general fund is transfered to the debt service fund to provide for the payment of $70,000 interest and ultimate payment of principal.
General fund:

Debt service fund:

General long-term debt account group:

b. On December 31, 20X8, the interest liability is recorded.
Debt service fund:

c. On December 31, 20X8, cash is transferred from the debt service fund to a bank that handles its interest and principal payments. A check for $320,000 is sent.
Debt service fund:

d. On January 10, 20X9, the bank notifies Southbridge that all interest payments for December 31, 20X8, have been made.
Debt service fund:

PART 4

On January 2, 20X7, the city of James Bay created an enterprise fund to account for the activities of its newly established public housing authority. Cash received as rent will be used to meet current operating expenses. Cash received as a security deposit is restricted since the deposit is refundable upon a tenant's departure. The city will contribute $750,000 to start the fund. The federal government will provide a $250,000 grant to subsidize the program.

1. **Instructions:** Record the journal entries for the following transactions in the enterprise fund.

    a.   The city and federal government contributions are received.

    b.   Housing units costing $700,000 are purchased with cash.

    c.   To prepare the units for rental, $200,000 is spent.

    d.   Security deposits of $20,000 are received.

    e. $50,000 from rentals is received.

    f.   Expenses of $45,000 for heat, light, and property taxes were paid.

    g.   Investments were purchased for $9,000 with cash from tenants' security deposits.

    h.   Building depreciation for a full year was recorded, using a 20-year life, no salvage value, and the straight-line method.

    i.   Investment income is $1,500 is received.

2. **Instructions:** Prepare the statement of revenues, expenses, and changes in retained earnings for the year 20X7.

City of James Bay
Public Housing Authority Enterprise Fund
Statement of Revenues, Expenses, and Changes in Net Assets
For Year Ended December 31, 20X7

Operating revenues:

Operating expenses:

Operating income (loss)
Nonoperating revenues (expenses):

Net income
Net assets, January 1, 20X7
Net assets, December 31, 20X7

3. **Instructions:** Prepare the public housing authority enterprise fund balance sheet as of December 31, 20X7.

City of James Bay
Public Housing Authority Enterprise Fund
Balance Sheet
December 31, 20X7

<u>Assets</u>   <u>Liabilities and Fund Equity</u>

PART 5

The city of Dunwood provides a pension retirement plan for its municipal employees, who also contribute to the plan. Employees who resign are entitled to a refund of their contributions.

Instructions: Record the journal entries for the following transactions in (#1-#7) the pension trust fund. Below #8, provide the requested statement.

1. Cash contributions of $50,000 and $25,000 are received from the city and from the employees, respectively.

2. Earnings on investments are accrued in the amount of $130,000.

3. Annuities that will be paid on January 1 are accrued in the amount of $74,000: $60,000 to retiring members and $14,000 to resigning employees.

4. Employees who have resigned are paid $7,500. This amount is not included in the amount accrued in question 3.

5. The fair value of pension plan investments increased by $10,500.

6. Investment fees of $500 are paid.

7. Pension fund books are closed at year end.

8. A statement of changes in plan net assets is prepared.

Chapter 17   Financial Reporting Issues

OUTLINE FOR REVIEW

In June 1999 the Governmental Accounting Standards Board (GASB) issued Statement No. 34, "Basic Financial Statements—and Management's Discussion and Analysis—for State and Local Governments."

I.   Statement No. 34 requires a new reporting model. It mandates several new financial statements including (1) government-wide financial statements, (2) funds-based financial statements, and (3) a management's discussion and analysis (MD&A) report.

   A.   Large governments (with $100 million or more in revenues) implemented the new standard in fiscal years beginning after June 15, 2001. Medium-sized governments (with between $10 and $100 million in revenues) implemented the new standard in fiscal years beginning after June 15, 2002. Smaller governments (with revenues of less than $10 million) implemented in fiscal years beginning after June 15, 2003.

   B.   A Comprehensive Annual Financial Report (CAFR) is prepared by government unit in order to demonstrate fiscal compliance. The CAFR has three sections: introductory, general-purpose financial statements, and statistical.

   C.   A complete set of general-purpose financial statements (GPFS) includes:

      1.   Management's discussion and analysis statement (MD&A)

      2.   Separate fund financial statements for governmental, proprietary, and fiduciary funds

      3.   Government-wide financial statements presenting the entire government

      4.   Notes to the financial statements

      5.   Required supplementary information (RSI) including a budgetary comparison statement or schedule, information about the condition of infrastructure assets, pension-related information, risk financing, and self-insurance activity

   D.   Management's discussion and analysis (MD&A) is required supplementary information presented with the basic financial statements. The purpose is to give a concise overview and analysis of the information in the government's financial statements.

II.   The reporting entity of the government consists of the primary government and one or more associated organizations (termed component units). A component unit is a legally separate organization for which the elected officials of the primary government are financially accountable or for which the nature and significance of the relationship with the primary government is such that exclusion would cause the financial statement to be misleading or incomplete.

   A.   Financial accountability is measured by (a) fiscal dependence or (b) the ability to appoint a voting majority and either impose will or have potential to receive specific benefit or burden.

   B.   Component units may be presented as discrete columns in the financial statements or blended into one or more funds of the government.

III.   Funds-based statements are almost exactly the same as the fund statements traditionally used in government accounting. They report detailed information about short-term spending and fiscal compliance using a modified accrual basis of accounting for governmental funds and a full accrual basis of accounting for proprietary funds.

   A.   The statements highlight major funds: a fund is considered major if assets, liabilities, revenues, or expenditures/expenses are at least 10% of all funds in that category or type AND at least 5% of all government and enterprise funds combined.

   B.   In addition, a government may designate as major any fund it believes is important to the users of its financial statements.

IV.   Separate funds-based statements are required for governmental, proprietary, and fiduciary funds.

   A.   Governmental funds statements include a balance sheet and statement of revenues, expenditures, and changes in fund balances.

   B.   Proprietary funds statements will include separate reporting of enterprise funds (labeled business-type activities) and internal service funds in a balance sheet and statement of revenues, expenses, and changes in fund net assets, and statement of cash flows.

   C.   Fiduciary funds statements include a statement of fiduciary net assets and a statement of changes in fiduciary net assets.

V.   Government-wide financial statements include a statement of net assets and a statement of activities. They are prepared for the government as a whole with one column for all governmental activities and one column for proprietary (business-type) activities.

   A.   The statement of net assets includes all assets, including infrastructure assets, and all liabilities of the government. The net assets (equity) is divided into three categories: unrestricted, restricted, and capital-related.

   B.   The statement of activities reports expenses by program (both direct and allocated indirect expenses) offset by revenue generated from grants, fees, and appropriations that are specifically connected to a program. The balance is the amount of expenses that are paid for by general governmental revenues.

      1.   The format of the statement of activities is unique.

      2.   Program revenues are broken down into three classifications: charges for services, program-specific operating and capital grants, and contributions.

   C.   Internal service funds are included as part of governmental activities after revenues and expenses are eliminated.

   D.   Infrastructure assets are reported. Governments have a 4-year delay (for years beginning after June 15, 2005) for retroactive reporting of the activity in the past 25 years. Prospective reporting is immediate upon adoption of GASB No. 34. Small governments are exempt from retroactive reporting.

   E.   Governments are required to report depreciation for all capital assets. They may use any conventional method for depreciation. They are also permitted to use a "modified preservation approach" to measuring the cost of using infrastructure assets rather than depreciation if they can demonstrate that the eligible infrastructure assets are being preserved at or above a condition level established by the government. If the condition of the assets falls below the target condition level, the government must depreciate.

VI.   Reconciliation from the funds-based statements to the government-wide statements is required. This reconciliation is necessary to convert from modified accrual basis of accounting and the detail of fund accounting to full accrual and summarized government-wide statements.

VII. Government auditing requirements include a financial audit and a performance audit.

   A.   Government auditing standards have been developed by the U.S. General Accounting Office (GAO). In addition, the AICPA publishes an Audit Guide that incorporates the GAO standards.

   B.   Governments who receive $300,000 or more of federal funds are also required to have a Single Audit that includes an audit of the financial statements and an audit of federal financial awards programs. A single audit expands testing of compliance with laws and regulations and internal controls.

VIII. The Government Accounting Standards Board recently adopted standards to clarify reports for officiated organizations (GASB No. 39), post-retirement benefits other than pensions (GASB No. 43 and 45), and new requests for note disclosures (GASB No. 38) and the statistical sections (GASB No. 44).

   A.   Other issues of concern to the Governmental Accounting Standards Board are service efforts and accomplishments–e.g., reporting of nonfinancial measures of efficiency and effectiveness, popular reports, and the conceptual framework.

PART 1

1.   What financial statements are required under Statement No. 34?

2.   How are major funds determined?

3. What basis of accounting is used to report governmental activities under Statement No. 34?

4. What is the management's discussion and analysis (MD&A)?

5. Explain budgetary reporting requirements in the new reporting model?

PART 2

Instructions: Based on the information presented in the City of Milwaukee, Wisconsin, financial statements on pages 125-165 of the Student Companion Book, complete the following:

1. Identify major funds for Milwaukee.

2. Identify the amount of internal service fund revenues and expenditures that are eliminated in converting from funds-based to government-wide statements.

3. What are the key items identified in reconciling the funds-based financial statements and the government-wide statements?

PART 3

Assume Spring Valley City has the following fund structure:

> General fund
> Special revenue fund (8)
> Capital projects fund (5)
> Debt service fund (1)
> Expendable trust funds (10)
> Internal service funds (7)
> Enterprise funds (4)
> General fixed assets account group
> General long-term debt account group

Spring Valley City determined that the debt service fund, capital projects funds A & C, and enterprise funds D & E are the only major funds.

Instructions:

1. Present the column headings that Spring Valley City must present in its governmental fund statement of revenues, expenditures, and changes in fund balance.

2. Present the column headings that Spring Valley City must present in its proprietary fund statement of revenues, expenses, and changes in net assets.

PART 4

Instructions: Indicate which section of the Comprehensive Annual Financial Report the following items will be presented:

A. The introductory section
B. The financial section
C. The statistical section

1. The MD&A   _____
2. The letter of transmittal   _____
3. The government-wide statement of activities   _____
4. Data on property tax collections for the past 10 years   _____
5. A certificate of achievement for excellence in financial reporting   _____
6. Notes to the financial statements   _____
7. Combining statements for nonmajor funds   _____
8. Information reported as required supplementary information (RSI)   _____
9. Component unit balance sheet   _____
10. Statement of revenues, expenses, and changes in net assets   _____
11. An analysis of factors underlying the financial statements   _____
12. Information on debt limit, debt margin, and debt trends   _____
13. A statement of activities   _____
14. Comparative data on general revenues, by source   _____
15. Component units that have been blended in the financial statements   _____

Chapter 18   Accounting for Private Not-for-Profit Organizations

OUTLINE FOR REVIEW

Both governmental and not-for-profit organizations have as their primary purpose the rendering of service without the profit motivation.

I.   Since not-for-profit organizations are devoted to service and not to profit generation, the success of a not-for-profit unit is difficult to evaluate. The lack of a profit motive is reflected in accounting and reporting practices. The general characteristics of not-for-profit organizations are as follows:

   A.   The budget is viewed as an essential tool for control and direction of the organization but often is not formally entered in the ledger.

   B.   All not-for-profit organizations use the accrual basis of accounting.

II.   Jurisdiction for accounting and financial reporting for not-for-profit organizations is shared by the Financial Accounting Standards Board (FASB) and the Governmental Accounting Standards Board (GASB). The GASB has jurisdiction over governmental not-for-profits (public colleges and universities and government hospitals). The FASB has jurisdiction over private not-for-profit organization accounting and financial reporting.

   A.   Five FASB standards have been directed at not-for-profits. Statement No. 93, Recognition of Depreciation by Not-for-Profit Organizations; Statement No. 116, Accounting for Contributions Received and Contributions Made; Statement No. 117, Financial Statements of Not-for-Profit Organizations; Statement No. 124, Accounting for Certain Investments Held by Not-for-Profit Organizations; and Statement No. 136, Transfers of Assets to a Not-for-Profit Organization or Charitable Trust that Raises or Holds Contributions for Others.

   B.   The FASB standards apply only to private not-for-profit organizations and have resulted in drastic changes in measurement and reporting for these organizations.

A voluntary health and welfare organization (VHWO) is characterized by receiving its primary sources of revenue from donors who do not directly benefit from the organization's programs in the area of health, welfare, or community service.

III.   Assets and liabilities of VHWOs are segregated into unrestricted and donor-restricted classifications.

   A.   Contributions received, including unconditional promises to give (pledges), are recognized as public support and as assets, decreases of liabilities, or expenses in the period received.

   B.   Contributions are measured at their fair market value and are reported as either unrestricted, temporarily restricted, or permanently restricted based on donor stipulations. Expiration of donor restrictions must be recognized in the period in which the restriction expires.

      1.   The expiration of a restriction may be based on the time period or the fulfillment of a stipulated purpose, or both.

      2.   Recognition of an expiration of a donor restriction is done by a reclassification entry. Reclassification results in an increase in the unrestricted class of net assets and a decrease in the temporarily restricted class of net assets.

      3.   The reclassification increases unrestricted net assets to "match" the decrease resulting from the stipulated expense.

   C.   Contributed collections of works of art, historical treasures, and similar assets need not be recognized as contributions; however, the choice of whether to capitalize collections must be applied to all collections.

   D.   Services are recognized if (1) the services received create or enhance nonfinancial assets or (2) the services received require specialized skills, are provided by individuals possessing those skills, and would typically need to be purchased if not provided by donation.

IV.   The full accrual basis of accounting is used in accounting and reporting for VHWOs.

   A.   Two major categories are used to record and communicate inflows of resources.

      1.   Public support is the inflow of resources from voluntary donors who receive no direct personal benefit from the organization's usual programs in exchange for their contribution. Receipts of assets in the public support category are recorded in the following accounts:

      a.   Contributions
      b.   Special events support
      c.   Legacies and bequests
      d.   Received from federated and nonfederated campaigns
    2.   Revenues are inflows of resources resulting from a charge for services or from financial activities.
      a.   Fees charged for services are credited to:
        (1)   Membership dues revenue
        (2)   Program services fees
        (3)   Sales of publications and supplies
      b.   Investment transactions involve the following revenue accounts:
        (1)   Investment revenue
        (2)   Realized gain on investment transactions
        (3)   Net increase (or decrease) in carrying value of investments (for the unrealized appreciation or depreciation of investments if they are carried at market value)

B.   An organization records its expenses incurred according to their function. However, the operating statements of a VHWO must show the cost of each program or service the organization provides. At the end of the fiscal year, the expenses are allocated to the programs conducted and to the supporting services of management, fund-raising, and member development. Allocation should be on a rational basis.

C.   After the expenses have been assigned, an entry is made to close the expense accounts and charge them to the programs and supporting services. The final closing entries close the support and revenue accounts as well as the program and supporting services accounts to the appropriate net asset class.

V.   Consistent with other not-for-profits, the three financial statements for VHWOs are a statement of financial position, a statement of activity, and a statement of cash flows. In addition, VHWOs must provide a statement of functional expenses, which presents the detailed expenses for each program and supporting service by natural expense categories.

VI.   To segregate resources and demonstrate compliance with restrictions, fund accounting may be used by VHWOs. If a VHWO chooses to use fund accounting, the following funds are described in the audit guide:

A.   The current unrestricted fund accounts for resources that have no external restrictions and are available for current operations at the discretion of the governing board. The governing board may make a decision to designate the unrestricted net assets. If such a decision is made, the process is similar to that of appropriating retained earnings. This is done by debiting unrestricted net assets—undesignated and crediting unrestricted net assets—designated.

B.   The current restricted fund accounts for assets received from outside sources for a current operating purpose that has been specified by the donor.

C.   The plant fund accounts for the activity related to fixed assets, including the accumulation of resources to acquire or replace them and the liabilities related to them as well as their acquisition, disposal, and depreciation.

D.   The endowment fund accounts for gifts or bequests with the legal restriction that the principal be maintained in perpetuity or until the occurrence of a specified event.
    1.   New gains and losses on the sale of endowment fund assets are increases or decreases in unrestricted net assets unless restricted by the donor or by law.
    2.   Distribution of endowment fund investment revenue may be restricted or unrestricted. Revenue not subject to restriction by the principal donor is recorded as unrestricted investment revenue and transferred to the current unrestricted fund. If the revenue is subject to restriction, it is recorded as temporarily restricted investment revenue and transferred to the appropriate restricted fund.

E.   A custodian fund is established to account for assets received by an organization to be held or disbursed only on instructions of the person or organization from whom they were received.
    1.   Assets are recorded when received. A liability to the donor is recorded at the same time.
    2.   When the assets are released by the contributor, they are recorded as revenue in the current fund.

F.   Investments may be carried at market value—provided that the market value is applied to all investments of all funds. An organization with substantial investments may pool the investments of various funds.
    1.   Once pooled, the individual investments lose their identity as to fund.
    2.   Before any additions or withdrawals may be made, the market value of the total portfolio must be determined. Realized and unrealized gains and losses are allocated to each participating fund on the basis of its share of the total market value at the previous valuation date.
    3.   Immediately after each addition and withdrawal, new equity percents must be determined.

4. When investments are pooled, each participating fund maintains an account, pooled investments, that is periodically adjusted to reflect its equity in the pool.

PART 1

Instructions: Use a check mark to indicate whether each of the following statements is true or false.

	True	False
1. In addition to recording depreciation by debiting depreciation expense and crediting accumulated depreciation, a VHWO records an entry to allocate depreciation to programs.	_____	_____
2. Fixed assets purchased by the unrestricted current fund are maintained in the unrestricted current fund of a VHWO using fund accounting.	_____	_____
3. A loss on the sale of a fixed asset by a VHWO is accounted for as miscellaneous expense.	_____	_____
4. When expenses are recorded for a donor-specified purpose, a "release" of the restriction is recorded as a reclassification from temporarily restricted to unrestricted net assets.	_____	_____
5. The entire amount of interest payments received, including the portions equal to the premium amortizations, on investments purchased by endowment funds are recognized as unrestricted revenue.	_____	_____
6. The modified accrual basis is used in accounting for VHWOs.	_____	_____
7. A unique aspect of the financial reports of a VHWO is that results are presented on a program basis in a functional expense statement.	_____	_____
8. Contributions of property are acknowledged as revenue in the amount of the donor's basis for the asset.	_____	_____
9. A donation that is not available until a future period is recorded as a deferred credit.	_____	_____
10. Substantial amounts of materials received by a not-for-profit organization as a donation should be recorded as inventory at market value.	_____	_____
11. Building facilities for which no rent is charged are not acknowledged in any form in the accounting for VHWOs.	_____	_____
12. Personal services donated by volunteers are recognized as contributions if the duties are of a skilled nature, are measurable and material, and the services donated would have been provided by a salaried person.	_____	_____
13. Investments of a VHWO may be maintained at either cost or market value.	_____	_____
14. Expenses of a VHWO must be allocated to benefiting programs to enable an analysis of each program's cost and the effectiveness with which resources have been managed	_____	_____
15. Not-for-profit organizations that are not hospitals, colleges and universities, VHWOs, or state and local government units can find guidance on financial reporting in the AICPA audit guide, *Not-for-Profit Organizations.*	_____	_____

PART 2 (Appendix)

Instructions: Complete the following statements by filling in the blanks.

1. The two current funds used by VHWOs are the _____ and the _____.

2. The four restricted funds traditionally used by a VHWO are the _____, _____, _____ , and _____.

3. The amounts designated at the discretion of the governing board of a not-for-profit organization are recorded by debiting _____ and crediting _____.

4. Permanently restricted net assets are recorded when the _____ is to be maintained as specified by the contributor and the _____ is expendable.

5. _____ is credited for the proceeds from the sale of a VHMO's monthly newsletter.

PART 3

The following closing entries were made on the books of the Lakeside Nature Center as of May 31, 20X5:

To close unrestricted net assets:		
Contributions	190,000	
Special events support	5,000	
Legacies and bequests	75,000	
Membership dues revenue	75,000	
Investment revenue	13,000	
Realized gain on sale of investments—unrestricted	1,200	
Reclassification in—unrestricted—satisfaction of program restrictions	63,400	
Reclassification in—unrestricted—satisfaction of plant acquisition restrictions	13,700	
Cost of special events		1,200
Wildlife preserve program		84,400
Children's activities		113,300
Planting program		153,900
Management and general services		16,600
Fund-raising services		3,700
Membership development services		2,000
Unrestricted net assets		61,200
To close temporarily restricted net assets:		
Contributions	94,000	
Investment revenue	6,500	
Reclassification out—temporarily restricted— satisfaction of program restrictions		63,400
Reclassification out—temporarily restricted— satisfaction of plant acquisition restrictions		13,700
Temporarily restricted net assets		23,400
To close permanently restricted net assets:		
Legacies and bequests	12,000	
Net increase in carrying value of investments	20,000	
Permanently restricted net assets		32,000
Additional data:		
Net assets on June 1, 20X4:		
Unrestricted		56,000
Temporarily restricted		54,600
Permanently restricted		160,000

Instructions: Prepare a statement of activities for the year ended May 31, 20X5.

Lakeside Nature Center
Statement of Activities
For Year Ended May 31, 20X5

	Unrestricted	Temporarily Restricted	Permanently Restricted	Total

Chapter 19   Accounting for Not-for-Profit Colleges and Universities and Health Care Organizations

OUTLINE FOR REVIEW

The responsibilities of a not-for-profit university may be classified as academic, financial, student services, and public relations. The effectiveness with which a university accomplishes its objectives in these areas depends upon the resources at its disposal.

Accounting procedures for public universities now also emphasize the flow of economic resources and full accrual accounts. Universities use fund accounts for internal control and decision-making. Two operating funds are used: the unrestricted current fund and the restricted current fund.

I.   The focus of accounting and financial reporting for *private* colleges and universities is on the organization as a whole. Organization-wide totals of assets, liabilities, and net assets as well as information concerning organization-wide changes in net assets classes and organization-wide cash flows are presented on the financial statements.

   A.   There is no requirement for financial statements to include fund group reporting.

   B.   Three net asset classes—unrestricted, temporarily restricted, and permanently restricted—are used instead of fund balances.

   C.   Only contributions with donor-imposed restrictions are considered restricted. Exchange transactions, that is, reciprocal transfers in which each party receives and sacrifices approximately equal value, are not considered restricted.

II.   All contributions received by a private university (or unconditional promises to give) are classified into one of three categories: unrestricted, temporarily restricted, or permanently restricted resources. Contributions may include cash, promises to give, investments, fixed assets, reduction of liabilities, donated professional services, and collections of art and historical treasures.

   A.   Contributions received and unconditional promises to give are recognized as revenues or gains in the period received. Donor-imposed restrictions have no bearing on the period in which contributions are recognized as revenue.

   B.   A restriction expires when the stipulated time has elapsed, when the stipulated purpose has been fulfilled, or over the useful life of the donated asset.

      1.   Expenditure or time restrictions are temporary and, when met, require a reclassification to unrestricted.

      2.   Gifts of long-lived assets (or long-lived assets acquired with restricted gifts of cash) are reported either as unrestricted when placed in service or as temporarily restricted with the expiration of the donor restriction recorded over the useful life of the asset.

      3.   This reporting of expirations of donor-imposed restrictions (reclassification) simultaneously decreases temporarily restricted net assets and increases unrestricted net assets in order to "match" the expenses they support (operating expenses, depreciation, etc., which decrease unrestricted net assets).

      4.   If an expense is incurred for a purpose for which both unrestricted and temporarily restricted net assets are available, a donor-imposed restriction is fulfilled first unless the expense is directly attributable to another specific external source of revenue.

      5.   Endowments are permanently restricted contributions. Realized and unrealized gains and losses on endowment investments are reported as increases or decreases in unrestricted net assets unless their use is temporarily or permanently restricted by the donor or by law. Endowment income may be unrestricted or temporarily restricted depending on donor specification.

III.   Financial statements of a *private* university classify the organization's net assets based on the existence or absence of donor-imposed restrictions: unrestricted, temporarily restricted, and permanently restricted. Changes in each of these three classes of net assets must also be reported. Reclassifications that simultaneously decrease temporarily restricted net assets and increase unrestricted net assets are reported separately.

   A.   External financial statements required are:

1. A statement of financial position (balance sheet) that reports organization-wide totals for assets, liabilities, and net assets, and net assets identified as unrestricted, temporarily restricted, and permanently restricted.
2. A statement of activities that reports revenues, expenses, gains, losses, and reclassifications (between classes of net assets). Minimum requirements are organization-wide totals, changes in net assets for each class of assets, and all expenses recognized only in the unrestricted classification. A display of a measure of operations in the statement of activities is permitted.
3. A statement of cash flows with categories (operating, financing, investing) similar to business organizations.

B. All expenses are changes in unrestricted net assets. Depreciation is recorded as an expense.
C. Information about liquidity is provided by sequencing assets and liabilities according to nearness of conversion to or use of cash on the statement of financial position.
D. Most authorities expect private colleges and universities to continue to use the traditional fund structure (detailed here for public colleges and universities) for internal management.

IV. Most public universities are required to report as special-purpose governments engaged in business-type activities; thus, the reporting requirements are similar to private colleges and universities.

A. The current unrestricted fund represents amounts that are available for any activity commensurate with the university's objectives.
1. Separate revenue accounts commonly are established to account for the fund resources, using the following classifications:
   a. Educational and general revenues group with accounts for specific revenue categories.
   b. Auxiliary enterprises revenues.
   c. Expired term endowment revenues.
2. Expense categories that are recommended are:
   a. Educational and general expenses group with accounts for specific expenditure categories.
   b. Auxiliary enterprises expenditures.
3. In addition to expenses, the unrestricted current fund is reduced by transfers.
4. The accrual basis of accounting is used.

B. The current restricted fund accounts for those resources available only for a specified purpose, which is designated by a party outside the university entity.
1. Restricted current fund revenues arise primarily from governmental grants and contracts, private gifts, and endowment income for government grants and contracts. Until the resources are expended properly, unrestricted current fund revenues are not recognized.
2. Public colleges and universities recognize contributions as revenue when eligibility requirements and time restrictions are met.

C. Loan funds are established to account for resources that are available for loans. Both principal and interest must be available for loan purposes in order for an item to be accounted for in a loan fund. Resources of loan funds consist mainly of gifts restricted for loan purposes and the unrestricted current fund resources transferred by authorization of the governing board.

D. Endowment and similar funds account for endowments received.
1. A college or university may have the following types of endowment funds:
   a. A regular or pure endowment is a fund whose principal has been specified as nonexpendable by the donor.
   b. A term endowment is a fund whose principal becomes expendable after a specified time period or after the occurrence of a specified event.
   c. A quasi-endowment is a fund set aside by the governing board.
2. Income from endowment assets is recorded in the proper donor-specified fund. Income on which there is no restriction should be recorded directly in the unrestricted current fund.

E. Annuity and life income funds account for resources received with the stipulation that periodic payments are to continue as an annuity to the donor or other designated beneficiary for an indicated time period.
1. The following procedures apply to annuity funds:
   a. The resources should be accounted for at their fair value on the date of receipt.
   b. A liability to the annuitant is recognized in the amount of the present value of the expected total annuity payments.
   c. The excess of resources received over the recorded liability is credited to annuity fund revenues.
   d. Periodically, the annuity liability is adjusted for interest on the balance.

2. A life income fund is used when all income received on contributed assets is to be paid to the donor or a designated beneficiary for life.
    a. The contributed assets are recorded at fair value with a credit to life income fund revenues.
    b. As income is received, a liability for its payment is accrued.
3. When the annuity payments or life income payments cease, the principal is transferred to the designated beneficiary fund or, if none is designated, to the current unrestricted fund.

F. Plant funds are designed to segregate the recording of various phases of activity related to fixed assets. There are four plant fund subgroups:
    1. The unexpended plant fund accounts for resources used to acquire properties or other fixed assets.
    2. The plant fund for renewals and replacements accounts for resources that are available to keep the physical plant in operating condition.
    3. The plant fund for retirement of indebtedness accounts for resources accumulated for the payment of interest and principal of plant fund indebtedness.
    4. The investment in plant subgroup controls all plant assets, except for those of the endowment fund.

G. Agency funds account for resources that are not the property of the university but that are held in the university's custody. The total amount of these resources represents a liability.

Expenditures for medical care now equal more than 10% of the gross national product. Health care entities include hospitals, clinics, continuing care retirement communities, health maintenance organizations, home health agencies, and nursing homes.

Modern health care facilities are complex entities with medical, surgical, research, and public service aspects. An unusual element in health care operations is the manner of payment by a third party on the basis of predetermined cost of providing services as defined by the third party, such as Blue Cross. With the many restrictions resulting from insurance companies, endowments, and governmental regulations for reimbursements, a health care facility my use fund accounting in order to demonstrate compliance; however, fund accounting is not required.

I. The net assets of the entire health care organization are divided into three classes—permanently restricted net assets, temporarily restricted net assets, and unrestricted net assets—based on the existence or absence of donor-imposed restrictions.

A. Revenues, expenses, gains, and losses increase or decrease the net assets of a health care entity.
B. Other events, such as expirations of donor-imposed restrictions, simultaneously increase one class of net assets and decrease another (reclassifications).
C. Revenues and gains may increase unrestricted net assets, temporarily restricted net assets, or permanently restricted net assets. Expenses reduce unrestricted net assets.

II. The following procedures are used in accounting for not-for-profit health care organizations:
A. Three controlling revenue accounts are used.
    1. Patient Service Revenue records gross revenues earned on an accrual basis for daily patient services, other nursing services, and other professional services.
    2. Other Operating Revenue records revenues from patients for nonmedical charges and revenues from nonpatient charges.
    3. Nonoperating Revenue records revenues that are not related to patient care or service, such as contributions and revenue from endowment investments.
B. Contractual adjustments and charity care are recorded as reductions from gross revenues. Net patient service revenue is shown on the operating statement. Net patient service revenue includes contractual adjustments for the difference between the gross revenue and the amount expected to be collected from third-party payors. It also includes other gross revenue adjustments made for charitable services and courtesy reductions granted to hospital employees. Estimated uncollectible amounts are recorded as an expense in the Provision for Uncollectibles.
C. The portion of payments made by third parties earmarked for reimbursement of depreciation charges is recorded as "assets whose use is limited: until they are expended.
D. Health care entities may receive gifts or donations that meet the definition of an unconditional contribution. These contributions may be unrestricted as to use or may be limited to a specific use.
    1. Unrestricted contributions are recognized at fair market value with a credit to Other Operating Revenue—Unrestricted or Nonoperating Revenue—Unrestricted depending on whether these

contributions are deemed to be ongoing major or central activities or peripheral or incidental transactions.

    2.   Bequests and gifts restricted by the donor as to use for (a) specific operating purposes, (b) additions to plant, (c) endowments, or (d) annuities or life incomes are recorded as a credit to Revenues (Other Operating or Nonoperating)—Temporarily Restricted, or Revenues (Other Operating or Nonoperating)—Permanently Restricted.

    3.   When expenditures are made consistent with the donor's stipulation, or when term endowments become available, a reclassification is made from the temporarily restricted net asset category to an unrestricted net asset category. Should resources from expired term endowments be restricted further, for example, to purchase equipment, they remain in the temporarily restricted net asset category.

    4.   Resources temporarily restricted for the purchase or construction of property, plant, and equipment may be released from restriction either in the period the asset is placed into service or over its useful life.

    5.   Donor-restricted contributions in which the restriction will be met in the current period may be classified as unrestricted revenues. Some promises to give are conditional and will not be recognized until the condition is met. Donated items may also be unrestricted or restricted. Examples of donated items in a health care entity are laboratory and pharmaceutical supplies donated by drug companies or associations of doctors; donated property, plant, and equipment; and contributed use of facilities.

    6.   Donated items are recognized at fair market value with a credit to Other Operating Revenue—Unrestricted or Nonoperating Revenue—Unrestricted, depending on whether the donations constitute the entity's ongoing major or central operations or are peripheral or incidental transactions.

    7.   Donated services must be recognized if the services received (a) create or enhance nonfinancial assets or (b) require specialized skills, are provided by individuals possessing those skills, and would typically need to be purchased if not provided by donation. Services provided by doctors, nurses, and other professionals in a health care entity may meet the above criteria.

  E. Operating expenses are reported by using a functional classification. In addition, information on natural classifications are discussed in the notes. The former would include the following accounts:
    1.   Nursing Services Expense
    2.   Other Professional Services Expense
    3.   General Services Expense
    4.   Fiscal Services Expense
    5.   Administrative Services Expense

  F. The ultimate costs of malpractice claims, including litigation costs, should be accrued when the incidents occur that give rise to the claims if it can be determined that it is probable that liabilities have been incurred and if the amounts of the losses can be reasonably estimated.

III. The financial statements of a health care provider include a statement of activities, a statement of financial position, and a statement of cash flows.

  A. The statement of activities presents organization-wide totals for changes in unrestricted net assets, temporarily restricted net assets, and permanently restricted net assets.

  B. The statement of financial position presents current assets, assets whose use is limited, property and equipment, and possibly other assets. Also shown are the current and other liabilities of the organization and the three classes of net assets.

  C. The statement of cash flows follows FASB Statement No. 95 guidance amended to include among the list of cash inflows from financing activities receipts from contributions and investment income that by donor stipulation are restricted for the purpose of acquisition, construction, or improving property, plant, and equipment or other long-lived assets or establishing or increasing a permanent endowment or term endowment.

IV. If funds are used by a health care organization, they are as follows:

  A. General funds, which account for resources available for general operations, with no restrictions placed upon those resources by an outsider, and other exchange transactions including resources from government grants and subsidies, tax support, and reimbursements from insurance contracts.

  B. Donor-restricted funds, which account for temporarily restricted and permanently restricted contributions. This class is subdivided into:
    1.   Specific purpose funds, which account for donor-restricted resources temporarily restricted for current but specified operations.
    2.   Plant replacement and expansion funds, which account for resources temporarily restricted by the donor for the acquisition, construction, or improvement of property, plant, and equipment.

3. Endowment funds, which account for permanently restricted endowment principal and temporarily restricted term endowments.
4. Other donor-restricted funds such as annuities, life income funds, or loan funds.

PART 1

Instructions: Use a check mark to indicate whether each of the following statements is true or false.

	True	False
1. Conditional pledges are recognized as revenue by a private university when the signed pledge card is received.	____	____
2. No revenue is recognized for noncash property contributed to a not-for-profit organization.	____	____
3. Daily activities of a public university are accounted for in the current funds using appropriate revenue and expense accounts.	____	____
4. Activities of public university noncurrent funds are recorded in a similar manner as the current funds.	____	____
5. Auxiliary enterprises revenues of a university are accounted for separately from daily operations to permit the evaluation of performance.	____	____
6. Depreciation is not recognized in accounting for private universities since plant assets are accounted for as expenditures in the year of acquisition.	____	____
7. In the current restricted fund of a public university, revenue is recognized in the exact amount of the expense at the time of an expenditure.	____	____
8. Investments of a public university are recorded at cost, and investments of a private university are recorded at fair value.	____	____

PART 2

Instructions: Circle the letter that identifies the best response for each question. (Item 5 is AICPA adapted.)

1. A gift that is made to a private university that is not restricted by the donor should be credited to
   a. Fund balance—unrestricted.
   b. Deferred revenue.
   c. Revenues—unrestricted contributions.
   d. Revenues—temporarily restricted.

2. The loan fund of a college or university would not normally grant loans to
   a. Students.
   b. Staff.
   c. Fulfillment of building requirements.
   d. Faculty.

3. Which one of the following must be used in accounting for not-for-profit private colleges and universities?
   a. Fund accounting and accrual accounting
   b. Fund accounting but not accrual accounting
   c. Accrual accounting but not fund accounting
   d. Neither accrual accounting nor fund accounting

4. Which one of the following receipts is properly recorded as restricted revenue on the books of a not-for-profit private university?
   a. Tuition
   b. Donor-restricted promises to give
   c. Dormitory fees
   d. Research grants

5. An alumnus donates securities to Rex Private College and stipulates that the principal be held in perpetuity and revenues be used for faculty travel. Dividends received from the securities should be recognized as
   a. Endowment income—temporarily restricted.
   b. Fund balance.
   c. Endowment income—unrestricted.
   d. Investment income—permanently restricted.

PART 3

Instructions: Record the journal entries for the following events, which took place at Hank Private University during the year 20X5. To the left of each entry indicate in which current fund these events should be recorded, using the designation "CUF" for the current unrestricted fund and "CRF" for the current restricted fund.

1. The budget is approved and is to be recorded. Estimated revenues are $1,000,000 and estimated expenditures are $750,000.

   _____

2. An unconditional pledge of $25,000 is contributed by an alumnus for accounting scholarships. All of the pledge is expected to be received.

   _____

3. The following educational and general revenues are billed but have not been received:

Student tuition and fees, of which $10,000 is considered uncollectible	$500,000
Approved governmental appropriations	100,000
State grants	200,000
Miscellaneous income	100,000
	$900,000

   _____

4. Revenues of $75,000 are billed for dormitory fees, which are accounted for as an auxiliary enterprise.

   _____

5. Cash totaling $965,000 is collected on receivables.

   _____

6. The $25,000 pledge (from question 2) is collected in full.

   _____

7. Invoices for purchases of materials and supplies of $65,000 are received. Perpetual inventory is maintained.

   _____

8. Scholarships totaling $7,500 are granted to students in accordance with the donor's specifications. Expenses are recorded to the extent of expenditures.

   _____

9. During the year, expenditures are paid with unrestricted monies and assigned to:

Instruction	$250,000
Research	50,000
Student services	25,000
Operation and maintenance of plant	50,000
Student aid (scholarships)	40,000
Auxiliary enterprises	70,000
Academic support	200,000
	$685,000

_____

10. Cash is transferred to the plant fund for:

Additions to plant (discretionary)	$10,000
Required payment of mortgage principal	20,000
	$30,000

_____

11. Materials and supplies are used for:

Instruction	$25,000
Student services	20,000
Auxiliary enterprises	15,000
	$60,000

_____

12. The board of trustees authorized an immediate transfer of $75,000 to the loan fund.

_____

13. A debt covenant requires an annual transfer of $35,000 to the plant fund for retirement of indebtedness. Cash is transferred.

_____

14. Term endowments expire, making $200,000 of cash available for unrestricted purposes.

_____

15. A cash gift of $30,000 is received with the stipulation that it be used for faculty research grants.

_____

16. Endowment income of $5,000 is received that is restricted to library operations.

_____

17. Expenditures of restricted funds are made for:

Research grants from private gifts	$25,000
Library operations from endowment income	4,000
	$29,000

Revenues are recognized to the extent of expenditures.

_____

18. The current unrestricted fund is closed (a) by reversing the budgetary entry, (b) by closing auxiliary enterprise items, (c) by closing operational revenues and expenses, and (d) by closing mandatory transfers.

_____

19. The current restricted fund is closed.

_____

PART 4

1. **Instructions:** Record the journal entries for the following events in the loan fund of Hable Public University, a not-for-profit school.

   a. A transfer of $75,000 from the current unrestricted fund and gifts of $10,000 from alumni were received for student loan purposes.

   b. Investments were purchased for $35,000 to generate additional student loan resources.

   c. Loans are made to students totaling $45,000.

   d. A student loan of $1,500 is determined to be uncollectible.

   e. Collections on student loans amounted to $27,000, which includes $2,000 of interest on the loans.

2. **Instructions:** Record the journal entries for the following events in Hable University's endowment and similar funds.

   a. The board of trustees approved a discretionary transfer of $40,000 from the current unrestricted fund. The transfer was made as a temporary endowment.

   b. Investments with a fair market value of $250,000 are received as a term endowment contribution. Income from the investments is to be transferred to the loan fund.

   c. Income of $40,000 received on investments is attributable to term endowment investments.

   d. Term endowment investments costing $50,000 are sold for $46,000.

3. **Instructions:** Record the journal entries for the following events in Hable University's annuity and life income fund.

   a. Joyce Walker, an alumnus, contributed $150,000 on the condition that she receive an annuity of $10,000 each year for life. The present value of the expected total annuity payments is $120,000.

   b. Another graduate contributed investments with a fair market value of $100,000 and is to receive the income from the investments for life.

   c. The interest adjustment on the annuity payable is $9,600 for the year. The annual annuity payment event a. is made.

   d. Income amounting to $12,000 is received on the investments in event b.

4. **Instructions:** Record the journal entries for the following events in Hable University's plant fund. To the left of each entry indicate in which subgroup the entry would be made.

   a. A gift of $60,000 cash is received. The donor specified that the gift is to be used to add to library collections.

   _____

   b. Cash in the amount of $210,000 is transferred from the current unrestricted fund for a possible building expansion project.

   _____

   c. Bonds are issued on an interest date at face value of $485,000. Proceeds will be used to construct a new library wing.

   _____

   d. The library wing is 50% completed. Costs of construction to date are $255,000, which will be paid only upon completion of the project.

   _____

   e. The library wing is completed at an additional cost of $240,000. Payment is made.

   _____

   f. Completed project costs for the library wing are transferred to the investment in plant subgroup.

   _____

   g. Library books costing $50,000 are purchased for cash with the restricted gift.

   _____

   h. An invoice for $45,000 for repairs made to the plant was received and paid.

   _____

PART 5

Instructions: Place a check mark in the appropriate column to indicate whether each of the following statements is true or false.

	True	False
1. The audit guide for providers of health care services recommends the use of two categories of funds—general and donor-restricted.	_____	_____
2. Contractual adjustments represent the excess of gross patient service revenues over the amount expected to be collectible from third-party payors.	_____	_____
3. Contractual adjustments, charity service allowances, and courtesy reductions granted to hospital employees are shown as contra-revenues in a not-for-profit hospital's statement of activities.	_____	_____
4. Payments made to hospitals by third-party payors may include reimbursement for depreciation.	_____	_____
5. The statement of cash flows for a not-for-profit hospital should be prepared using the indirect method.	_____	_____

PART 6

Instructions: Prepare the necessary journal entries to record the following transactions, for not-for-profit St. Jo's Hospital for the year 20X4. (Assume fund accounting is not used.)

1. Revenues are billed as follows:

For patient services	$220,000
For nursing services	40,000
For other professional services	60,000
Cafeteria revenue	25,000
	$345,000

Estimated uncollectibles are $12,000. Discounts to employees are $8,000.

2. An analysis of patients' accounts shows:

Cash collected	$300,000
Contractual adjustments with third-party payors	7,000
Uncollectible accounts written off	8,000

3. Salaries earned and paid are chargeable to the following functional expenses:

Nursing services	$100,000
Other professional services	200,000
General services	25,000
Fiscal services	30,000
Administrative services	10,000
	$365,000

4. The following items were paid:

Current principal of the mortgage	$40,000
Note payable	20,000
Interest expense	31,000
	$91,000

5. Reclassified $90,000 of donor-specified contributions to cover current operating expenses.

6. Purchased a new CT-SCAN unit of equipment at a cost of $150,000 to be paid in 90 days.

7. Depreciation expense of $18,000 was recognized on equipment.

8. Board-designated investments received $10,000 cash earnings, which is to remain a part of board-designated cash.

PART 7

The accountant for Grand Rapids Hospital, a private not-for-profit organization, is not familiar with FASB Statement No. 95, Statement of Cash Flows. The board of directors has requested your professional assistance, and you have accepted.

Instructions: From the data provided, prepare the Statement of Cash Flows under the direct method and the necessary supporting reconciliation for the year ended July 31, 20X6.

The following condensed cash account was furnished:

Cash Account

August 1, 20X5 Balance	$ 137,950	To employees and suppliers	$3,675,500
From patients and third-party payors	4,280,950	To physicians consultation service	100,000
From flower shop	258,850	Payment of bond principal	300,000
Unrestricted gifts	81,750	To First Bank for payment of note due in 20X9	121,150
Endowment income	80,000	For total interest paid	73,500
		For purchase of operating room equipment	250,600
		Transfer assets whose use is limited to plant	
	4,839,500	replacement and expansion	114,000
July 31, 20X6 balance	$ 204,750		$4,634,750

The following is the condensed statement of revenues and expenses for the year ended July 31, 20X6:

Total operating revenues (including the increase in patient accounts receivable of $113,700)	$4,641,650
Total operating expenses (including decrease in supplies inventory of $5,900; depreciation of $216,250, increase in liability for estimated malpractice costs of $6,150; increase in accounts payable of $15,050)	4,090,050
Income from operations	$ 551,600
Nonoperating revenue (which includes an unrestricted gain from the sale of investments of $8,750)	180,050
Excess of revenues over expenses	$ 731,650

Grand Rapids Hospital
Statement of Cash Flows
For Year Ended July 31, 20X6

Grand Rapids Hospital
Reconciliation of Excess of Revenues over Expenses
To Net Cash Provided by Operating Activities and Nonoperating Revenue
For Year Ended July 31, 20X6

Chapter 20   Estates and Trusts: Their Nature and the Accountant's Role

OUTLINE FOR REVIEW

An estate consists of the net assets of an individual at the time of his/her death, and a trust is a separate distinct entity into which estate assets are often distributed in order to satisfy some purpose. Persons responsible for the management of an estate and/or trust have a fiduciary responsibility. Accountants are often involved in accounting for the activities of an estate or trust and reporting the results to the responsible fiduciary.

I.   Estate planning has a primary goal of reflecting the desires of the decedent. Proper estate planning for individuals with sizable asset values involves income tax and gift-giving strategies. Estate planning may become extremely complex and require the specialized talents of accountants and attorneys.

   A.   The goals of more complex estates include the following:

      1.   Discover and clearly communicate the desires and wishes of the decedent.

      2.   Ensure that the estate is properly administered or managed in order to satisfy the desires and wishes of the decedent.

      3.   Maximize the economic value of the estate's net assets.

      4.   Minimize the taxes that may be assessed against the assets and income of the estate.

      5.   Define the necessary liquidity of the estate's assets so that desired conveyances and distributions may be achieved.

      6.   Provide a proper and timely accounting of the activities of the estate and its fiduciary.

   B.   A will is used to communicate, prior to death, the wishes of a decedent. When an individual dies with a will, that person is said to have died testate. Individuals with no will or an invalid will are said to have died intestate.

      1.   A probate court determines the validity of a will and identifies a fiduciary responsible for its administration.

         a.   If a will names the person responsible for administering the estate, s/he is referred to as an executor or personal representative.

         b.   If the probate court appoints a person responsible for administering the estate, s/he is referred to as an administrator.

      2.   Although a Uniform Probate Code does exist, generally, probate law is developed by each state.

      3.   If an individual dies intestate, the probate court appoints an administrator and distributes the assets of the estate according to state inheritance laws.

      4.   An inter vivos trust is a popular way of passing property to one's heirs without a will and, therefore, avoiding the probate process.

   C.   The fiduciary of an estate must identify the principal, or corpus, of the estate. The estate is measured at fair value at the date of death. However, for federal estate tax purposes, an alternative date of valuation may be used.

      1.   A decedent may have two types of estates.

         a.   The probate estate includes all of the decedent's assets passing to others by means of a will.

         b.   The gross estate is the one that is used to determine the federal and state estate tax liabilities. This estate includes all assets owned by the decedent at the moment of death regardless if they pass to others by means of the will, by joint tenancy, or by community property laws.

      2.   The principal, or corpus, of the estate includes assets that were the legal property of the decedent at the time of the decedent's death and, therefore, should include accrued items.

         a.   The principal is not reduced by the obligations or liabilities of the decedent. These items are recognized when paid or otherwise satisfied.

         b.   Subsequently discovered assets are also included in the principal.

         c.   Some state probate laws exempt certain real property from the estate principal. Other assets may be excluded through a homestead or family allowance.

3. The inventory of the probate estate principal must be accounted for by debiting the various assets and crediting an estate principal account. Gains and losses resulting from the sale of principal assets increase and decrease, respectively, the estate principal.

D. The fiduciary of the probate estate must identify the claims against the estate, evaluate their validity, and prioritize these for payment purposes.

1. The order of priority of claims varies from state to state; however, an example might be to observe the following order of priority:

a. Claims having a special lien against property—not to exceed the value of the property

b. Funeral and administrative expenses

c. Income, estate, and inheritance taxes

d. Debts due the United States and various states

e. Judgments of any court of competent jurisdiction

f. Wages due domestic servants for a period of not more than one year prior to date of death and medical claims for the same period.

g. All other claims

2. This order is generally observed, noting that within a class each claim is satisfied on a pro rata basis if funds are inadequate to accomplish total payment for that class.

II.   An estate is considered to be a separate distinct taxable entity during the period of administration, or settlement. Major claims against many estates consist of federal estate taxes and state inheritance taxes.

A. During one's lifetime, serious consideration should be given to how various divestiture and trusts could be used to manage one's taxable estate. Minimizing taxes imposed on an estate is a complex topic that should address the following considerations:

1. Maximizing benefits of the marital deduction.

2. Making gifts during one's lifetime.

3. Taking actions to accomplish a step-up in property basis.

4. Taking actions to benefit from a loss in property values.

5. Utilization of charitable deductions.

6. Planning estate liquidity in order to pay estate taxes and probate costs.

B. In order to calculate the federal estate tax, the gross estate must first be determined. The gross estate consists of the fair market value of property owned by the decedent at the date of death and also may include other assets that were transferred by the decedent during his/her lifetime. The value of certain "qualified family-owned business interests" may be excluded from the taxable estate. The taxable estate is determined by reducing the gross estate by the following allowable deductions:

1. Allowable expenses, such as funeral expenses and costs of administrating the estate

2. Indebtedness against property included in the gross estate, such as a mortgage and other debts of the decedent

3. Unpaid property and income taxes of the decedent to date of death

4. Uninsured losses from casualty or theft of estate assets during the period of settlement

5. Transfers to charity specified by the will

6. Marital deduction, which is unlimited in amount, for estate property that passes to the surviving spouse if he/she is a U.S. citizen

C. The taxable estate may be increased by taxable gifts made by the decedent.

1. Post-1976 annual gifts per donee made by a donor are taxable to the extent that they exceed proscribed amounts. Currently, annual gifts are not taxable to the extent that they do not exceed $11,000 per donee per donor.

2. In addition to the above annual limit, a lifetime gift(s) exclusion also exists. Currently, the first $1 million of lifetime gifting per donor is not taxable.

D. Estate tax rates are progressive, and the tentative estate tax is reduced by a unified credit that exempts a portion of the taxable estate from taxation. For years 2006 through 2008, a maximum of $2,000,000 of taxable estate is excluded from tax for a maximum credit of $780,800. Additional credits are available for state death or inheritance taxes paid and taxes paid on taxable gifts made after 1976.

E. A marital deduction is allowed for property passing to a decedent's spouse. This deduction can significantly reduce and/or defer estate taxes, but it must be used with careful planning.

1. It is important to note that the marital deduction will not eliminate estate taxes but will defer them until the death of the remaining spouse.

2. In some instances, it may be better to use the decedent's unified credit rather than the marital deduction.

        3.   Credit shelter trusts may also be used to shelter a portion of the estate from tax by placing a portion of the gross estate into a trust.

   F. The use of annual gifts in amounts less than the taxable limits is an effective way to reduce one's taxable estate.

        1.   Currently, the first $11,000 ($22,000 for consenting spousal gifts) to any one person during any calendar year is subtracted in determining taxable gifts.

        2.   An individual's lifetime gift tax exclusion additionally could also be used as the amount of a tax-free gift.

   G. Assets are included in the taxable estate at their fair market value at the date of the decedent's death.

        1.   Value at an alternate date (6 months after death) may be used for all assets existing at that date if the value is less than at date of death. Property sold, distributed, or disposed of during the 6-month period is valued at the date of disposition.

        2.   Recipients of estate assets measure their tax basis in such assets as the fair market value at date of decedent's death or the alternate valuation date. Generally, this results in a stepped-up basis and avoids income (versus estate) tax on the gain in asset appreciation.

        3.   If assets in the estate have a current value that is less than the decedent's tax basis, the lower value becomes the new tax basis. In this case, neither the decedent nor his beneficiaries receive an income tax benefit from the decline in value. Therefore, it may be better to sell assets with a tax loss prior to death.

   H. Estates or the decedent's heirs may be subject to taxes in addition to estate tax.

        1.   Most states assess an inheritance tax on the value of estate assets transferred to heirs. Unlike the estate tax, the inheritance tax is levied on the heirs rather than the estate. Certain transfers are exempt, and reductions are allowed for certain expenses and debts of the decedent.

        2.   To the extent an estate generates income that was not originally included in the inventory of principal assets, a tax will be imposed on the income. If taxable income is distributed to a beneficiary, the income will be taxed to the beneficiary. The income that passes to the beneficiary retains the same character it had in the hands of the estate. If taxable income is not distributed but is accumulated by the estate, the income is taxable to the estate.

   I. Estate income must be accounted for separately and also may be the subject of special provisions of a decedent's will.

        1.   A will might stipulate that the income accrue to a particular party, referred to as an income beneficiary, while the principal be ultimately distributed to a party referred to as the remainderman.

        2.   If a will does not clearly address the question of income, many states have adopted the Revised Uniform Principal and Income Act, which provides guidance on this issue.

        3.   The determination of income for estate purposes does not always parallel generally accepted accounting principles.

            a.   Gains and losses on the sales of estate principal are generally not considered part of income but rather part of principal.

            b.   Generally, the premium or discount on bonds is not amortized except in the case of a premium on bonds subsequently purchased using estate assets.

            c.   Generally, depreciation is not considered in determining estate income, although including depreciation may serve to preserve estate principal. However, depletion is charged to income.

III.   After estate assets and debts have been identified and applicable taxes have been paid, the provisions of the decedent's will must be carried out and accounted for. If the decedent dies intestate, distribution of the probate estate is governed by applicable state law.

   A. Distribution of probate estate assets is a devise if real property is involved and a legacy if personal property is involved. The recipients of real and personal property are referred to as devisees and legatees, respectively.

   B. The process of abatement requires that legacies be satisfied to whatever extent possible given the following order of priority:

        1.   A specific legacy is a gift of a particular, specified thing that is distinguishable from others.

        2.   A demonstrative legacy is a gift of an amount from a specific source with the will stipulating that, if the amount cannot be satisfied from that source, it shall be satisfied from the general estate. If proceeds are inadequate to meet the amount, the difference shall constitute a general legacy.

        3.   A general legacy is a gift of an indicated amount or quantity of something. However, the specific source of the payment is not designated.

    4.   A residuary legacy is composed of all estate property remaining after assigning the specific, demonstrative, and general legacies.

  C. If a general legacy cannot be satisfied in its entirety, the available amount is abated proportionately among the recipients.

  D. A charge and discharge statement is prepared that accounts for the fiduciary's activities with respect to estate principal and income.

    1.   The charge and discharge statement provides a separate accounting for both principal and income.

    2.   It is important to understand which activities and/or transactions affect estate principal versus estate income.

IV.   A trust is a separate distinct entity that receives assets from an individual for the purpose of managing and distributing the trust's income and assets.

  A. Trusts may be created to serve a variety of purposes, such as serving to reduce estate taxes. An inter vivos, or living, trust becomes operative while the grantor is alive, and a testamentary trust is created through a will. Some further examples of trusts include:

    1.   A charitable remainder trust, which distributes income to beneficiaries for a period of time after which point the remaining assets are distributed to a charitable remainderman.

    2.   A bypass, or credit shelter trust, which is used to split assets between a surviving spouse and the trust so that the values of the marital deduction and unified credit are maximized.

    3.   A qualified terminable interest property trust (Q-TIP trust), which is similar in nature to a bypass or credit trust.

  B. Accounting for a trust is similar to that for an estate and requires a distinction between principal and income. A charge and discharge statement is used to account for the activities of a trust.

PART 1

Instructions: Use a check mark to indicate whether each of the following statements is true or false.

	True	False
1. Accrued interest at the time of a decedent's death would be interest income and considered part of estate income rather than principal.	_____	_____
2. The gain realized from the sale of stocks should also be included in estate principal.	_____	_____
3. Certain assets of decedents can pass directly to their heirs and not be included in the probate estate.	_____	_____
4. When recording the inventory of an estate, the assets of the estate are recorded net of the decedent's debts.	_____	_____
5. A fiduciary's claim against an estate for administrative expenses is generally satisfied before claims for unpaid taxes.	_____	_____
6. The unified credit has the effect of exempting a portion of estate assets from estate taxes.	_____	_____
7. Annual gifts per donee in excess of established amounts will be added to the taxable estate of a decedent.	_____	_____
8. Property acquired by an heir to an estate retains the same tax basis as when held by the decedent.	_____	_____
9. If an estate consists of wasting assets such as timber, it would be appropriate to include depletion in the calculation of estate income.	_____	_____
10. The payment of legacies by an estate must follow an order of priority that requires general legacies to be satisfied before specific legacies.	_____	_____
11. Generally speaking, both estates and trusts must maintain the distinction between principal and income.	_____	_____
12. Trusts may be used to shelter assets of an estate from taxation.	_____	_____

PART 2

Instructions: Beside each of the following statements, write the letter that corresponds to the term that best characterizes the statement.

A. Intestate
B. Marital deduction
C. Unified credit
D. Alternate valuation date
E. Charge and discharge statement

F. Estate principal
G. Estate income
H. Charitable remainder trust
I. Bypass or credit shelter trust
J. Inter vivos trust

Term

1. A component of the estate tax calculation that, in substance, defers versus eliminates estate taxes   _____

2. A trust that is created and operable before an individual's death   _____

3. A component of the estate tax calculation that is designed to prevent tax inequities resulting from declining market values subsequent to a decedent's death   _____

4. Unless otherwise stipulated, the classification normally given to interest earned since a decedent's death on bonds held at the time of death   _____

5. A trust that is required to specify a charitable organization as the recipient of the trust's principal   _____

6. Unlike a discount on bonds purchased subsequent to the decedent's death, the amortization of a premium on such bonds generally affects this amount   _____

PART 3

Instructions: Circle the letter that identifies the best response to each question.

1. You have been informed that, under your late aunt's will, you are a legatee. Technically, this means that you will receive
   a. Cash.
   b. Real property.
   c. Personal property.
   d. The face value of a life insurance policy.

2. Tim Mietrich, a single man, has accumulated a considerable amount of assets. He wishes to reduce his ultimate estate tax. Over the next 12 years, the maximum total gifts that he could make through the annual gift tax exclusion without incurring any gift tax is
   a. $11,000 × 12
   b. $22,000 × 12
   c. $11,000 × 12 × 12
   d. Not determinable from the facts provided.

3. Carlotta Lopez wishes to donate $10,000 to her church this year. Her estate is large and will be subject to estate tax. She is undecided whether to give $10,000 in cash, donate shares of stock that cost $40,000 but with a current market value of $10,000 and little hope of recovery, or sell these shares and donate the proceeds. Considering only these facts, she should do which of the following?
   a. Sell the stock and donate the proceeds.
   b. Donate $10,000 cash and keep the stock.
   c. Donate the shares of stock.
   d. Make no donation until the market value of the shares has recovered.

4. Julio Doro received 400 shares of stock from his mother after her death on February 1. Her basis for the stock was $12,000. The stock had a market value of $20,000 on February 1; $23,000 6 months later; and $25,000 when the estate tax return was filed. The alternative valuation date was not applicable. Julio's basis for the stock is
   a. $25,000   b. $23,000   c. $20,000   d. $12,000

5. Which one of the following statements in regard to the marital deduction is correct?
   a. It cannot be split between the decedent and his/her surviving spouse.
   b. It should not be combined with a gift program.
   c. It is of greater tax benefit to the surviving spouse than to the deceased.
   d. It is of greater benefit to taxable estates equal to or less than the amount that corresponds to the unified credit.

6. The valid will of Ginger Hill said, "I leave my friend Chien Yang $10,000." This is an illustration of a
   a. Specific legacy.
   b. General legacy.
   c. Demonstrative legacy.
   d. Residuary legacy.

7. Which of the following would not reduce the unified tax base upon which estate taxes are based?
   a. Funeral expenses.
   b. Unpaid income taxes of the decedent to date of death.
   c. Transfers to charity specified in a will.
   d. Taxable gifts made after 1976.

PART 4

Pete Mitchell died on February 28, 20X7. The following trial balance was prepared by the executor of Mitchell's estate as of December 31, 20X7:

	As to Principal		As to Income	
	Debits	Credits	Debits	Credits
Cash—principal	$ 45,000			
Cash—income			$25,000	
Corporation stock	100,000			
Assets subsequently discovered		$ 25,000		
Loss on realization of principal assets	5,000			
Funeral and administrative expenses	10,000			
Debts of decedent paid	25,000			
Legacies distributed	10,000			
Devises distributed	15,000			
Estate principal		185,000		
Expenses chargeable against income			4,000	
Distributions to income beneficiaries			5,000	
Estate income				$34,000
	$ 210,000	$ 210,000	$34,000	$34,000

Instructions: Prepare a charge and discharge statement.

Estate of Pete Mitchell
Charge and Discharge Statement
For the Period February 28, 20X7, to December 31, 20X7

PART 5

The following transactions are typical of those incurred by an estate:
1. Recording of the original assets of the estate.
2. Sale of capital stock in the original estate at a gain.
3. Recording receipt of interest (partly accrued at date of death) on bonds in the original estate.
4. Recording assets subsequently discovered.
5. Purchase of bonds at a premium along with accrued interest.
6. Receipt of first interest check on bonds in 5.
7. Payment of property taxes on a rental apartment. (The taxes became a lien after the date of death.)

Instructions: Assuming no stipulation to the contrary is made in the will, indicate whether the typical accounting treatment of each of the items would affect principal accounts only, income accounts only, or both. Use the following columnar format for your answers, placing an "X" in the appropriate column.

Would Affect

# of Item	Principal Only	Income Only	Principal and Income
1.			
2.			
3.			
4.			
5.			
6.			
7.			

Chapter 21   Debt Restructuring, Corporate Reorganizations, and Liquidations

OUTLINE FOR REVIEW

The going concern assumption may not hold true for all business entities due to business difficulties and/or uncertainties. Several corrective actions may be available to a troubled or insolvent company, including a troubled debt restructuring, reorganization, or liquidation.

I.   A business is considered to be insolvent if it is unable to service its liabilities or, technically, has liabilities in excess of assets. There are several remedies available to insolvent companies that do not require court action or approval.

   A.   Seeking relief outside of a bankruptcy court has several advantages, including:

      1.   A more timely solution.

      2.   A less public and more discreet solution that may not adversely affect future business.

   B.   A troubled debt restructuring is a process whereby creditors grant concessions to the debtor in order to maximize their recovery on the debt. Such restructurings generally involve one of the following:

      1.   Transferring assets to the debtor in settlement of the debt.

         a.   The debtor records a gain on restructuring, which is measured as the difference between the carrying basis of the debt and the fair market value of the assets transferred.

         b.   The difference between the book value of the assets transferred and their fair market value is recognized as a separate gain or loss.

      2.   Granting an equity interest in order to satisfy the debt. A gain is recorded as the difference between the carrying basis of the debt and the fair market value of the equity interest.

      3.   Modifying the terms of the debt in a way that involves principal and/or interest.

         a.   If future payments of principal and interest specified by the restructuring are less than the carrying basis of the debt, a gain is recognized. All subsequent cash payments are recognized as principal, and no interest expense is recognized.

         b.   If future payments of principal and interest specified by the restructuring are more than the carrying basis of the debt, no gain is recognized. However, interest expense based on an effective interest rate is recognized until maturity.

      4.   Combining the restructuring alternatives discussed in (1), (2), and (3) above.

         a.   The carrying basis of the debt should first be reduced to the extent of the fair market value of assets transferred and/or equity interests granted. This step does not result in any gain on restructuring.

         b.   The remaining carrying basis of the debt is compared against the "modification of terms" portion of the restructuring and accounted for accordingly.

   C.   A restructuring generally involves a formal agreement between the debtor and the debtor's creditors.

      1.   A creditor agreement is used to extend the terms of a debt or to make other concessions regarding future interest rates.

      2.   A composition agreement is used to scale down a creditor's claims against the debtor.

   D.   A quasi-reorganization may be used to eliminate a large deficit in retained earnings and to revalue assets to reflect lower fair market values.

      1.   The decreases in recorded amounts of assets resulting from the revaluation are charged against retained earnings and thus increase the deficit.

      2.   The deficit in retained earnings is eliminated by charges against paid-in capital in excess of par value. If such paid-in capital is not adequate, par values may be adjusted in order to generate additional capital in excess of par value.

      3.   Retained earnings balances subsequent to the reorganization should be dated to indicate the starting point of new accumulations.

   E.   A corporation may decide to liquidate its business. Shareholders receive any net assets remaining after fully satisfying the claims of creditors. A general assignment for the benefit of creditors must be agreed to by all creditors. If creditors are not fully satisfied, they share assets according to this general assignment.

II.   Legal proceedings for bankruptcy may be initiated under the Bankruptcy Reform Act and the Bankruptcy Code Amendments.

    A.   A bankruptcy case may be filed under several chapters of the Bankruptcy Code Reform Act. Chapter 7, "Liquidation," and Chapter 11, "Reorganization," are applicable to business enterprises.

    B.   A bankruptcy may be initiated voluntarily by the debtor seeking an order for relief or involuntarily by creditor(s) with a specified level of claim(s).

III.   The goal of a corporate reorganization under Chapter 11 is to restructure the debt and/or capital of a company so that it may continue its business purpose.

    A.   A petition seeking a reorganization may be voluntarily or involuntarily filed to seek an order for relief.

        1.   A plan of reorganization must be filed with the court detailing the proposed arrangements to reorganize the company.

        2.   The plan must be approved by the parties that are impaired.

            a.   A plan affecting creditors is approved if it is accepted by creditors representing at least two-thirds in amount and more than one-half in number of a class of claims.

            b.   A plan affecting shareholders is approved if it is accepted by holders representing at least two-thirds in amount of allowed claims.

        3.   Once approved by the impaired parties, the reorganization plan must be confirmed by the bankruptcy court. Before confirmation, the court verifies that under the plan each holder of a claim will receive or retain property of a value that is at least the amount such holder would receive under a Chapter 7 liquidation.

        4.   If the reorganization plan is not accomplishing its intended purpose, it may be modified or converted to a Chapter 7 liquidation.

    B.   A plan of reorganization may involve debt restructurings and/or quasi-reorganizations that must be accounted for.

        1.   Debt restructurings in a reorganization are accounted for differently than restructurings that do not require court approval.

            a.   The gain on restructuring is measured as the difference between the net present value of the restructured consideration to be received and the carrying basis of the debt.

            b.   Interest to be recognized on the restructured debt is imputed at market rates; it represents the difference between the net present value of the consideration to be received and the total of all principal and interest payments to be received.

        2.   The courts require periodic reports detailing operations, cash flows, and other information that the court may request. If a trustee is appointed, a new set of books may be established by the trustee.

IV.   For certain companies, the only solution to their financial difficulties is to liquidate the entity under Chapter 7. The commencement of a liquidation may be voluntary or involuntary.

    A.   The court appoints a trustee to administer the liquidation of the entity.

        1.   In order to assist the trustee, the company must file a statement of affairs, which provides certain information regarding the debtor company.

        2.   The trustee must begin to dispose of assets in order to meet the claims of secured and unsecured creditors.

    B.   The claims of unsecured creditors must be satisfied to whatever extent possible in the following order of priority:

        1.   Class 1—Expenses to administer the estate. Those who administer the estate should be assured of payment; otherwise, competent attorneys and accountants would not be willing to participate.

        2.   Class 2—Debts incurred after the commencement of a case of involuntary bankruptcy but before the order for relief or appointment of a trustee. These items, referred to as "gap" creditors, are granted priority in order to permit the business to carry on its operations during the period of legal proceedings.

        3.   Class 3—Wages up to $4,000 per individual earned within 90 days before the filing of the petition or the cessation of the debtor's business, whichever occurs first.

        4.   Class 4—Unpaid contributions to employee benefit plans arising from services performed during 180 days prior to filing the petition—to the extent of $4,000 per employee covered by the plan.

        5.   Class 5—Deposits up to $1,800 each for goods or services never received from the debtor.

        6.   Class 6—Tax claims of a governmental unit. Since these taxes are nondischargeable (that is, they still must be met by the debtor after the termination of the case), the arrangement favors the debtor. Whatever funds are available for this priority will reduce the amount the debtor will have to pay later.

        7.   Class 7—Claims of general creditors not granted priority. All remaining unsecured claims fall into this category.

    C. An accounting statement of affairs must be prepared that estimates the net realizable value of assets and indicates how the assets will be made available to secured and unsecured creditors.

        1. The statement categorizes assets into assets pledged with fully secured creditors, assets pledged with partially secured creditors, and free assets available to unsecured creditors.

        2. The liability and owners' equity sections of the statement divide claims between various categories of secured and unsecured creditors.

        3. The ratio of assets received by a class of creditors compared to the total amount of their claims is referred to as a dividend.

    D. A trustee may also be required to prepare a report, referred to as a statement of realization and liquidation, which states actual rather than expected results.

PART 1

Instructions: Use a check mark to indicate whether each statement is true or false.

                                                                                   True   False

1. A debt restructuring is a method of dealing with a troubled company that may or may not be part of a court-approved plan.

2. If in a troubled debt restructuring assets are transferred to creditors in full settlement of a debt, a gain is recognized to the extent that the fair market value of the assets transferred is less than the basis of the debt.

3. A debt restructuring that involves a modification of terms and does not require court approval may not require the recognition of subsequent interest expense.

4. Interest expense associated with a modification of terms under a debt restructuring is measured differently, depending on whether or not the modification is part of a plan under a Chapter 11 reorganization.

5. In a quasi-reorganization, if paid-in capital in excess of par value is not sufficient to absorb a deficit in retained earnings, the par value for stock may be reduced.

6. A reorganization under Chapter 11 of the Bankruptcy Code Amendments will be approved by the courts even if creditors receive less than would be the case with a Chapter 7 liquidation.

7. Under the Bankruptcy Code, a reorganization may be either voluntary or involuntary, yet a liquidation may be only voluntary.

8. A Chapter 11 reorganization plan must be approved by those creditors representing at least one-half of the total dollar amount due that class.

9. Under a corporate liquidation, all unsecured creditors have equal rights to claim available assets of the corporation.

10. A statement of affairs measures a deficiency—traceable to unsecured creditors without priority—as the difference between the estimated net realizable value of the assets and the amount due those creditors.

11. The dividend to general unsecured creditors is the dividend rate declared on common stock multiplied by the amount due to unsecured creditors.

12. The statement of realization and liquidation reports the actual results of a liquidation whereas a statement of affairs reports estimated results.

PART 2

Instructions: Circle the letter that identifies the best response to each question based on the following situation.

Radco Industries is seeking to restructure its debt and eliminate its retained earnings deficit. Relevant account balances are as follows:

Equipment (net)	$700,000
Commercial loan payable	600,000
Paid-in capital in excess of par value	400,000
Common stock ($10 par)	200,000

1. Assuming assets with a cost of $400,000 and a fair market value of $520,000 are transferred in total satisfaction of the commercial loan payable, the total gain to be recognized is
   a. $120,000   b. $80,000   c. $200,000   d. $150,000

2. Assuming the terms of the commercial loan are modified to provide for six payments of $90,000 each with a present value of $428,989 based on a market interest rate of 7%, the gain on restructuring is
   a. $171,011   b. $60,000   c. $0   d. $40,000

3. Given the facts of question 2, the interest expense recognized over the life of the restructuring is
   a. $171,011   b. $60,000   c. $10,000   d. $0

4. Given the facts of question 2, except that the restructuring is part of a Chapter 11 reorganization, the interest expense recognized in the first year after modification is
   a. $10,000   b. $0   c. $28,502   d. $30,029

5. Assume assets with a fair market value of $220,000 and a cost of $200,000 are transferred in satisfaction of a portion of the commercial loan. In addition, the balance of the debt is to be repaid over 5 years in annual payments of $78,000, which have a present value of $319,815 based on a market interest rate of 7%. The gain on restructuring is
   a. $0   b. $20,000   c. $10,000   d. $60,185

6. Assuming the deficit in retained earnings is $320,000, including the effect of the debt restructuring, a quasi-reorganization would result in a balance for paid-in capital in excess of par value of
   a. $400,000   b. $280,000   c. $80,000   d. $720,000

7. Given the facts of question 6 and assuming that the equipment has a fair value of $550,000, a quasi-reorganization would result in an adjusted par value per share of common stock of
   a. $6.50   b. $10.00   c. $2.50   d. $8.40

PART 3

Instructions: Circle the letter that identifies the best response to each question based on the following situation.

The D. A. Norman Company has decided to seek a Chapter 7 liquidation after previous restructuring attempts failed. The company has the following condensed balance sheet as of April 1, 20X9:

Assets		Liabilities and Stockholders' Equity	
Cash	$ 12,000	Accounts payable	$ 60,000
Receivables (net)	280,000	Loans from officer	80,000
Inventory	70,000	Equipment loan payable	360,000
Plant assets (net)	340,000	Accrued payroll	10,000
		Business loan payable	180,000
		Common stock	60,000
		Retained earnings deficit	(48,000)
Total assets	$702,000	Total liabilities and stockholders' equity	$702,000

The noncash assets shown have the following fair market values (FMV): receivables (net), $230,000; inventory, $76,000; plant assets (net), $350,000. A loan from the officer in the amount of $30,000 was incurred after commencement of the bankruptcy case but before the appointment of a trustee. The liabilities are secured as follows:

Liabilities	Amount Secured	Secured by	Securities Book Value	FMV
Accounts payable	$ 40,000	Inventory	$ 40,000	$ 44,000
Equipment loan payable	360,000	Plant assets	340,000	350,000
Business loan payable	180,000	Receivables	100,000	80,000

1. Assuming trustee expenses of $12,000 in addition to the recorded liabilities, which of the remaining unsecured creditors has the next-highest order of priority?
   a. Accrued payroll
   b. Equipment loan payable
   c. Loan from officer
   d. Business loan payable

2. The realizable value of assets pledged with fully secured creditors is
   a. $459,000   b. $44,000   c. $40,000   d. $489,000

3. Of those creditors who are partially secured, their unsecured amounts are
   a. $430,000   b. $110,000   c. $540,000   d. $120,000

4. The realizable value of free assets available to unsecured creditors is
   a. $628,000   b. $232,000   c. $220,000   d. $198,000

5. The dividend to Class 7 unsecured creditors is
   a. 90%   b. 100%   c. 88%   d. 76%

PART 4

Instructions: Circle the letter that identifies the best response to each question.

1. The primary difference between a balance sheet and an accounting statement of affairs is that
   a. A balance sheet reflects book values, while a statement of affairs emphasizes realization values.
   b. Assets are arranged in a different sequence.
   c. Liabilities are arranged in a different sequence.
   d. Owners' equity is not considered in the statement of affairs.

2. An accounting statement of affairs of a corporation in financial difficulty indicates that unsecured creditors would receive $0.40 on the dollar. Which one of the following assets is most likely to realize the smallest percentage of its book value?
   a. Accounts receivable
   b. Inventories
   c. Plant and equipment
   d. Goodwill

3. Immediately after the recording of a quasi-reorganization, there will be no balance in the account
   a. Accumulated depreciation.
   b. Capital stock.
   c. Paid-in capital from reorganization.
   d. Retained earnings.

4. If a dividend of 80% is allocable to Class 7 unsecured creditors based on an accounting statement of affairs, it correctly may be concluded that
   a. All unsecured claims will receive the same percentage of return.
   b. All unsecured claims will be paid in full.
   c. Classes 1 through 6 unsecured claims will be paid in full.
   d. Stockholders will receive 20% of their equity.

5. Which of the following is not correct?
   a. The difference between the fair market value of assets transferred to a creditor and the book value of such assets is not considered as part of the gain on restructuring.
   b. It is possible to convey both assets and equity interest as part of a restructuring.
   c. If the terms of a debt are modified under a bankruptcy reorganization, no interest expense will be recognized in subsequent periods if the total of all future cash payments exceeds the carrying value of the debt.
   d. If equity is conveyed in satisfaction of a debt, the equity is valued at an amount equal to its fair market value rather than the carrying value of the debt.

6. In a liquidation proceeding, if the proceeds on the realization of an asset exceed the lien against that asset, the excess is assigned to
   a. The holder of the lien.
   b. Other lien holders whose assets will not realize a sufficient amount to cover their liens.
   c. Meet the claims of the unsecured creditors.
   d. The stockholders of the corporation.

PART 5

J. Wachs, CPA, has prepared a statement of affairs. Assets against which there are no claims or liens are expected to produce $70,000, which must be allocated to unsecured claims of all classes totaling $105,000. The following are some of the claims outstanding:

(a) Accounting fees for Wachs, $1,500.
(b) An unsecured note for $1,000, on which $60 of interest has accrued, held by S. Bart.
(c) A note for $3,000, secured by $4,000 of receivables, estimated to be 60% collectible, held by J. Gamble.
(d) A $1,500 note, on which $30 of interest has accrued, held by B. Land. Property with a book value of $1,000 and a market value of $1,800 is pledged to guarantee payment of principal and interest.
(e) Unpaid income taxes of $3,500.

Instructions: From the information given above, calculate the following.

1. The total amount allocable to unsecured claims with priority.
2. The dividend per each dollar of Class 7 unsecured claims.
3. The amount each of the claimants may expect to realize.

Solutions

CHAPTER 1

PART 1

1. F   It is higher. Less depreciation
2. F   The separate statements must be consolidated.
3. T
4. T
5. T
6. T
7. F   The tax loss carryforward is recorded less an allowance for lack of realization.
8. F   Only since acquisition date
9. F   Extraordinary gain recorded if price is below sum of priority accounts.
10. T
11. T
12. F   Fixed assets will be allocated the amount available.
13. T
14. T   Caused by higher depreciation on assets
15. F   DTL is $50 x tax rate.
16. T

PART 2

1. b   Price paid $3,000,000
       Market value of net assets   2,440,000
       Goodwill $ 560,000

2. c   Common stock issued, 100,000 x $36 $3,600,000
       Direct acquisition costs   160,000
       Total cost $3,760,000

3. d   The appraised fair market value is recorded, along with a separate deferred tax liability of $11,600 [40% x ($85,000 − $56,000)].

4. b   Registration fees are deducted from paid-in capital. Direct costs are added to price and could mean higher cost for depreciable assets.

5. a   In a purchase, where the price exceeds book value, assets are increased to market value. This results in greater expenses in periods subsequent to the purchase. This means purchase income will be lower than pooling income.

6. d   Include S for only half the year and greater fixed asset depreciation.

Common analysis for 7–9:

		Total
Priority (inventory less note)	$ 50,000	$ 50,000
Nonpriority (machinery, building and patents)	320,000	370,000

7. c   All accounts at fair value + goodwill

8. c   Allocate $250,000 to nonpriority accounts, 50/320 of 250,000 = 39,063, 40/320 of 250,000 = 31,250.

9. d   Amount is less than sum of priority accounts, no amount available for other accounts, extraordinary gain recorded.

PART 3

1. Account groups are as follows:

    Priority—Current assets, investments (except those under equity method), assets to be disposed of, deferred tax assets, prepaid assets relating to pension and other post retirement plans.

    Nonpriority—All other identifiable assets

    > A price higher than sum of fairer value of all priority and nonpriority accounts results in goodwill.

    > A price higher than sum of fairer value of only the priority accounts allocates balance to nonpriority accounts.

    > A price below sum of fairer value of only priority accounts results in extraordinary gain.

2. Pooling had the following advantages over purchase accounting:

    - Included income for entire year even if acquisition is during year
    - Brought accounts over at book value, less depreciation and amortization expenses
    - Brought over retained earnings of company acquired

3. A company is sold as a "nontaxable exchange." The buyer must record fair value of assets included in purchase, but can use only book value for future depreciation for tax return. The excess of the assigned fair value over the book value cannot be depreciated for tax purposes. The excess multiplied by the tax rate is the lost future tax savings, and it is recorded as the deferred tax liability. In future years, the deferred tax liability will be paid off each year as the tax liability exceeds the tax provision (based on fair value depreciation).

4. Goodwill is no longer amortized. Instead, it is impairment tested annually. If impaired, goodwill is written down.

PART 4

Comparison of Income

	Purchase Method	Pooling Method
Revenue	$650,000	$650,000
Less:		
All expenses except depreciation and other adjustments resulting from business combination	(215,000)	(215,000)
Depreciation of buildings:		
Purchase: 1/15 of $210,000 market value	(14,000)	—
Pooling: 1/15 of $170,000 book value	—	(11,333)
Depreciation of equipment:		
Purchase: 1/6 of $185,000 market value	(30,833)	—
Pooling: 1/6 of $150,000 book value	—	(25,000)
Other adjustments:		
Purchase, increase in cost of goods sold	(10,000)	
Pooling, expense direct acquisition costs		(10,000)
Net income	$380,167	$388,667

PART 5

1.

Assets	Group Amount	Cumulative Total
Priority	15,000	15,000
Nonpriority	250,000	265,000

a. A price in excess of $265,000 results in goodwill.

b. A price below $15,000 results in recording an extraordinary gain.

2.

Current assets	100,000	
Land	40,000	
Buildings	80,000	
Equipment	80,000	
Liabilities		85,000
Cash		215,000

Allocation:

Consideration (cash)		$215,000
Less market value of net current assets:		
Current assets	$100,000	
Liabilities	(85,000)	15,000
Value available for plant assets		$200,000

Asset	Fair Value	Percent of Nonpriority Total	x	Value Available	=	Assigned Value
Land	$ 50,000	20%		$200,000		$40,000
Buildings	100,000	40%		200,000		80,000
Equipment	100,000	40%		200,000		80,000
Total	$250,000	$100%				$200,000

PART 6

1. Zone Analysis for the Rocky Company:

	Group Amount	Cumulative Total
Priority accounts	40,000	40,000
Nonpriority accounts	550,000	590,000

2. Entry for $600,000:

Accounts receivable	20,000	
Inventory	80,000	
Marketable investments	100,000	
Land	110,000	
Buildings	275,000	
Equipment	82,500	
Patent	44,000	
Employee training	38,500	
Goodwill	10,000	
Accounts payable		60,000
Bonds payable		100,000
Cash		600,000

3. Entry for $400,000:

Accounts receivable	20,000	
Inventory	80,000	
Marketable investments	100,000	
Land	72,000	
Buildings	180,000	
Equipment	54,000	
Patent	28,800	
Employee training	25,200	
Accounts payable		60,000
Bonds payable		100,000
Cash		400,000

Allocation:

Price paid $400,000
Priority accounts   40,000
Available   360,000

Asset	Fair Value	Percent of Nonpriority Total	x	Value Available	=	Assigned Value
Land	$ 110,000	20%		$360,000		$ 72,000
Buildings	275,000	50%		360,000		180,000
Equipment	82,500	15%		360,000		54,000
Patents	44,000	8%		360,000		28,800
Employee training	38,500	7%		360,000		25,200
Total	$550,000	100%				$360,000

4. Entry for $20,000:

Accounts receivable	20,000	
Inventory	80,000	
Marketable investments	100,000	
Extraordinary gain		20,000
Accounts payable		60,000
Bonds payable		100,000
Cash		20,000

PART 7

1. Price $800,000
    Sum of assets at fair value   600,000
    Goodwill $200,000

2. Estimated fair value of business $700,000
    Book value of assets at 12/31/X3   800,000 (includes $200,000 goodwill)
    Deficiency $100,000 goodwill is impaired

3. Estimated fair value of business $700,000
    Fair value of identifiable assets   640,000
    New estimate of goodwill $ 60,000
    Original goodwill   200,000
    Impairment loss $140,000

PART 8

Computation of assigned values for long-lived assets:

Total consideration:		
Market value of securities issued (14,000 x $30)		$420,000
Direct acquisition costs		13,000
Total price		$433,000
Less assignment to identifiable assets and liabilities:		
Current assets	$150,000	
Inventory	35,000	
Accounts payable	(90,000)	
Bonds payable	(85,000)	
Land	28,000	
Buildings	200,000	
DTL .3 (200,000 – 85,000)	(34,500)	
Equipment	78,000	
DTL .3 (78,000 – 70,000)	(2,400)	279,100
Available for goodwill net of DTL		$153,900
Goodwill (153,900/7)	$219,857	
DTL (.3 x 219,857)	$ (65,957)	

Entries to Record Purchase of King Corporation

Current assets	150,000	
Inventory	35,000	
Land	28,000	
Building	200,000	
Equipment	78,000	
Goodwill	219,857	
Cash (direct acquisition costs)		13,000
Accounts payable		90,000
Bonds payable		85,000
Deferred tax liability (34,500 + 2,400 + 65,957)		102,857
Common stock (14,000 shares x $2)		28,000
Paid-in capital in excess of par		392,000
Professional services expense	9,800	
Cash		9,800
Paid-in capital in excess of par	22,000	
Cash		22,000

CHAPTER 2

PART 1

1. F They are made only on the worksheet and are not recorded on the books of either company.
2. T
3. F These accounts are adjusted regardless of the price paid.
4. F The excess increases.
5. F It is a separate item within the stockholders' equity section.
6. T
7. T But it is less than fair value
8. F Assets are only adjusted for the parent ownership interest.
9. T If effective control can be shown to exist
10. T
11. F The total amount available must be allocated based on estimated fair value.
12. F It is shown, in total, as a component of consolidated equity.

PART 2

1. d $1,300,000 existing for Poe + 200,000 shares x $8

2. a
Price paid	$60,000
Equity, $50,000 x 90%	45,000
Excess cost	$15,000
Inventory, add $9,000	9,000
Balance to goodwill	$ 6,000

   Current assets = $70,000 + $20,000 + $9,000

3. c (none of the payments under new borrowing included)

   Noncurrent assets = $90,000 + $40,000 + $6,000

4. b $30,000 + $10,000 + $6,000 payment

5. c (includes $54,000 long-term portion of new debt)

6. a

7. b

8. d

9. d Since the price paid exceeds fair market value of the net assets, assets and liabilities are recorded at full market value.

10. d

PART 3

100% Interest

1. a. Zone Analysis

	Group Total	Cum. Total
Priority accounts	$105,000	$105,000
Nonpriority accounts	250,000	355,000

b. D&D of excess

Price paid		$650,000		$360,000		$295,000		$100,000
Less interest acquired:							
Common stock	$100,000		$100,000		$100,000		$100,000
Paid-in capital in excess of par	150,000		150,000		150,000		150,000
Retained earnings	95,000		95,000		95,000		95,000
Total equity	$345,000		$345,000		$345,000		$345,000
Ownership interest	100%	345,000	100%	345,000	100%	345,000	100%	345,000
Excess of cost (book)		$305,000		$ 15,000		$(50,000)		$(245,000)
Adjustments:							
Inventory		$ 10,000		$ 10,000		$ 10,000		$ 10,000
Equipment		30,000		30,000		(30,000)		(220,000)
Goodwill (net adjustment)		265,000		(25,000)		(30,000)		(30,000)
Extraordinary gain		0		0		0		(5,000)
Total adjustments		$305,000		$ 15,000		$ (50,000)		$(245,000)

80% Interest

2. a. Zone Analysis

	Group Total	Ownership Portion	Cum. Total
Priority accounts	$105,000	$ 84,000	$ 84,000
Nonpriority accounts	250,000	200,000	284,000

b. D&D of excess

Price paid		$650,000		$360,000		$295,000		$100,000
Less interest acquired:							
Common stock	$100,000		$100,000		$100,000		$100,000
Paid-in capital in excess of par	150,000		150,000		150,000		150,000
Retained earnings	95,000		95,000		95,000		95,000
Total equity	$345,000		$345,000		$345,000		$345,000
Ownership interest	80%	276,000	80%	276,000	80%	276,000	80%	276,000
Excess of cost (book)		$374,000		$ 84,000		$ 19,000		$(176,000)
Adjustments:							
Inventory		$ 8,000		$ 8,000		$ 8,000		$ 8,000
Equipment		24,000		24,000		24,000		(160,000)
Goodwill (net adjustment)		342,000		52,000		(13,000)		(24,000)
Extraordinary gain		0		0		0		0
Total adjustments		$374,000		$ 84,000		$ (19,000)		$(176,000)

PART 4

1. Zone analysis:

	Group Total	Ownership Portion	Cumulative Total
Priority accounts	70,000	56,000	56,000
Nonpriority accounts	600,000	480,000	536,000

2.

		a.	b.	c.
Price paid		$720,000	$592,000	$336,000
Less book value of interest purchased:				
Common stock	$ 50,000			
Paid-in capital in excess of par	130,000			
Retained earnings	370,000			
Total stockholders' equity	$550,000			
Ownership interest	80%	440,000	440,000	440,000
Excess cost over book value (book value over cost)		$280,000	$152,000	$(104,000)
Adjustments: Inventory [($300,000 – $200,000) x 80%]		80,000	80,000	80,000
Land ($100,000 – $80,000) x 80% 16,000		16,000		
$280,000 available x 1/6 – .8 x $80,000)				(17,333)
Plant and equipment				
[($500,000 – $400,000) x 80% for parts a and b]		80,000	80,000	
$280,000 available x 5/6 – .8 x $400,000				(86,667)
Goodwill (new)		104,000	(24,000)	(80,000)
Total adjustments		$280,000	$152,000	$(104,000)

3. Elimination Entries:

a.	Common stock	40,000	
	Paid-in capital in excess of par	104,000	
	Retained earnings	296,000	
	Investment in Wright		440,000

To eliminate 80% of the stockholders' equity against the investment (same for all prices)

b. (1)	Inventory	80,000	
	Land	16,000	
	Plant and equipment	80,000	
	Goodwill (net)	104,000	
	Investment in Wright		280,000

To distribute the excess of cost over book value for $720,000 price

b. (2)	Inventory	80,000	
	Land	16,000	
	Plant and equipment	80,000	
	Goodwill (net)		24,000
	Investment in Wright		152,000

To distribute the excess of cost over book value for $592,00 price

c.	Inventory	80,000	
	Investment in Wright	104,000	
	Goodwill		80,000
	Land		17,333
	Plant and equipment		86,667

To eliminate the excess of book value over cost for $336,000 price

PART 5

Zone Analysis:

	Group Total	Ownership Portion	Cumulative Total
Priority accounts	10,000	8,000	8,000
Nonpriority accounts	500,000	400,000	408,000

Price Analysis:
Price paid (including any direct acquisition costs) $380,000
Assign to priority accounts, controlling share $8,000
Assign to nonpriority accounts, controlling share   372,000
Goodwill   0
Extraordinary gain   0

D & D of Excess:

Price paid		$380,000
Less book value of interest purchased:		
Common stock	$ 50,000	
Paid-in capital in excess of par	150,000	
Retained earnings	190,000	
Total stockholders' equity	$390,000	
Ownership interest	80%	312,000
Excess of cost over book value		$ 68,000
Adjustments:		
Current assets (80% x $30,000)		$ 24,000 Dr.
Land		21,200 Dr.
Buildings		42,000 Dr.
Equipment		(19,200) Cr.
Goodwill		0
Total adjustments		$ 68,000

Allocation Schedule

Asset	Fair Value	Percent	Amount to Allocate*	Allocated Amount	Book Value (80%)	Adjustment Increase (Decrease)
Land	$ 50,000	10.0%	$372,000	$ 37,200	$ 16,000	$ 21,200
Buildings	250,000	50.0%	372,000	186,000	144,000	42,000
Equipment	200,000	40.0%	372,000	148,800	168,000	(19,200)
Total	$500,000			$372,000	$328,000	$ 44,000

*$400,000 share of fair value – $28,000 bargain

PART 6

1.   Zone Analysis:

	Group Total	Ownership Portion	Cumulative Total
Priority accounts	(145,000)	(116,000)	(116,000)
Nonpriority accounts	1,000,000	800,000	684,000

     Price Analysis:
     Price paid (including any direct acquisition costs) $ 750,000
     Assign to priority accounts, controlling share   (116,000)
     Assign to nonpriority accounts, controlling share   800,000
     Goodwill   66,000
     Extraordinary gain   0

2.   Determination and distribution of excess schedule:

     Price paid for investment in subsidiary
       (including direct acquisition costs) $750,000
     Less book value of interest purchased:
       Common stock $100,000
       Paid-in capital in excess of par   110,000
       Retained earnings   335,000
         Total stockholders' equity $545,000
       Ownership interest   80%   436,000
     Excess of cost over book value $ 314,000
     Adjustments:
       Inventory ($40,000 x 0.80) $ 32,000 Dr.
       Land ($85,000 x 0.80)   68,000 Dr.
       Buildings ($120,000 x 0.80)   96,000 Dr.
       Equipment ($65,000 x 0.80)   52,000 Dr.
       Goodwill (new)   66,000 Dr.
     Total adjustments $314,000 Dr.

3.

Yankee Corporation and Subsidiary Gary Corporation
Worksheet for Consolidated Balance Sheet
December 31, 20X0

	Trial Balance		Eliminations and Adjustments		NCI	Consolidated Balance Sheet	
	Yankee	Gary	Dr.	Cr.		Dr.	Cr.
Cash	115,000	60,000				175,000	
Accounts receivable	290,000	160,000				450,000	
Inventory	520,000	80,000	(D) 32,000			632,000	
Land	1,000,000	100,000	(D) 68,000			1,168,000	
Buildings	700,000	230,000	(D) 96,000			1,026,000	
Equipment	1,500,000	400,000	(D) 52,000			1,952,000	
Investment in Gary	750,000			(EL) 436,000			
				(D) 314,000			
Goodwill			(D) 66,000			66,000	
Current liabilities	(500,000)	(85,000)					585,000
Bonds payable		(400,000)					400,000
							600,000
Common stock—Yankee	(600,000)						600,000
Paid-in capital in excess—Yankee	(1,400,000)						1,400,000
Retained earnings—Yankee	(2,375,000)						
Common stock—Gary		(100,000)	(EL) 80,000		20,000		
Paid-in capital in excess—Gary		(110,000)	(EL) 88,000		22,000		
Retained earnings—Gary		(335,000)	(EL) 268,000		67,000		
Total	0	0	750,000	750,000			
Total NCI					109,000		109,000
						5,469,000	5,469,000

4.

Yankee Corporation and Subsidiary Gary Corporation
Consolidated Balance Sheet
December 31, 20X0

Assets

Current assets:		
Cash	$ 175,000	
Accounts receivable	450,000	
Inventory	632,000	
Total current assets		$1,257,000
Property, plant, and equipment:		
Land	$1,168,000	
Buildings	1,026,000	
Equipment	1,952,000	4,146,000
Goodwill		66,000
Total assets		$ 5,469,000

<u>Liabilities and Stockholders' Equity</u>

Current liabilities		$ 585,000
Bonds payable		400,000
Total liabilities		$ 985,000
Stockholders' equity:		
Noncontrolling interest		109,000
Controlling interest:		
Common stock	$ 600,000	
Paid-in capital in excess of par	1,400,000	
Retained earnings	2,375,000	4,375,000
Total liabilities and stockholders' equity		$ 5,469,000

CHAPTER 3

PART 1

1. T
2. T
3. F Dividends are recorded as income and do not increase the investment under the cost method.
4. T
5. F Only the parent's share is affected.
6. F The parent may use a different method and remaining life.
7. F All eliminations and adjustments are made on the worksheet and would not affect trial balances.
8. F The cost method maintains an investment at original cost and makes no adjustment for subsidiary equity changes.
9. T
10. T
11. T
12. F Consolidated net income is distributed to controlling and noncontrolling interests.
13. F The investment account remains at cost, and the dividends are recorded as income.

PART 2

1. a Under the cost method, dividends are income; under the equity method, they reduce investment account.

2. c Determination and distribution of excess schedule:

Price paid	$600,000
Equity, $660,000 assets less $160,000 liabilities	500,000
Excess of cost over book value	$100,000
Patent (10-year life, $10,000 per year)	$100,000

$210,000 + $100,000 − $10,000 patent amortization = $300,000.

3. b

Current assets	$ 730,000
Property, plant, and equipment	760,000
Patent, $100,000 less $10,000 amortization	90,000
Total consolidation assets	$1,580,000

4. c Retained earnings include only that of the controlling interest. $660,000 less $10,000 patent amortization.

5. d (see #3)

6. c Determination and distribution of excess schedule:

Price paid		$ 975,000
Equity, net assets of $1,000,000 x 80%		800,000
Excess of cost over book value		$ 175,000
Plant assets, 80% x $100,000		80,000
Goodwill		$ 95,000

7. b

Net assets, Jan. 1, 20X8	$1,000,000
Income less dividends	65,000
Total equity	$1,065,000
NCI (20% x $1,065,000)	$ 213,000

8. c. Consolidated net income includes only parent share of subsidiary for the entire year.

Post income for 20X7	$2,100,000
Ship income last 6 months of 20X7	500,000
Consolidated net income for 20X7	$2,600,000

9. c Building goes down and goodwill is recorded. There will be decrease in depreciation, and there will be no goodwill amortization.

PART 3

1. Purchased income exists in an intraperiod purchase when subsidiary books are not closed. It is the income of the subsidiary earned by outside interests, prior to the parent's acquiring control.

2. Noncontrolling interest in consolidated net income exists when the parent owns less than 100% of the subsidiary's voting common stock. Calculated on an income distribution schedule, it is the NCI percentage multiplied by the subsidiary reported net income.

3. Consolidated net income is the income of the consolidated company before allocation to the NCI and controlling interest. It is computed by combining the adjusted nominal accounts of the constituent companies.

4. The controlling interest is consolidated net income less the NCI share.

PART 4

Event		(A) Simple Equity Method		(B) Sophisticated Equity Method		(C) Cost Method	
20X5							
To record investment in Mars Company	Investment in Mars Company Cash	160,000	160,000	160,000	160,000	160,000	160,000
Subsidiary income of $45,000 reported to parent	Investment in Mars Company Subsidiary income	36,000	36,000	34,000*	34,000		
Dividends of $12,000 paid by Mars	Cash Investment in Mars Company (A) and (B) Subsidiary (dividend) income (C)	9,600	9,600	9,600	9,600	9,600	9,600
20X6							
Subsidiary income of $52,000 reported to parent	Investment in Mars Company Subsidiary income	41,600	41,600	39,600*	39,600		
Dividends of $18,000 paid by Mars	Cash Investment in Mars Company (A) and (B) Subsidiary (dividend) income (C)	14,400	14,400	14,400	14,400	14,400	14,400

*Amortization of equipment excess deducted from simple equity income amount = $2,000.

2.

Nitro Corporation and
Partial Worksheets
For Year Ended 20X6

	(a) Simple Equity Method					
	Trial Balance		Eliminations and Adjustments			
	Nitro	Mars	Dr.		Cr.	
Equipment (net)	640,000	320,000	(D₁)	16,000	(A)	4,000
Investment in Mars Company	213,600		(CY₂)	14,400	(CY₁)	41,600
					(EL)	153,600
					(EL)	32,800
Goodwill			(D₂)	16,800		
Common stock—Nitro	(60,000)					
Paid-in capital in excess—Nitro	(185,000)					
Retained earnings—Nitro (1/1/X6)	(703,500)		(A)	2,000		
Common stock—Mars		(24,000)	(EL)	19,200		
Paid-in capital in excess—Mars		(41,600)	(EL)	33,280		
Retained earnings—Mars (1/1/X6)		(126,400)	(EL)	101,120		
Expenses	250,000		(A)	2,000		
Subsidiary income*	(41,600)		(CY₁)	41,600		
Dividends declared	45,000	18,000			(CY₂)	14,400
Totals				246,400		246,400

Subsidiary Mars Company
Under Three Methods
December 31, 20X6

(b) Sophisticated Equity Method

	Trial Balance — Nitro	Trial Balance — Mars	Eliminations and Adjustments Dr.	Eliminations and Adjustments Cr.
Equipment (net)	640,000	320,000	(D₁) 14,000	(A) ***2,000
Investment in Mars Company	209,600		(CY₂) 14,400	(CY₁) 39,600
				(EL) 153,600
				(D) **30,800
Goodwill			(D₂) 16,800	
Common stock—Nitro	(60,000)			
Paid-in capital in excess—Nitro	(185,000)			
Retained earnings—Nitro (1/1/X6)	(701,500)			
Common stock—Mars		(24,000)	(EL) 19,200	
Paid-in capital in excess—Mars		(41,600)	(EL) 33,280	
Retained earnings—Mars (1/1/X6)		(126,400)	(EL) 101,120	
Expenses	250,000		(A) 2,000	
Subsidiary income*	(39,600)		(CY₁) 39,600	
Dividends declared	45,000	18,000		(CY₂) 14,400
Totals			240,400	240,400

(c) Cost Method

	Trial Balance — Nitro	Trial Balance — Mars	Eliminations and Adjustments Dr.	Eliminations and Adjustments Cr.
Equipment (net)	640,000	320,000	(D₁) 16,000	(A) 4,000
Investment in Mars Company	160,000		(CV) ****26,400	(EL) 153,600
				(D) 32,800
Goodwill			(D₂) 16,800	
Common stock—Nitro	(60,000)			
Paid-in capital in excess—Nitro	(185,000)			
Retained earnings—Nitro (1/1/X6)	(677,100)		(A) 2,000	(CV) 26,400
Common stock—Mars		(24,000)	(EL) 19,200	
Paid-in capital in excess—Mars		(41,600)	(EL) 33,280	
Retained earnings—Mars (1/1/X6)		(126,400)	(EL) 101,120	
Expenses	250,000		(A) 2,000	
Subsidiary income*	(14,400)		(CY₂) 14,400	
Dividends declared	45,000	18,000		(CY₂) 14,400
Totals			231,200	231,200

The following information applies to sections a, b, and c.

* "Dividend income" under the cost method.
** $32,800 less one year's amortization of $2,000.
*** Amortization is for the current year only since the prior year's amount has been amortized through the investment account.
**** $33,000 increase in retained earnings x 80%.

Eliminations and adjustments:
(EL) Eliminate 80% of Mars' beginning-of-the-year equity balances.
(D) Distribute excess as required by the determination and distribution of the excess schedule.
(A) Amortize equipment for the current and prior year (not under sophisticated equity method).
(CV) Convert equity (cost method only).
(CY₁) Eliminate current year equity income (not applicable to cost method).
(CY₂) Eliminate intercompany dividends.

PART 5

Payrol Company and Subsidiary Johnson Company
Worksheet for Consolidated Balance Sheet
For Year Ended December 31, 20X7

	Trial Balance Payrol	Trial Balance Johnson	Eliminations and Adjustments Dr.	Eliminations and Adjustments Cr.	Consolidated Income Statement	NCI	Controlling Retained Earnings	Consolidated Balance Sheet
Cash	654,000							1,159,000
Equipment (net)	1,290,000	940,000	40,000	15,000				2,255,000
Patents	195,000	35,000	80,000	24,000				286,000
Other assets	1,720,000	730,000						2,450,000
Investment in Johnson Company	1,500,000		144,000	1,504,000 / 140,000				
Goodwill			12,000					12,000
Accounts payable	(550,000)	(205,000)						(755,000)
Common stock—Payrol ($5 par)	(2,000,000)							(2,000,000)
Paid-in capital in excess—Payrol	(1,200,000)							(1,200,000)
Retained earnings in excess—Payrol 1/1/X7	(1,255,000)		8,000 / 10,000 / 16,000	144,000			(1,365,000)	
Common stock—Johnson		(1,000,000)	800,000			(200,000)		
Paid-in capital in excess—Johnson		(300,000)	240,000			(60,000)		
Retained earnings—Johnson 1/1/X7		(580,000)	464,000			(116,000)		
Sales	(1,100,000)	(425,000)			(1,525,000)			
Costs of goods sold	470,000	170,000			640,000			
Other expenses	250,000	100,000	5,000 / 8,000		363,000			
Dividend income	(24,000)		24,000					
Dividends declared	50,000	30,000		24,000		6,000	50,000	
Total	0	0	1,851,000	1,851,000				
Consolidated net income					(522,000)			
To NCI					31,000	(31,000)		
To controlling interest					491,000		(491,000)	
NCI						(401,000)		(401,000)
Controlling retained earnings, December 31, 20X7							(1,806,000)	(1,806,000)

Subsidiary Johnson Company Income Distribution

		Internally generated net income	$155,000
		Adjusted income	$155,000
		NCI share	20%
		NCI	$ 31,000

Parent Payrol Company Income Distribution

Equipment depreciation	$5,000	Internally generated net income	$380,000
Patent amortization	8,000	80% x Johnson Company adjusted income	124,000
		Controlling interest	$491,000

Eliminations and adjustments:
(CV) Convert from the cost to the equity method as of January 1, 20X7.
      [$580,000 January 1, 20X7 – $400,000 January 1, 20X5 = $180,000 x 0.80 = $144,000.]
(CY$_2$) Eliminate intercompany dividends.
(EL) Eliminate subsidiary equities.
(D)   Distribute the excess cost as given by the determination and distribution schedule:
      (1) Decrease parent's retained earnings by $8,000 for inventory sold.
      (2) Increase equipment $40,000.
      (3) Increase patents $80,000.
      (4) Increase goodwill $12,000.
(A)   Record amortizations resulting from the revaluations:
      (1) No amortization necessary.
      (2) Record $5,000 annual increase in equipment depreciation for the current and past two years.
      (3) Record $8,000 annual increase in patent depreciation for the current and past two years.

PART 6

1.	Price paid		$148,500
	Less interest acquired:		
	Common stock ($1 par)	$ 10,000	
	Paid-in capital in excess of par	40,000	
	Retained earnings, January 1, 20X5	84,000	
	Income of Ripley Co., January 1–September 1	18,000	
	Total interest, September 1, 20X5	$152,000	
	Interest acquired	85%	129,200
	Excess of cost over book value attributed to equipment, 10-year life		$19,300

2.

Liberty Inc. and Subsidiary Ripley Company
Worksheet for Consolidated Financial Statements
For Year Ended December 31, 20X5

	Trial Balance		Eliminations and Adjustments		Consolidated Income Statement	NCI	Controlling Retained Earnings	Consolidated Balance Sheet
	Liberty	Ripley	Dr.	Cr.				
Current assets	427,000	118,000						545,000
Land	62,000							62,000
Equipment	285,000	154,000	(D) 19,300					458,300
Accumulated depreciation	(145,000)	(41,000)		(A) 643				(186,643)
Investment in Ripley Company	160,400			(CY₁) 11,900				
				(EL) 129,200				
				(D) 19,300				
Liabilities	(126,500)	(65,000)						(191,500)
Common stock—Liberty	(100,000)							(100,000)
Paid-in capital in excess of par —Liberty	(250,000)							(250,000)
Retained earnings— Liberty	(180,000)						(180,000)	
Common stock— Ripley		(10,000)	(EL) 8,500			(1,500)		
Paid-in capital in excess of par —Ripley		(40,000)	(EL) 34,000			(6,000)		
Retained earnings— Ripley		(84,000)	(EL) 71,400			(12,600)		
Sales	(460,000)	(156,000)			(616,000)			
Cost of goods sold	216,000	82,000			298,000			
Expenses	123,000	42,0000	(A) 643		165,643			
Subsidiary income	(11,900)		(CY₁) 11,900					
Purchased income*			(EL) 15,300		15,300			
	0	0	161,043	161,043				
Consolidated net income					(137,057)			
To NCI					4,800	(4,800)		
Consolidated net income					132,257		(132,257)	
Total NCI						(24,900)		(24,900)
Retained earnings, controlling interest							(317,257)	(312,257)
								0

Eliminations and adjustments:

(CY₁) Eliminate the current-year entries in the investment account and the subsidiary income account.

(EL) Eliminate 85% of subsidiary equity balances at the beginning of the year, plus 85% of the undistributed subsidiary income as of September 1, 20X5.

(D) Distribute $19,300 excess of cost over book value.

(A) Record annual increase in equipment depreciation: ($19,300/ 10 years x 1/3 year = $643).

Subsidiary Ripley Company Income Distribution

	Internally generated net income (entire year)	$ 32,000
	Adjusted income	$ 32,000
	NCI share	15%
	NCI	$ 4,800

Parent Liberty Inc. Income Distribution

Equipment depreciation	$ 643	Internally generated net income	$121,000
Purchased income	15,300	80% x Ripley Company adjusted income of $32,000	27,200
		Controlling interest	$ 132,257

PART 7 (APPENDIX A)

1.

Paxton Company and Subsidiary Saxton Company
Determination and Distribution of Excess Schedule
January 1, 20X4

Price Analysis

		Amortization Periods	Amortization
Price paid for investment including acquisition costs	$692,000		
Assign to priority accounts, controlling share (90,000 x 80%)	72,000		
Assign to nonpriority accounts, controlling share (750,000 x 80%)	600,000		
Goodwill	20,000		

			Amortization Periods	Amortization
Price paid for investment		$692,000		
Less book value of interest purchased:				
Common stock, (par)	$100,000			
Paid-in capital in excess of par	200,000			
Retained earnings	400,000			
Total stockholders' equity	$700,000			
Ownership interest	80%	560,000		
Excess of cost over book value		$132,000		
Adjustments:				
Building [$160,000 x 80%]		$128,000 Dr.	20	6,400
Equipment [($20,000) x 80%]		(16,000) Cr.	10	(1,600)
Goodwill		20,000 Dr.		
Total adjustments		$132,000		

2.

Worksheet for the Paxton Company

	Trial Balance		Eliminations and Adjustments		NCI	Consolidated
	Paxton	Saxton	Dr.	Cr.		
Sales	(250,000)	(200,000)				(450,000)
Cost of goods sold	150,000	120,000				270,000
Expenses	50,000	40,000	(A1) 6,400	(A2) 1,600		94,800
Dividend income	(8,000)		(CY₂) 8,000			
Net income	(58,000)	(40,000)				(85,200)
NCI					(8,000)	
Controlling interest						(77,200)
Retained earnings Jan. 1, Paxton	(670,000)		(A1) 12,800	(CV) 80,000		
				(A2) 3,200		
Retained earnings Jan. 1, Saxton		(500,000)	(EL) 400,000		(100,000)	
Dividends declared		10,000		(CY₂) 8,000	2,000	
Net income (from above)	(58,000)	(40,000)			(8,000)	(77,200)
Retained earnings, Dec. 31	(728,000)	(530,000)				
Current assets	246,000	230,000				476,000
Investment in Saxton	692,000		(CV) 80,000	(EL) 640,000		
				(D) 132,000		
Land	100,000	100,000				200,000
Building	300,000	400,000	(D1) 128,000			828,000
Accumulated depr. (building)	(100,000)	(90,000)		(A1) 19,200		(209,200)
Equipment	150,000	300,000		(D2) 16,000		434,000
Accumulated depr. (equipment)	(60,000)	(90,000)	(A2) 4,800			(145,200)
Goodwill			(D3) 20,000			20,000
Current liabilities	(300,000)	(20,000)				(320,000)
Common stock, par—Paxton	(300,000)					(300,000)
Common stock, par—Saxton		(100,000)	(EL) 80,000		(20,000)	
Paid-in capital in excess—Saxton		(200,000)	(EL) 160,000		(40,000)	
Retained earnings Dec. 31—Paxton (from above)	(728,000)					(817,600)
Retained earnings Dec. 31—Saxton (from above)		(530,000)			(106,000)	(166,000)
Total NCI					(166,000)	(166,000)
Total	0	0	900,000	900,000		0

Subsidiary Saxton Company Income Distribution

Internally generated net income	$40,000
Adjusted income	$40,000
NCI share	20%
NCI	$ 8,000

Parent Paxton Company Income Distribution			
Building depreciation	$6,400	Internally generated net income	$50,000
		Equipment depreciation	1,600
		80% x Saxton adjusted income of $40,000	32,000
		Controlling interest	$77,200

Eliminations and adjustments:
(CV) Convert from the cost to the equity method as of January 1, 20X6 ($100,000 increase in retaining earnings x 80%).
(CY$_2$) Eliminate intercompany dividends.
(EL) Eliminate the pro rata share of Saxton Company equity balances at the beginning of the year against the investment account.
(D)   Distribute the excess cost as given by the determination and distribution schedule:
         (1) Increase building
         (2) Decrease equipment
         (3) Increase goodwill
(A)   Record amortizations resulting from the revaluations:
         (1) Record annual increase in building depreciation for the current and past two years.
         (2) Record annual decrease in equipment depreciation for the current and past two years.

PART 8 (APPENDIX B)

Price Analysis:
    Price paid (including direct acquisition costs) $736,000
    Assign to priority accounts, controlling share   (18,000)
    Assign to nonpriority accounts, controlling share   687,000
    Goodwill   49,000 ($24,000 more than $25,000 recorded)

Determination and Distribution of Excess:		
Price paid for investment		$736,000
Less book value of interest purchased		
Common stock	$200,000	
Paid-in capital in excess of par	300,000	
Retained earnings	100,000	
Total stockholders' equity	600,000	
Ownership interest	100%	600,000
Excess cost over book value (debit)		136,000
Priority accounts:		
Inventory	($ 10,000)	
DTL on inventory, 30%	(3,000)	
Nonpriority accounts:		
Building	50,000	
DTL on building, 30%	(15,000)	
Equipment	100,000	
DTL on equipment, 30%	(30,000)	112,000
New goodwill net of DTL		$ 24,000

Gross new goodwill, $24,000/0.7 = $34,286
DTL, 30% =   10,286

CHAPTER 4

PART 1

1. T
2. F Eliminations are the same under both methods.
3. T
4. F Amount of sales and cost eliminated are equal.
5. T
6. F Consolidated net income is lowered.
7. T
8. F There is no profit recorded, so none must be eliminated.
9. F The gain or loss remains because it is a transaction with an unrelated party.
10. T
11. T
12. F The gain also is realized as the asset is depreciated.
13. F Loss is not deferred if it reflects market value.
14. F Adjustments must be made for intercompany profits and for amortizations of excess.
15. T

PART 2

1. a All sales are eliminated. No impact on net income since all goods are sold to outside parties.
2. a

	20X3	20X4
Internally generated net income	$80,000	$90,000
Less ending inventory profit	(2,000)	—
Add beginning inventory profit	—	2,000
Adjusted income	$78,000	$92,000
NCI share	30%	30%
NCI	$23,400	$27,600

3. a Based on original cost and depreciation rate.
4. c $24,000 gain less $2,000 ($4,000 per year x 1/2 year) recognized during 20X6. No effect on NCI retained earnings since the parent company was the internal seller.
5. c
6. a (30% x $65,000) – $7,000 adjustment.
7. d All intercompany balances are eliminated.

PART 3

1.	Sales	60,000	
	Cost of goods sold		60,000
2.	Retained earnings—Von	1,600	
	Retained earnings—Gary	400	
	Cost of goods sold		2,000
	$10,000 x 20% gross profit = $2,000		
3.	Cost of goods sold	3,000	
	Inventory		3,000
	$15,000 x 20% gross profit = $3,000		
4.	Accounts payable	40,000	
	Accounts receivable		40,000
5.	Retained earnings—Von	20,000	
	Land		20,000

PART 4

Mannix Corporation and Subsidiary Raun Company
Partial Worksheet
For Year Ended December 31, 20X8

	Trial Balance		Eliminations and Adjustments		Consolidated Income Statement
	Mannix	Raun	Dr.	Cr.	
Accounts receivable (net)	200,000	71,000		(IA) 10,000	
Inventory	281,000	175,000		(EI) 4,000	
Accounts payable	(230,800)	(102,000)	(IA) 10,000		
Retained earnings—Mannix	(827,000)		(BI) 2,400		
Retained earnings—Raun		(260,000)	(BI) 600		
Sales	(1,800,000)	(700,000)	(IS) 50,000		(2,450,000)
Cost of goods sold	750,000	400,000	(EI) 4,000	(BI) 3,000	
				(IS) 50,000	1,101,000
Other expenses	240,000	98,000			338,000
			67,000	67,000	
Consolidated net income					(1,011,000)
To NCI					40,200
To controlling interest					970,800

Eliminations and adjustments:
(BI) 30% x $10,000. The decrease is shared 20% by minority interest.
(IS) Eliminate intercompany sales.
(EI) Ending inventory profit of $6,000 less $2,000 writedown.
(IA) Eliminate intercompany debt.

Subsidiary Raun Company Income Distribution

Unrealized profit in ending inventory	$ 4,000	Internally generated net income	$202,000
		Realized profit in beginning inventory	3,000
		Adjusted income	$201,000
		NCI share	20%
		NCI	$ 40,200

Parent Mannix Corporation Income Distribution

	Internally generated net income	$810,000
	80% x Raun Company adjusted income	160,800
	Controlling interest	$970,800

PART 5

Hayes Inc. and Subsidiary Barney Company
Partial Worksheet
For Year Ended December 31, 20X3

	Trial Balance		Eliminations and Adjustments			
	Hayes	Barney	Dr.		Cr.	
Land	103,000	95,000			(LA)	20,000
Machinery	317,000	190,000			(F1)	7,000
Accumulated depreciation	(185,000)	(73,000)	(F1)	700		
			(F2)	1,400		
Retained earnings—Hayes	(921,000)		(LA)	20,000		
			(F1)	5,040		
Retained earnings—Barney		(219,000)	(F1)	1,260		
Depreciation expense	15,600	7,100			(F2)	1,400
				28,400		28,400

Eliminations and adjustments:
(LA) Eliminate the intercompany gain on the sale of the land as reflected in Hayes' beginning retained earnings.
(F1) Eliminate the intercompany gain on the sale of the machinery as reflected in beginning retained earnings. $7,000 profit on date of sale, less 1/2 year's depreciation of $700 ($7,000 gain ÷ 5 years x 1/2 year). The unrealized gain at the beginning of the year (now $6,300) is shared 20% by the minority interest.
(F2) Reduce current depreciation expense and accumulated depreciation $1,400 per year.

PART 6

	Trial Balance		Eliminations and Adjustments			
	Park	May	Dr.		Cr.	
Assets under construction		250,000	(LT3)	70,000		
Contracts receivable	250,000	190,000			(LT1)	250,000
Construction in progress	400,000	(73,000)			(LT2)	80,000
					(LT3)	320,000
Payables (to outsiders)	(230,000)					
Contracts payable		(250,000)	(LT1)	250,000		
Billings on construction in progress	(250,000)		(LT3)	250,000		
Earned income on long-term contracts	(80,000)		(LT2)	80,000		
				650,000		650,000

Eliminations and adjustments:
(LT1) Eliminate intercompany debt.
(LT2) Eliminate the income recorded on long-term contracts and remove profit from construction in progress.
(LT3) Eliminate balance of construction in progress and billings on construction in progress, and increase assets under construction for unbilled costs.

PART 7

Paul Company and Subsidiary Sara Inc.
Worksheet for Consolidated Financial Statements
For Year Ended December 31, 20X7

	Trial Balance		Eliminations and Adjustments				Consolidated Income Statement	NCI	Controlling Retained Earnings	Consolidated Balance Sheet
	Paul	Sara	Dr.		Cr.					
Cash	21,400	18,700								40,100
Accounts receivable	80,000	76,000			(IA)	21,000				135,000
Inventories	54,800	85,600			(EI)	7,500				132,900
Other current assets	15,000	10,200			(LN1)	10,000				
					(LN2)	1,000				14,200
Investment in Sara Inc.	120,000		(CV)	23,200	(EL)	127,200				
					(D)	16,000				
Notes receivable	20,000				(LN2)	20,000				
Land	25,000	15,000								40,000
Building and equipment	200,000	100,000			(F1)	20,000				280,000
Accumulated depreciation	(102,000)	(17,500)	(F1)	2,500						(116,000)
			(F2)	1,000						
Goodwill			(D)	16,000						16,000
Accounts payable	(35,500)	(81,000)	(IA)	21,000						(95,500)
Dividends payable										
Other current liabilities	(24,500)	(12,000)	(LN1)	10,000						
Notes payable		(20,000)	(LN2)	20,000						
Common stock—Paul	(300,000)									(300,000)
Retained earnings, Jan. 1, 20X7—Paul	(27,000)				(CV)	23,200				
			(BI)	5,000						
			(F1)	17,500					(27,700)	
Common stock—Sara		(100,000)	(EL)	80,000				(20,000)		
Retained earnings—Sara		(59,000)	(EL)	47,200				(11,800)		
Sales	(420,000)	(300,000)	(IS)	100,000			(620,000)			
Cost of goods sold	315,000	240,000	(EI)	7,500	(BI)	5,000				
					(IS)	100,000	457,500			
Expenses	65,000	35,000			(F2)	1,000	99,000			
Dividend income	(7,200)		(CY2)	7,200						
Dividends declared		9,000			(CY2)	7,200		1,800		
	0	0		359,100		359,100				
Consolidated net income							(63,500)			
To NCI							5,000	(5,000)		
To controlling interest							58,500		(58,500)	
Total NCI								(35,000)		(35,000)
Retained earnings—Controlling interest, Dec. 31, 20X7									(86,200)	(86,200)
										0

Eliminations and adjustments:
(CV)   Convert to equity, 80% x ($59,000 – $30,000) = $23,200.
(CY2) Eliminate intercompany dividends.
(EL)   Eliminate pro rata share of Sara's equity balances.

(D)   Distribute excess cost according to determination and
       distribution of excess schedule.
(BI)   Eliminate intercompany profit from beginning inventory: Gross profit = ($420,000 – $315,000) ÷ $420,000 = 25%; profit in beginning inventory =
       25% x $20,000 = $5,000.
(IS)   Eliminate intercompany sales.
(EI)   Eliminate profit in ending inventory: 25% x $30,000 = $7,500.
(IA)   Eliminate intercompany trade balances resulting from the intercompany sales.
(LN1) Eliminate cash advance.
(LN2) Eliminate intercompany mortgage and interest due to sale of building: accrued interest = $20,000 x 10% x 1/2 year = $1,000. No entry necessary
       for interest revenue and expense since revenue is credited to expense.
(F1)   Eliminate gain on sale of building remaining at the beginning of the period: reduction of accumulated depreciation = $20,000 ÷ 20 years = $1,000
       per year; $1,000 x 2 1/2 years = $2,500 for 2 1/2 prior years.
(F2)   Reduce depreciation for current year, $1,000.

Subsidiary Sara Inc. Income Distribution

	Internally generated net income	$25,000
	Adjusted income	$25,000
	NCI share	20%
	NCI	<u>$5,000</u>

Parent Paul Company Income Distribution

Unrealized gross profit in ending inventory	$7,500	Internally generated net income	$40,000
		Realized gross profit in beginning inventory	5,000
		Gain realized through use of building sold to Sara	1,000
		Share of subsidiary income	20,000
		Controlling interest	<u>$58,500</u>

CHAPTER 5

PART 1

1.   F   The gain or loss is reflected in retained earnings.
2.   T
3.   F   The gain or loss on retirement of bonds is absorbed by the issuer of the bonds.
4.   T
5.   T
6.   F   The leased asset must be reclassified as a normal productive asset. Accrued rent receivable and payable also must be
         eliminated.
7.   T
8.   F   These payments are recorded as rent revenue and expense as paid.
9.   F   The lessor's implicit rate usually is used.
10. T
11. T

PART 2

1. a The asset is recorded on Greale's balance sheet.

2. a

3. b

4. a The rental expense eliminated equals the rental income eliminated.

5. e $1,000 sales profit eliminated less $250 depreciation expense eliminated due to current-year recognition of sales profit.

6. a Price paid exceeded book value which is a loss.

7. b $100,000 gain is shared by subsidiary.

PART 3

Skeleton elimination entries:

1. Advance from parent   XXX
     Advance to sub   XXX

2. Interest revenue   XXX
   Bonds payable   XXX
   Loss on bond retirement   XXX
     Discount on bonds payable   XXX
     Investment in sub bonds   XXX
     Interest expense   XXX

3. Interest revenue   XXX
   Bonds payable   XXX
   Retained earnings   XXX
     Discount on bonds payable   XXX
     Investment in sub bonds   XXX
     Interest expense   XXX

4. Rent revenue—equipment lease   XXX
   Rent payable   XXX
     Rent receivable   XXX
     Rent expense—equipment lease   XXX

5. Equipment   XXX
   Acc. depr. equipment under financing lease   XXX
   Capital lease   XXX
   Unearned interest income   XXX
     Minimum lease payments receivable   XXX
     Equipment under capital lease   XXX
     Accumulated depreciation   XXX
   Interest income   XXX
     Interest Expense   XXX

6. Machine   XXX
   Acc. depr. machine under capital lease   XXX
   Sales   XXX
   Profit on sales-type lease   XXX
   Obligation under capital lease   XXX
   Interest payable—capital lease   XXX
   Unearned interest income   XXX
     Minimum lease payments receivable   XXX
     Machine under capital lease   XXX
     Acc. depr. machine   XXX

PART 4

1. Interest expense   7,800
   Premium on bonds payable   200
     Interest payable   8,000

2. Investment in Slinger bonds   97,000
      Cash   97,000
      Interest receivable   8,000
      Investment in Slinger bonds   1,000
      Interest income   9,000

3.

Pat Inc. and Subsidiary Slinger Company
Partial Consolidated Worksheet
For Year Ended December 31, 20X3

	Trial Balance		Eliminations and Adjustments	
	Pat	Slinger	Dr.	Cr.
Interest receivable	8,000			(B2) 8,000
Investment in Slinger bonds	98,000			(B1) 98,000
Interest payable		(8,000)	(B2) 8,000	
Bonds payable		(100,000)	(B1) 100,000	
Premium on bonds payable		(400)	(B1) 400	
Interest income	(9,000)		(B1) 9,000	
Interest expense		7,800		(B1) 7,800
				(B1) 3,600
			117,400	117,400

Supporting calculation:

Gain remaining:

Carrying value of bonds at December 31, 20X3	$100,400	
Investment in bonds, December 31, 20X3	98,000	$ 2,400
Gain amortized during the year:		
Interest income	$ 9,000	
Interest expense	7,800	1,200
Gain at January 1, 20X3		$ 3,600

4.

Pat Inc. and Subsidiary Slinger Company
Partial Consolidated Worksheet
For Year Ended December 31, 20X4

	Trial Balance		Eliminations and Adjustments	
	Pat	Slinger	Dr.	Cr.
Interest receivable	8,000			(B2) 8,000
Investment in Slinger bonds	99,000			(B1) 99,000
Interest payable		(8,000)	(B2) 8,000	
Bonds payable		(100,000)	(B1) 100,000	
Premium on bonds payable		(200)	(B1) 200	
Retained earnings—Pat				(B1) 1,920
Retained earnings—Slinger				(B1) 480
Interest income	(9,000)		(B1) 9,000	
Interest expense		7,800		(B1) 7,800
			117,200	117,200

Supporting calculation:
Gain remaining:

Carrying value of bonds at December 31, 20X3	$100,200	
Investment in bonds, December 31, 20X3	99,000	$1,200
Gain amortized during the year:		

Interest income	$ 9,000	
Interest expense	7,800	1,200
Gain at January 1, 20X3		$2,400

The remaining gain will be split 80% to the parent, 20% to the sub.

PART 5
(Part 4 with Effective Interest)

Amortization tables:

1.   Bond payable at 7.75%:

5-Year Amortization Schedule
for Bonds Issued by Slinger

Date	Payment	7.5% Interest	Amortization	Balance
1/1/X1				101,005
1/1/X2	8,000	7,828	172	100,833
1/1/X3	8,000	7,815	185	100,648
1/1/X4	8,000	7,800	200	100,448
1/1/X5	8,000	7,785	215	100,233
1/1/X6	8,000	7,768	233*	100,000

* rounding difference.

2.   Investment in bonds at 7.5%:

3-Year Amortization Schedule
for Bonds Purchased by Pat Inc.

Date	Payment	7.75% Interest	Amortization	Balance
1/1X3				101,300
1/1X4	8,000	7,598	402	100,898
1/1X5	8,000	7,567	433	100,465
1/1X6	8,000	7,535	465	100,000

3.   Entries for Slinger for 20X3:

Interest expense	7,800	
Premium on bonds	200	
Interest payable		8,000

4.   Entries for Pat Inc. for 20X3:

Investment in bonds	101,300	
Cash		101,300
Interest receivable	8,000	
Interest revenue		7,598
Investment in bonds		402

5.

Pat Inc. and Subsidiary Slinger Company
Partial Consolidated Worksheet
For Year Ended December 31, 20X3

	Trial Balance		Eliminations and Adjustments	
	Pat	Slinger	Dr.	Cr.
Interest receivable	8,000			(B2) 8,000
Investment in Slinger bonds	100,898			(B1) 100,898
Interest payable		(8,000)	(B2) 8,000	
Bonds payable		(100,000)	(B1) 100,000	
Premium on bonds payable		(448)	(B1) 448	
Interest income*	(7,598)		(B1) 7,598	
Interest expense*		7,800		(B1) 7,800
			(B1) 652	
			116,698	116,698

Supporting calculation:

Loss remaining:

Carrying value of bonds at December 31, 20X3	$100,448	
Investment in bonds, December 31, 20X3	100,898	$450
Loss amortized during the year:		
Interest income	$ 7,578	
Interest expense	7,800	202
Loss at January 1, 20X3		$652

6.

Pat Inc. and Subsidiary Slinger Company
Partial Consolidated Worksheet
For Year Ended December 31, 20X4

	Trial Balance		Eliminations and Adjustments	
	Pat	Slinger	Dr.	Cr.
Interest receivable	8,000			(B2) 8,000
Investment in Slinger bonds	100,465			(B1)100,465
Interest payable		(8,000)	(B2) 8,000	
Bonds payable		(100,000)	(B1) 100,000	
Premium on bonds payable		(233)	(B1) 233	
Retained earnings—Pat			(B1) 360	
Retained earnings—Slinger			(B1) 90	
Interest income*	(7,567)		(B1) 7,567	
Interest expense*		7,785		(B1) 7,785
			116,250	116,250

Supporting calculation:

Loss remaining:

Carrying value of bonds at December 31, 20X4	$100,233	
Investment in bonds, December 31, 20X4	100,465	$232
Loss amortized during the year:		
Interest income	$ 7,567	
Interest expense	7,785	218
Loss at January 1, 20X4		$450

The remaining loss will be split 80% to the parent, 20% to the sub.

PART 6

Gorski Inc. and Subsidiary Kovcic Inc.
Partial Consolidated Worksheet
For Year Ended December 31, 20X4

	Trial Balance		Eliminations and Adjustments	
	Gorski	Kovcic	Dr.	Cr.
Rent receivable	2,000			(OL2) 2,000
Equipment	700,000	200,000		
Accumulated depreciation—equipment	(350,000)	(50,000)		
Rent payable		(2,000)	(OL2) 2,000	
Rent income	(12,000)		(OL1) 12,000	
Rent expense		12,000		(OL1) 12,000
Depreciation expense	30,000			
			14,000	14,000

PART 7

1.

	Annual Lease Payment	Interest	Reduction of Principal	Principal Balance
Jan. 1, 20X0	6,000	—	6,000	19,119
Jan. 1, 20X1	6,000	2,868	3,132	15,987
Jan. 1, 20X2	6,000	2,398	3,602	12,385
Jan. 1, 20X3	6,000	1,858	4,142	8,243
Jan. 1, 20X4	6,000	1,236	4,764	3,479
Jan. 1, 20X5	6,000	521*	3,479	0
	34,000	8,881	25,119	

*Includes rounding error.

2.
Minimum lease payments receivable	28,000	
Cash	6,000	
Unearned interest income		8,881
Asset (cost to lessor)		20,119
Sales profit on lease		5,000
Unearned interest income	2,868	
Interest income		2,868

3.
Asset under capital lease	25,119	
Cash		6,000
Obligation under capital lease		19,119
*Depreciation expense	3,588	
Accumulated depreciation—asset under capital lease		3,588
Interest expense	2,868	
Interest payable		2,868

*$25,119 \div 7 = \$3,588$.

4.

Jo Company and Subsidiary Miller Corporation
Partial Consolidated Worksheet
For Year Ended December 31, 20X0

	Trial Balance		Eliminations and Adjustments	
	Jo	Miller	Dr.	Cr.
Minimum lease payments receivable	28,000			(CL2) 28,000
Unearned interest income	(6,013)		(CL2) 6,013	
Assets under capital lease		25,119		(CL3) 25,119
Accumulated depreciation—assets under capital lease		(3,588)	(CL3) 3,588	
Property, plant, and equipment	680,000	320,000	(CL3) 25,119	(F1) 5,000
Accumulated depreciation—property, plant, and equipment	(240,000)	(160,000)	(F2) 714	(CL3) 3,588
Obligations under capital lease		(19,119)	(CL2) 19,119	
Interest payable		(2,868)	(CL2) 2,868	
Interest income	(2,868)		(CL1) 2,868	
Interest expense		2,868		(CL1) 2,868
Sales profit on lease	(5,000)		(F1) 5,000	
Depreciation expense	19,000	10,500		(F2) 714
			65,289	65,289

PART 8

Steady Winds, Inc. and Subsidiary Rigging Ltd.
Worksheet for Consolidated Balance Sheet
For Year Ended December 31, 20X6

	Trial Balance		Eliminations and Adjustments		Consolidated Income Statement	NCI	Controlling Retained Earnings	Consolidated Balance Sheet
	Steady Winds	Rigging	Dr.	Cr.				
Cash	105,000	45,000						150,000
Accounts receivable	87,500	78,000						165,000
Inventory	88,000	58,860						146,860
Investment in bonds	98,200			(B) 98,200				
Plant and equipment (net)	642,000	345,990						987,990
Investment in Rigging	326,295			(CY$_1$)24,795				
				(EL) 301,500				
Accounts payable	(102,500)	(62,000)						(164,500)
Bonds payable (10%)		(100,000)	(B)100,000					
Premium on bonds payable		(3,300)	(B) 3,300					
Common stock—Steady (no par)	(450,650)							(450,650)
Paid-in capital—Steady								
Retained earnings— Steady 1/1/X6	(683,750)			(B) 5,355			(689,105)	
Common stock—Rigging (no par)		(75,000)	(EL) 67,500			(7,500)		
Paid-in capital—Rigging								
Retained earnings— Rigging 1/1/X6		(260,000)	(EL)234,000	(B) 595		(26,595)		
Sales	(800,000)	(305,000)			(1,105,000)			
Cost of goods sold	525,000	183,000			708,000			
Selling and general expense	100,000	85,000			185,000			
Interest income	(10,300)		(B) 10,300					
Interest expense		9,450		(B) 9,450				
Subsidiary income	(24,795)		(CY$_1$)24,795					
Dividends declared	100,000						100,000	
Total	0	0	439,895	439,895				
Consolidated net income					(212,000)			
To NCI					(2,670)	(2,670)		
To controlling interest					(209,330)		(209,330)	
Total NCI						(36,765)		(36,765)
Retained earnings, controlling interest, Dec. 31, 20X6							(798,435)	(798,435)
								0

Subsidiary Rigging Ltd. Income Distribution

Interest adjustment	$850	Internally generated net income	$ 27,550
		Adjusted net income	$ 26,700
		NCI share	10%
		NCI	$2,670

Parent Steady Winds Income Distribution

		Internally generated net income	$185,300
		90% x Rigging adjusted income	24,030
		Controlling interest	$209,330

Eliminations and Adjustments:
(CY$_1$) Eliminate the entry recording the parent's share of the subsidiary net income.
(EL) Eliminate the parent's investment in the subsidiary and the parent's share of the subsidiary equity as of the beginning of the year.
(B) Eliminate intercompany interest revenue and expense. Eliminate the balance in the investment in bonds against the bonds payable. The gain on retirement at the start of the year is calculated as follows:

Gain remaining at year end:			
Carrying value of bonds at December 31, 20X6	$103,300		
Investment in bonds at December 31, 20X6	98,200	$5,100	
Gain amortized during the year:			
Interest revenue eliminated (amort. = $25/month)	$ 10,300		
Interest expense eliminated (amort. = $550/year)	9,450	850	
Remaining gain at January 1, 20X6		$5,950	

The remaining unamortized gain is allocated 90% to the controlling retained earnings and 10% to the minority retained earnings.

CHAPTER 6

PART 1

1. T
2. F The purchase is considered an investing activity.
3. F It is shown in a schedule of noncash activities.
4. T
5. F The NCI is disclosed in the schedule of noncash activities.
6. F The purchase of additional subsidiary stock from the NCI shareholders is an outflow of cash and would appear in the consolidated statement of cash flows as an investing transaction.
7. T
8. T
9. T
10. F Tax return is based on separate incomes.
11. F Deferred tax assets are created.
12. T
13. F Only the investor's portion of the gain need be deferred.
14. T

PART 2

1. b   Share of income = 30% of 6/12 of $120,000 = $18,000. The dividends received ($12,000) are a distribution of the income earned. There is no information on amortization of excess.

2. d   Income increases the investment account; losses and dividends received reduce the investment account.

3. d   Dividends are distribution of income already reported.

4. c   Income is equal to dividends on the preferred stock.

5. c   30% of 20X2 income, 10% of 20X1 income – dividends included in 20X1.

6. a $600,000 undistributed income x 30% ownership x 20% inclusion x 30% tax

7. c   Intercompany receivables are not eliminated and are not part of the investment.

8. c   Since there is influence by year end, the equity method is applied to the 10% interest for 20X2.

PART 3

1.

December 31, 20X2 consolidated cash	$130,000
December 31, 20X1 parent-company-only cash	400,000
Decrease in cash	$270,000

2.

Money Inc. and Subsidiary Fastbuck Company
Consolidated Statement of Cash Flows
For Year Ended December 31, 20X2

Cash flows from operating activities:		
Controlled interest in consolidated net income		$ 154,000
Adjustments to reconcile net income to net cash:		
NCI portion of net income	$ 21,000	
Depreciation expense	50,000	
Increase in inventory ($400,000 – $290,000)	(110,000)	
Decrease in current liabilities	(100,000)	
Total adjustments		(139,000)
Net cash provided by operating activities		$ 15,000
Cash flows from investing activities:		
Payment for purchase of Fastbuck Company, net of cash acquired	$(215,000)	
Increase in property, plant, and equipment (710,000 – 650,000 – 40,000 + 50,000)	(70,000)	
Net cash used for investing activities		(285,000)
Net decrease in cash		$(270,000)
Cash at beginning of year		400,000
Cash at year end		$ 130,000

Schedule of noncash investing and financing activity:

Money Inc. purchased 80% of the capital stock of Fastbuck Company for $275,000. In conjunction with the acquisition, liabilities were assumed and a noncontrolling interest was created as follows:

Adjusted value of assets acquired ($400,000 book value plus $75,000 excess)	$475,000	
Cash paid for capital stock	275,000	$200,000
Liabilities assumed		150,000
NCI ($250,000 x 20%)		$ 50,000

PART 4

1.

Consolidated Income Statement Worksheet

	Wond	Ellen	Adjustments			Consolidated Income Statement
			Dr.	**Cr.**		
Sales	(600,000)	(350,000)	(IS) 88,000			(862,000)
Cost of goods sold	300,000	200,000	(EI) 12,500	(IS) 88,000		
				(BI) 10,500		414,000
Gross profit	(300,000)	(150,000)				(448,000)
Less:						
Operating expenses	175,000	110,000	(A) 8,000	(F) 5,000		288,000
Operating income	(125,000)	(40,000)				(160,000)

(IS) Intercompany sales.
(BI) Beginning inventory profit.
(EI) Ending inventory profit.
(F)   Depreciation adjustment related to intercompany fixed asset sales.
(A)   Patent amortization.

Consolidated Tax Provision

Consolidated income before tax	$160,000	(Includes patent amortization.)
Consolidated tax liability (30%)	48,000	
Consolidated income after tax	$112,000	

Subsidiary Ellen Company Income Distribution

Ending inventory profit	$12,500	Internally generated net income	$ 40,000
		Beginning inventory profit	10,500
		Adjusted income before tax	$ 38,000
		Ellen's share of taxes	11,400
		Ellen's net income	$ 26,600
		NCI (10%)	$ 2,660

Parent Wond Company Income Distribution

Patent amortization	$ 8,000	Internally generated income	$125,000
		Gain realized on equipment through use	5,000
		Adjusted income before tax	$122,000
		Wond's share of taxes	36,600
		Wond's net income	85,400
		Share of Ellen's net income	23,940
		Controlling interest	$109,340

2.   Ellen's Books:
      Provision for income tax   11,400
        Income tax payable   11,400
          To record the subsidiary's allocated
      portion of consolidated income
      tax expense.

      Wond's Books:
      Provision for income tax   36,600
        Income tax payable   36,600
          To record the parent's allocated
      portion of consolidated income
      tax expense.
      Subsidiary income   10,260
        Investment in Ellen   10,260
      To adjust subsidiary income for tax
        expense recorded by subsidiary
        (90% x $11,400)

3.   Ellen's Books:
      Provision for income tax   12,000
        Income tax payable   12,000
          To record Ellen's tax
      provision (30% x $40,000).

      Wond's Books:
      Provision for income tax (30% x $125,000)   37,500
        Income tax payable   37,500
          To record Wond's tax provision on
      Wond's internally generated income

      Note: There is no second tax since the 100% dividend exclusion applies.

PART 5

1.   Paxton deferred tax asset (liability)
        Increase in Saxton's retained earnings, $50,000 x 60% interest x 20% x 30% tax $ 1,800
        Current year undistributed income, $11,000 x 60% interest x 20% x 30% tax   396
        Total $ 2,196

      Paxton provision for tax
        Internally generated income, $70,000 x 30% tax $21,000
        Tax on Saxton income, $21,000 x 60% interest x 20% x 30% tax   756
        Total $21,756

      Notice: All intercompany profits recorded by the separate companies have been taxed.

2.   Determination and distribution of excess schedule:

      Price paid $481,000
      Interest acquired:
        Common stock $100,000
        Paid-in excess   300,000
        Retained earnings   235,000
        Total equity   635,000
      Ownership interest   60%   381,000
      Patents, 20-year life, $5,000 per year amortization $100,000

3.   Explanations for eliminations with tax allocation schedules:

      (CY$_1$) Eliminate subsidiary income.
      (CY$_2$) Eliminate intercompany dividends.
      (EL)   Eliminate 60% of subsidiary equity on January 1, 20X7.

(D) Distribute excess to patents.
(A) Amortize patents, $5,000 per year, for 2 prior years and the current year.
(IS) Eliminate intercompany sales of $80,000.
(BI) Eliminate beginning inventory profit from cost of goods sold and parent beginning retained earnings.
(EI) Eliminate ending inventory profit from cost of goods sold and inventory account.
(F) (1) Eliminate $54,000 remaining fixed-asset profit at start of year.
      (2) Reduce current-year depreciation by $6,000.

(T1) Adjust the beginning retained earnings balances and create a deferred tax asset (DTL) on prior period adjustments as follows:

DTA/DTL adjustments	Total Tax	Parent	Sub.
To beginning retained earnings			
Subsidiary transactions:			
Beginning inventory			
Remaining fixed asset profit:		$54,000	
Total		$54,000	
First tax (30% x 54,000)	$16,200	9,720	$6,480
Second tax (20% x 30% x 60% x			
(54,000 – 16,200 first tax))	1,361	1,361	
Parent transactions			
Beginning inventory	4,000		
Amortizations of excess	10,000		
Total	$14,000		
First tax (30% x 14,000)	4,200	4,200	
Total increase in retained earnings and DTA	$21,761	$15,281	$6,480

(T2) Adjust current-year tax provision and adjust deferred tax asset (DTA) for the tax effects of current year income adjustments.

Subsidiary transactions:	Total Tax	Parent	Sub.
Beginning inventory			
Ending inventory			
Fixed asset sale			
Realized fixed asset	$(6,000)		
Total			
First tax (30% x 6,000)	(1,800)	$(1,080)	$(720)
Second tax (20% x 30% x	(151)	(151)	
60% x (6,000 – 1,800 first tax)			
Parent transactions:			
Beginning inventory	(4,000)		
Ending inventory	8,000		
Fixed asset sale			
Remaining fixed asset profit			
Amortization of excess	5,000		
Total	9,000		
First tax (30% x 9,000)	2,700	2,700	
Increase (decrease) in DTA	$ 749	$ 1,469	$(720)

Subsidiary Saxton Company Income Distribution

			Internally generated income (before tax)		$ 30,000
			Realized gain on fixed asset	F2	6,000
			Total income before tax		$ 36,000
			Tax provision (30%)		(10,800)
			Net income		$ 25,200
			NCI share (40%)		**$ 10,080**
			Controlling share (60%)		$ 15,120

Parent Paxton Company Income Distribution

Ending inventory profit	EI	8,000	Internally generated income (before tax)		$70,000
Amortization of patents	A	5,000	Realized beginning inventory profit	BI	4,000
			Total income before tax		$61,000
			Tax provision (30%)		(18,300)
			Net income		$42,700
			Controlling share of subsidiary income (net of first tax)		15,120
			Second tax on share of controlling subsidiary income ($15, 120 x 20% x 30%)		(907)
			Total controlling interest		$56,913

Paxton Company and Subsidiary Saxton Company
Worksheet for Consolidated Financial Statements
For the Year Ended December 31, 20X7

	Trial Balance		Eliminations and Adjustments		Consolidated Income		Controlling Retained	Consolidated Balance
	Paxton	Saxton	Dr.	Cr.	Statement	NCI	Earnings	Sheet
Cash	166,360	91,000						257,360
Accounts receivable	188,000	145,000						333,000
Inventory	150,000	120,000		(EI) 8,000				262,000
Investment in Saxton	517,600		(CY₂) 6,000	(CY₁) 12,600				
				(EL) 411,000				
				(D) 100,000				
Land	100,000	50,000						150,000
Building and equipment	430,000	450,000		(F1) 60,000				820,000
Accum. deprec., bldg. and equip.	(160,000)	(180,000)	(F1) 6,000					(328,000)
			(F2) 6,000					
Patents		20,000	(D) 100,000	(A) 15,000				105,000
Deferred tax asset (liability)	(2,196)		(T1) 21,761					20,314
			(T2) 749					
Common stock—Paxton	(900,000)							(900,000)
Retained earnings—Paxton	(428,920)		(A) 10,000	(T1) 15,281			(397,801)	
			(BI) 4,000					
			(F1) 32,400					
Common stock—Saxton		(100,000)	(EL) 60,000			(40,000)		
Paid-in capital in excess of par—Saxton		(300,000)	(EL) 180,000			(120,000)		
Retained earnings—Saxton		(285,000)	(EL) 171,000	(T1) 6,480		(98,880)		
			(F1) 21,600					
Dividends declared		10,000		(CY₂) 6,000		4,000		
Sales	(400,000)	(250,000)	(IS) 80,000		(570,000)			
Cost of goods sold	230,000	160,000	(EI) 8,000	(IS) 80,000	314,000			
				(BI) 4,000				
Expenses	100,000	60,000	(A) 5,000	(F2) 6,000	159,000			
Subsidiary income	(12,600)		(CY₁) 12,600					
Provision for tax	21,756	9,000		(T2) 749	30,007			
	0	0	725,110	725,110				
Consolidated net income					(66,993)			
To NCI					10,080	(10,080)		
To controlling interest					56,913		(56,913)	
Total NCI						(264,960)		(264,960)
Retained earnings, controlling interest, December 31, 20X7							(454,714)	(454,714)
								0

PART 6

Rick Company and Subsidiary Plann Inc.
Worksheet for Consolidated Balance Sheet
For Year Ended December 31, 20X4

	Trial Balance Rick	Trial Balance Plann	Eliminations and Adjustments Dr.	Eliminations and Adjustments Cr.	Consolidated Income Statement	NCI	Controlling Retained Earnings	Consolidated Balance Sheet
Inventory	200,000	80,000		(EI) 15,000				265,000
Other current assets	198,400	295,000						493,400
Buildings (net)	500,000	320,000	(F2) 1,000	(F1) 19,000				802,000
Investment in Plann	496,750			(CY₁) 36,750				
				(EL) 434,000				
				(D) 26,000				
Patents			(D) 26,000	(A) 5,200				20,800
Common stock—Rick	(600,000)							(600,000)
Retained earnings—Rick	(600,000)		(A) 2,600	(T1) 10,310				
			(BI) 11,200					
			(F1) 19,000				(577,510)	
Common stock—Plann		(200,000)	(EL)140,000			(60,000)		
Retained earnings—Plann		(420,000)	(EL)294,000	(T1) 1,440				
			(BI) 4,800			(122,640)		
Sales	(900,000)	(600,000)	(IS) 100,000		(1,400,000)			
Cost of goods sold	500,000	400,000	(EI) 15,000	(BI) 16,000				
				(IS) 100,000	799,000			
Expenses	250,000	125,000	(A) 2,600	(F2) 1,000	376,600			
Provision for income tax	47,205	22,500		(T2) 151	69,554			
Subsidiary income	(36,750)		(CY₁)36,750					
Income taxes payable	(45,000)	(22,500)						(67,500)
Deferred tax asset (liability)	(10,605)		(T1) 11,750					1,296
			(T2) 151					
Total	0	0	664,351	664,351				
Consolidated net income					154,846			
To NCI					15,960	(15,960)		
To controlling interest					138,886		(138,886)	
Total NCI						(198,600)		(198,600)
Controlling retained earnings							(716,396)	(716,396)
								0

(T1) Adjust the beginning retained earnings balances and create a deferred tax asset (DTL) on prior period adjustments
        as follows:

DTA/DTL adjustments	Tax	Parent	Sub.
To beginning retained earnings			
Subsidiary transactions:			
Beginning inventory	$16,000		
Total	$16,000		
First tax (30% x 16,000)	$ 4,800	$ 3,360	$1,440
Second tax (20% x 30% x 70% x			
(16,000 – 4,800 first tax))	470	470	
Parent transactions:			
Remaining fixed asset profit	$19,000		
Amortization of excess	2,600		
Total	$21,600		
First tax (30% x 21,600)	6,480	6,480	
Total increase in retained earnings and DTA	$11,750	$10,310	$1,440

(T2) Adjust current year tax provision and adjust deferred tax asset (DTA) for the tax effects of current year income adjustments:

Subsidiary transactions:	Tax	Parent	Sub.
Beginning inventory	(16,000)		
Ending inventory	15,000		
Total	1,000		
First tax (30% x 1,000)	(300)	(210)	(90)
Second tax (20% x 30% x 70% x			
(1,000 – 300 first tax))	(29)	(29)	
Parent transactions:			
Realized fixed asset profit (building)	(1,000)		
Amortization of excess (parent)	2,600		
Total	1,600		
First tax (30% x 1,600)	480	480	
Increase (decrease) in DTA	151	241	(90)

Subsidiary Plann, Inc. Income Distribution

			Internally generated income (before tax)		$75,000
Unrealized gain on ending inventory	EI	15,000			
			Realized gain on beginning inventory	BI	16,000
			Total income before tax		$76,000
			Tax provision (30%)		(22,800)
			Net income		$53,200
			NCI share (30%)		**$15,960**
			Controlling share (70%)		$37,240

Parent Rick Company Income Distribution

			Internally generated income (before tax)		$150,000
Amortization of patent	A	2,600	Realized profit on fixed beginning inventory profit	F2	1,000
			Total income before tax		$148,400
			Tax provision (30%)		(44,520)
			Net income		$103,880
			Controlling share of subsidiary income (net of first tax)		37,240
			Second tax on share of controlling subsidiary income ($37,240 x 20% x 30%)		(2,234)
			Total controlling interest		$138,886

PART 7

1.   Determination and distribution schedule:

Price paid:	$350,000	
Equity purchased, 30% x $800,000	240,000	
Excess	110,000	
Equipment, 30% x $50,000, 5-year life	15,000	3,000/year
Goodwill	$ 95,000	

2.   Information table:

	20X5	20X6
Investment account balance, January 1	$350,000	$368,375
Share of adjusted income—from IDS schedule (prior to amortization adjustment)	24,375	17,475
Amortization adjustment	(3,000)	(3,000)
Dividend received	(3,000)	(3,000)
Investment account balance, December 31	$368,375	$379,850
Able Company deferred profit		
Balance, January 1	$	$6,750
Adjustment	6,750	(1,500)
Balance, December 31	$6,750	$5,250

Income Distribution Schedule: 20X5

End inventory profit (net of tax) ($50,000 x 25% x 70%)	$8,750	Reported income	$90,000
		Adjusted income	$81,250
		Ownership %	30%
		Share of income	$24,375

Income Distribution Schedule: 20X6

End inventory profit (net of tax) ($60,000 x 25% x 70%)	$10,500	Reported income	$60,000
		Beginning inventory profit (net of tax)	8,750
		Adjusted income	$58,250
		Ownership %	30%
		Share of income	$17,475

(3)   Schedule of deferred tax asset (liability)—investment in Baker:

	20X5	20X6
Balance, January 1	0	742
Subsidiary income, 20% taxed at 30%	(1,463)	(1,049)
Less: tax paid on dividends ($3,000 x 20% x 30%)	180	180
Deferred profit on machine sale	2,025	(450)
Balance, December 31	742	(577)

CHAPTER 7

PART 1

1.   T

2.   T

3.   F   Only 70% of Company S income from January 1–July 1 belongs to the controlling interest. Controlling interest in subsidiary income from July 1–December 31 is 90%.

4.   T

5.   F   Once control is achieved, the amortization of excess can be recorded on the consolidated worksheets.

6.   T

7.   T

8.   T

9. F   All intercompany transactions and balances must be eliminated. The preferred stock is viewed as having been retired.

10. F   Only voting common stock holdings are used to determine effective control over a subsidiary.

11. T

12. F   Only the retained earnings available to common stockholders is to be included in the determination and distribution of excess schedule.

13. T

14. F   It flows through the paid-in capital from stock retirement and/or retained earnings.

PART 2

1. c   A separate determination and distribution schedule is calculated for each purchase. Each schedule would calculate a separate amount for goodwill.

2. a   An equity adjustment is calculated by comparing the price paid to the equity adjusted cost (including adjustment for amortizations of excess). The entire interest would have to be sold to qualify as a discontinued operation.

3. c   The preferred stock is retired with an adjustment to paid-in capital.

4. b   Income is recorded on each interest during the period that it was owned.

5. a   20% of preferred shares of $10,000 and 80% of common shares of $50,000.

PART 3

1. a. If the parent acquires all the stock from the subsidiary, no excess will result, since the price paid will equal the total interest in stockholders' equity.
    b. If the parent achieves control and is consolidating the investment, the determination and distribution of excess schedule will result in excess cost or book value, since the portion of equity owned by the parent will not equal the price paid for ownership interest.

2. When the original purchase results in control, the original purchase and the subsequent purchase should each be accompanied by a separate determination and distribution of excess schedule. The excess of cost or book value on each purchase should be distributed and amortized separately.

3. Two situations must be addressed in this case. If the original investment is maintained under the sophisticated equity method, at the time of the second block purchase the investment account will reflect the proportionate share of subsidiary income net of amortization of any excess. Upon achieving control, the amortization need no longer be deducted directly from the subsidiary earnings. Since consolidation procedures are in effect upon achieving control, the amortization may now be made on the consolidated worksheet.

    If the original investment is maintained under the cost method, the original investment should be converted to the simple equity method. This conversion may be made directly on the parent's books, so as to make the original investment compatible with the later investment. If the conversion is not made directly to the parent's books, each period a "cost conversion" entry will be necessary to bring the investment balance to the simple equity method.

    Under both situations, each block purchased must maintain its own determination and distribution of excess schedule, and excesses must be amortized separately.

4. If the subsidiary has preferred stock outstanding, retained earnings must be apportioned between preferred shareholders and common shareholders on the basis of their claims against retained earnings. The determination and distribution of excess schedule prepared on the date of the parent's investment in common stock includes only that portion of retained earnings available to common shareholders. If the parent holds some of the subsidiary's preferred stock, the stock is viewed as retired.

PART 4

1.

	10% Purchase		
Price paid			$60,000
Less interest acquired:			
Common stock		$200,000	
Retained earnings		250,000	
Total stockholders' equity		$450,000	
Interest acquired		10%	45,000
Excess of cost over book value (building), 20-year amortization, $750 per year			$15,000

50% Purchase		
Price paid		$450,000
Less interest acquired:		
Common stock	$200,000	
Retained earnings, Jan. 1, 20X5	500,000	
Income of Dune, Jan. 1 to June 30	70,000	
Total stockholders' equity	$770,000	
Interest acquired	50%	385,000
Excess of cost over book value		$ 65,000
Attributable to equipment:		
50% x $50,000 (5-year		
amortization, $5,000 per year)		25,000
Goodwill		$ 40,000

2. Investment in Dune   25,000

      Retained earnings   25,000

      10% ($500,000 − $250,000)

3.

Port Corporation and Subsidiary Dune Company
Partial Consolidated Worksheet
For Year Ended December 31, 20X5

	Trial Balance		Eliminations and Adjustments		Minority
	Port	Dune	Dr.	Cr.	Interest
Investment in Dune	657,200			(CY₁) 122,200	
				(EL₁) 70,000	
				(D₁) 15,000	
				(EL₂) 385,000	
				(D₂) 65,000	
Building and equipment	600,000	250,000	(D₁) 15,000		
			(D₂ₐ) 25,000		
Accumulated depreciation	(300,000)	(125,000)		(A₁) 3,000	
				(A₂) 2,500	
Goodwill			(D₂ᵦ) 40,000		
Common stock—Port	(800,000)				
Retained earnings—Port	(900,000)		(A₁) 2,250		
Common stock—Dune		(200,000)	(EL₁) 20,000		
			(EL₂) 100,000		
Retained earnings—Dune		(500,000)	(EL₁) 50,000		
			(EL₂) 250,000		
Sales	(600,000)	(557,000)			(1,157,000)
Cost of goods sold	420,000	215,000			635,000
Expenses	120,000	80,000	(A₂) 2,500		
			(A₁) 750		203,250
Subsidiary income	(122,200)		(CY₁) 122,200		
Purchased income			(EL₂) 35,000		35,000
			662,700	662,700	
Consolidated net income					(283,750)
To NCI					104,800
To controlling interest					178,950

Subsidiary Dune Company Income Distribution

	Internally generated net income	$262,000
	Adjusted net income	$262,000
	NCI share	40%
	NCI	$104,800

Parent Port Corporation Income Distribution

Less amortizations:		Internally generated net income	$ 60,000
Building—Block 1	(A₁)	$ 750	
Equipment—Block 2	(A₂)	2,500	
		Adjusted net income	$ 56,750
		Share of first 1/2 year Dune income, $70,000 x 10%	7,000
		Share of second 1/2 year Dune income, $192,000 x 60%	115,200
		Controlling interest	$178,950

PART 5

1. Investment in Salt Company   318,800
        Retained earnings   318,800
        80% ($437,500) – (3 x $10,400)
        amortizations.
    Cash   1,250,000
        Investment in Salt Company   1,193,800
        Gain on sale of Subsidiary   56,200
        To record the sale of the
        investment.

2. Retained earnings   318,800
        Investment in Salt Company   318,800
        To adjust the investment and controlling retained earnings accounts. Since Pepper has lost control, all future
        amortizations will be made directly through the investment account.
    Cash   910,000
        Investment in Salt Company   895,350*
        Gain on sale of subsidiary   14,650
        To record sale of investment.

    *75% ($1,193,800)

3. Retained earnings (25% x $318,800)   79,700
        Investment in Salt Company   79,700
        To adjust the investment and controlling retained earnings accounts. Only adjust for interest sold using the
        sophisticated equity method.
    Cash   300,000
        Investment in Salt Company   298,450*
        Paid-in capital in excess of par   1,550
        To record the sale of the
        investment.

    *Adjusted cost is 25% ($875,000) + $79,700.

PART 6

1.

Price paid		$35,000
Less preferred interest acquired:		
Preferred stock	$100,000	
Dividends in arrears	12,000	
Total preferred stockholders' equity	$112,000	
Interest acquired	30%	33,600
Increase (decrease) on retirement		$(1,400)

2.

	Trial Balance		Eliminations and Adjustments	
	Carry	Kelley	Dr.	Cr.
Investment in Kelley common stock	300,000		(CV) 255,000	(EL) 540,000
				(D) 15,000
Investment in Kelley preferred stock	35,000			(ELP) 35,000
			(D) 15,000	
Common stock—Carry	(800,000)			
Retained earnings—Carry	(1,500,000)			(CV) 255,000
			(ELP) 1,400	
Preferred stock—Kelley		(100,000)	(ELP) 30,000	
R. E. allocated to pref. stock			(ELP) 3,600	(P) 12,000
Common stock—Kelley		(300,000)	(EL) 180,000	
Retained earnings—Kelley		(612,000)	(P) 12,000	
			(EL) 360,000	
Dividend income—common				
Dividend income—preferred	(1,800)		(CYP) 1,800	
Dividends declared—common				
Dividends declared—preferred		6,000		(CYP) 1,800
			858,800	858,800

Explanations of eliminations and adjustments:
(CV) (60% ($600,000 – $175,000)).
(ELP) The loss on retirement flows through the controlling retained earnings.

PART 7 (Appendix)

Pam Corporation and Subsidiary Sy Corporation
Worksheet for Consolidated Balance Sheet
For Year Ended December 31, 20X6

	Trial Balance		Eliminations and Adjustments		NCI	Consolidated Balance Sheet
	Pam	Sy	Dr.	Cr.		
Cash	65,000	25,000				90,000
Accounts and other receivables	360,000	120,000		(LN) 105,000		285,000
				(IA) 90,000		
Merchandise inventory	920,000	670,000		(EI) 3,000		1,587,000
Property, plant, and equipment (net)	1,000,000	400,000	(D) 530,000	(A) 26,500		
				(F) 22,500		1,881,000
Investment in Sy Corporation	1,250,000		(CV) 90,000	(EL) 810,000		
				(D) 530,000		
Accounts payable and other current liabilities	(130,000)	(315,000)	(LN)105,000			(250,000)
			(IA) 90,000			
Common stock—Pam	(500,000)					(500,000)
Retained earnings—Pam	(2,965,000)		(A) 26,500	(CV)90,000		(3,005,250)
			(EI) 3,000			
			(F) 20,250			
Common stock—Sy		(200,000)	(EL)180,000		(20,000)	
Retained earnings—Sy		(700,000)	(EL)630,000		(67,750)	
			(F) 2,250			
Total	0	0	1,677,000	1,677,000		
NCI					(87,750)	(87,750)
						0

<u>Determination and Distribution of Excess Schedule</u>

Price paid		$1,250,000
Less interest acquired:		
Sy equity	$800,000	
Interest acquired	90%	720,000
Excess of cost over book value attributable to building		
(20-year life, $26,500 per year)		$ 530,000

Eliminations and adjustments:
(CV) Equity conversion is 90% of $100,000 increase in retained earnings = $90,000. Total adjustment to retained earnings is $90,900.
(EL) Eliminate Sy equity owned by Pam.
(D) Distribute the excess to building.
(A) Amortize building increase for one year.
(LN) Eliminate the intercompany note and $5,000 accrued interest.
(IA) Eliminate the $90,000 intercompany trade debt.
(EI) Defer the ending inventory profit, 5% x $60,000.
(F) Defer the unamortized profit on equipment sale, $25,000 – 1/2 of $5,000 depreciation = $22,500. Allocate 90%/10% to controlling and NCI in retained earnings.

CHAPTER 8

PART 1

1. F   The parent merely makes a memo entry to acknowledge the number of shares received.
2. T
3. T
4. F   This was done in the past if the sale was a public offering.
5. F   Additional equity adjustments are necessary when the number of subsidiary shares outstanding is altered. An equity adjustment is not necessary when the parent purchases additional shares to maintain its ownership interest.
6. F   The treasury stock at cost is carried on the books of the subsidiary. The parent prepares a determination and distribution of excess schedule and treats the treasury stock as an added investment.
7. T
8. T
9. F   The treasury stock method views the parent's shares as retired.
10. T
11. F   The determination and distribution of excess schedule is prepared for the number of shares acquired beyond those needed to maintain the parent's former ownership interest.

PART 2

1. c   The subsidiary transfers equity from retained earnings to paid-in excess. There is no change in the total equity to paid-in excess. There is no change in total equity owned by the parent.
2. a   The equity of the subsidiary increases by a greater percentage than the number of shares. The parent's interest increases. The increase goes to paid-in excess.
3. b   Baker can only record 80% of the market value as its share. Able can only record 70% of any asset adjustment on a Baker asset. The investment in Cable is a Baker asset.
4. b   Ninety percent of Pride shares are owned externally. Twenty percent of Simba shares are owned externally.
5. a   The shares are treated either as an investment for Sun or as treasury shares. In either case, no gain or loss is recorded on the transaction.
6. b   Gasson owned the $400,000 Able equity, plus 90% of Baker ($27,000). Able assets include $3,000 Baker equity, which was purchased at a price $1,000 in excess of book value. This decreases the $427,000 interest by $1,000.

PART 3

1.		
Common stock ($25 par)	$131,250	
Paid-in capital in excess	1,250	
Retained earnings	492,500	
Total stockholders' equity	$625,000	

5% dividend:
  $125,000 ÷ $25 par = 5,000 shares
  5% x 5,000 = 250 shares
  250 x $30 = $7,500 market value

2.		
Investment in Kern Company	$200,000	
Retained earnings		$200,000
Retained earnings, January 20X6		$542,500
Retained earnings, January 20X3		300,000
Change in retained earnings balance		$242,500
Retained earnings transferred to common stock and paid-in capital ($30 x 250)		7,500
Total change in retained earnings		$250,000
Ownership interest		80%
Simple equity conversion		$200,000

PART 4

1.

	Case 1	Case 2	Case 3
Sales price per share	$5	$12.50	$15
Jacklin equity prior to sale	$750,000	$750,000	$750,000
Add to common stock ($5 par)	20,000	20,000	20,000
Add to paid-in capital in excess of par	—	30,000	40,000
Jacklin equity subsequent to sale	$770,000	$800,000	$810,000
Controlling interest subsequent to sale: 48,000 = 75% 64,000	$577,500	$600,000	$607,500
Prior controlling interest (80% x $750,000)	600,000	600,000	600,000
Net change in controlling interest	$ (22,500)	$ 0	$ 7,500

2.

		(1) Maintain Interest	(2) Increase Interest	(3) Decrease Interest
Shares purchased		3,200	4,000	2,000
Total shares after purchase		51,200	52,000	50,000
Subsidiary equity after sale		$810,000	$810,000	$810,000
Ownership percent		80%	81.25%	78.125%
Ownership amount		$648,000	$658,125	$632,813
Subsidiary equity prior to sale		$750,000	$750,000	$750,000
Ownership percent		80%	80%	80%
Ownership amount		$600,000	$600,000	$600,000
Change in interest resulting from purchase		$ 48,000	$ 58,125	$ 32,813
Price paid ($15 per share)		48,000	60,000	30,000
Excess of price over change in interest		$ 0	$ 1,875	$ (2,813)

1.	Investment in Jacklin	48,000		
	Cash		48,000	
2.	Investment in Jacklin	60,000		
	Cash		60,000	
	Determination and distribution schedule:			
	Price paid for 800 shares	$ 12,000		
	Equity = $810,000 x 0.0125	10,125		
	Excess	$ 1,875		
3.	Investment in Jacklin	32,813		
	Paid-in capital in excess of par		2,813	
	Cash		30,000	

PART 5

1. Treasury stock (at cost)   128,000
       Cash   128,000

2. Determination and Distribution of Excess Schedule for Treasury Stock
    Price paid $128,000
    Interest acquired (20% x $610,000)   122,000
    Goodwill $ 6,000

    60% interest eliminations:
    Investment in Isle
      [60% x ($450,000 – $300,000)]   90,000
        Retained earnings   90,000

    Common stock   60,000
    Paid-in capital in excess of par   36,000
    Retained earnings   270,000
        Investment in Isle   366,000
    Goodwill   30,000
        Investment in Isle   30,000
    Treasury stock eliminations:
    Common stock   20,000
    Paid-in capital in excess of par   12,000
    Retained earnings   90,000
        Treasury stock (at cost)   122,000
    Goodwill   6,000
        Treasury stock (at cost)   6,000

PART 6

1. Price paid $325,000
    Equity interest:
      Common stock, $5 par $150,000
      Paid-in capital in excess of par   90,000
      Retained earnings   165,000
        Total equity   405,000
        Ownership interest   70%   283,500
    Excess of cost over book value (debit balance) $ 41,500
    Allocate to:
      Sub-land, 0.7 x 0.6 x $10,000   4,200 Dr.
      Sub-par equipment, 0.7 x $15,000   10,500 Dr.
      Additional goodwill $ 26,800 Dr.

2. Accumulated depreciation (2 x $2,000)   4,000
      NCI—sub (40%)*   3,200
      NCI—sub-par (30% x 60%)*   1,440
      Controlling interest (70% x 60%)*   3,360
        Machine   10,000
        Depreciation expense   2,000

    *Retained earnings ($8,000 profit remaining on Jan. 1, 20X5).

PART 7

Subsidiary Basket Income Distribution

Profit in ending inventory	(EI)	$6,000	Internally generated net income	$25,000
			Adjusted income	$19,000
			NCI share	25%
			NCI	$ 4,750

Parent Ott Income Distribution

Equipment depreciation	(A)	$4,000	Internally generated net income	$60,000
			75% of Basket adjusted income	14,250
			Total controlling interest	$70,250

Ott Corporation and Subsidiary Basket Company
Partial Consolidated Worksheet—Treasury Stock Method
For Year Ended December 31, 20X5

	Trial Balance		Eliminations and Adjustments		Consolidated Income Statement	Controlling Retained Earnings	Consolidated Balance Sheet
	Ott	Basket	Dr.	Cr.	NCI		
Current assets	738,750	545,833		(EI) 6,000			1,278,583
Investment in Basket (75%)	590,000			(CY1)18,750			
				(EL)531,250			
				(D) 40,000			
Investment in Ott (15%)		187,500		(TS)187,500			
Equipment (net)			(D) 40,000	(A) 12,000			28,000
Common stock—Ott	(750,000)						(750,000)
Retained earnings—Ott	(500,000)		(A) 8,000			(492,000)	
Common stock—Basket		(500,000)	(EL)375,000		(125,000)		
Retained earnings—Basket		(208,333)	(EL)156,250		(52,083)		
Sales	(250,000)	(175,000)	(IS) 60,000				
Cost of goods sold	160,000	100,000	(EI) 6,000	60,000			
Expenses	30,000	50,000	(A) 4,000				
Subsidiary income	(18,750)		(CY₁)18,750				
Treasury stock			(TS)187,500				187,500
	0	0	855,500	855,500			
Consolidated net income							
To NCI					(4,750)		
To controlling interest						(70,250)	
Total NCI					(181,833)		(181,833)
Retained earnings, controlling interest, Dec. 31, 20X5						(562,250)	(562,250)
							0

SPECIAL APPENDIX 1

PART 1

1. 8,000 shares for $35 cash $280,000
    500 shares from continuing stockholders not
    a part of the control group at $35 fair value 17,500
    1,500 shares from members of the new control
    group at $30 simple-equity-adjusted cost 45,000
    Total $342,500
    Note: 80% test is passed.

2. Determination and Distribution of Excess Schedule for 8,500 Shares at Fair Value
    Price paid ($280,000 + $17,500) $297,500
    Equity ($200,000 x 85%) 170,000
    Goodwill $127,500

    Determination and Distribution of Excess Schedule for 1,500 shares at Equity-Adjusted Cost
    Price paid (1,500 x $30) $45,000
    Equity ($200,000 x 15%) 30,000
    Goodwill $15,000

3. Entry to record the formation of Pry:
    Cash 60,000
       Common stock ($1 par) 2,000
       Paid-in capital in excess of par 58,000

4. Entry to record assumption of debt:
    Cash 240,000
       Long-term debt 240,000

5. Entry to record acquisition of interest in Nail Inc.:
    Current assets 80,000
    Equipment (net) 120,000
    Building (net) 150,000
    Goodwill 142,500
       Long-term debt 150,000
       Cash (8,000 shares x $35) 280,000
       Common stock ($1 par) 2,000
       Paid-in capital in excess of par 60,500

SPECIAL APPENDIX 2

PART 1

1. Price paid is $750,000

Zone Analysis
Price paid	$750,000
Fair value of net priority assets	28,000
Available for nonpriority accounts	722,000

New Rules:
Price paid	$ 750,000
Fair value of net assets	1,028,000
Gain on purchase	278,000

Existing Rules	Dr.	Cr.	Proposed Rules	Dr.	Cr.
Accounts receivable	50,000		Accounts receivable	50,000	
Inventory	120,000		Inventory	120,000	
Equipment (net) .3 x $722,000	216,600		Equipment (net)	300,000	
Building (net) .5 x $722,000	361,000		Building (net)	500,000	
Patent .2 x $722,000	144,400		Patent	200,000	
Accounts payable		40,000	Accounts payable		40,000
Bonds payable		100,000	Bonds payable		100,000
Premium on bonds payable		2,000	Premium on bonds payable		2,000
Cash		750,000	Cash		750,000
			Gain on purchase		278,000
	892,000	892,000		1,170,000	1,170,000

2. Price paid is $ 20,000.

Zone Analysis
Price paid	$ 20,000
Fair value of net priority assets	28,000
Extraordinary gain	8,000

New Rules:
Price paid	$ 20,000
Fair value of net assets	1,028,000
Gain on purchase	1,008,000

Existing Rules	Dr.	Cr.	Proposed Rules	Dr.	Cr.
Accounts receivable	50,000		Accounts receivable	50,000	
Inventory	120,000		Inventory	120,000	
Equipment (net)	0		Equipment (net)	300,000	
Building (net	0		Building (net)	500,000	
Patent	0		Patent	200,000	
Accounts payable		40,000	Accounts payable		40,000
Bonds payable		100,000	Bonds payable		100,000
Premium on bonds payable		2,000	Premium on bonds payable		2,000
Cash		20,000	Cash		20,000
Extraordinary gain		8,000	Gain on purchase		1,008,000
	170,000	170,000		1,170,000	1,170,000

PART 2

1. Price paid is $900,000 for 80% interest.

Value Analysis Schedule	Parent Price (80%)	NCI Value (20%)	Implied Company Value
1. Company fair value*	$900,000	$225,000	$1,125,000
2. Fair value of net assets excluding goodwill	712,000	178,000	890,000
3. Goodwill—Fair value of company exceeds fair value of net assets excluding goodwill.	188,000	47,000	235,000
4. Gain—Parent price is less the parent share of fair value of net assets excluding goodwill.	n/a		

* $900,000 ÷ 80% = $1,125,000 implied company value; $1,125,000 x 20% = $225,000 NCI Value

Determination and Distribution of Excess Schedule	Implied Company Value	Parent Price	NCI Value	Worksheet Distribution
Fair value of subsidiary	1,125,000	900,000	225,000	
Less book value interest acquired:				
Common stock, $1 par	100,000			
Paid-in excess of par	200,000			
Retained earnings	400,000			
Total equity	700,000			
Interest acquired		80.00%	20.00%	
Book value		560,000	140,000	
Excess of fair value over book value	425,000	340,000	85,000	
Adjustment of identifiable accounts:				Amort. per year
Land ($120,000 – $100,000 book value)	20,000			
Buildings ($380,000 – $240,000 net book value)	140,000			7,000
Equipment ($300,000 fair – $270,000 net book value)	30,000			3,000
Goodwill	235,000			
Gain (not applicable)				
Total	425,000			

2. Price paid is $580,000 for 80% interest.

Value Analysis Schedule	Parent Price (80%)	NCI Value (20%)	Implied Company Value
1. Company fair value*	$580,000	$178,000	$ 758,000
2. Fair value of net assets excluding goodwill	712,000	178,000	$890,000
3. Goodwill—Fair value of company exceeds fair value of net assets excluding goodwill.			
4. Gain—Parent price is less the parent share of fair value of net assets excluding goodwill.	132,000		132,000

Determination and Distribution of Excess Schedule	Implied Company Value	Parent Price	NCI Value	Worksheet Distribution
Fair value of subsidiary	758,000	580,000	178,000	
Less book value interest acquired:				
Common stock, $1 par	100,000			
Paid-in excess of par	200,000			
Retained earnings	400,000			
Total equity	700,000			
Interest acquired		80.00%	20.00%	
Book value		560,000	140,000	
Excess of fair value over book value	58,000	20,000	38,000	
Adjustment of identifiable accounts:				Amort. per year
Land ($120,000 – $100,000 book value)	20,000			
Buildings ($380,000 – $240,000 net book value)	140,000			7,000
Equipment ($300,000 fair – $270,000 net book value)	30,000			3,000
Goodwill	n/a			
Gain	(132,000)			
Total	58,000			

* $580,000 ÷ 80% = $725,000; $725,000 x 20% = $145,000; but NCI Value must be at least 20% x fair value of net assets excluding goodwill; thus NCI Value = $890,000 x 20% = $178,000 and Implied Company Value = $580,000 + $178,000 = $758,000.

PART 3

1. Prepare a revised determination and distribution of excess schedule under the proposed rules.

Determination and Distribution of Excess Schedule	Implied Company Value	Parent Price	NCI Value	Worksheet Distribution
Fair value of subsidiary	1,875,000	1,500,000	375,000	
Less book value interest acquired:				
Common stock, $1 par	1,000,000			
Paid-in excess of par	300,000			
Retained earnings	400,000			
Total equity	1,700,000			
Interest acquired		80.00%	20.00%	
Book value		1,360,000	340,000	
Excess of fair value over book value	175,000	140,000	35,000	
Adjustment of identifiable accounts:				Amort. per year
Inventory	10,000			
Equipment	50,000			6,250
Patent	100,000			10,000
Goodwill	15,000			
Gain (not applicable)				
Total	175,000			

2.

Payrol Company and Subsidiary Johnson Company
Worksheet for Consolidated Balance Sheet
For Year Ended December 31, 20X7

	Trial Balance		Eliminations and Adjustmer.ts		Consolidated Income		Controlling Retained	Consolidated Balance
	Payrol	Johnson	Dr.	Cr.	Statement	NCI	Earnings	Sheet
Cash	654,000	505,000						1,159,000
Equipment (net)	1,290,000	940,000	(D2) 50,000	(A2) 18,750				2,261,250
Patents	195,000	35,000	(D3) 100,000	(A3) 30,000				300,000
Other assets	1,720,000	730,000						2,450,000
Investment in Johnson Company	1,500,000		(CV) 144,000	(EL)1,504,000				
				(D) 140,000				
Goodwill			(D4) 15,000					15,000
Accounts payable	(550,000)	(205,000)						(755,000)
Common stock—Payrol ($5 par)	(2,000,000)							(2,000,000)
Paid-in capital in excess—Payrol	(1,200,000)							(1,200,000)
Retained earnings—Payrol 1/1/X7	(1,255,000)		(D1) 8,000	(CV) 144,000				
			(A2) 10,000					
			(A3) 16,000					
							(1,365,000)	
Common stock—Johnson ($1 par)		(1,000,000)	(EL) 800,000			(200,000)		
Paid-in capital in excess—Johnson		(300,000)	(EL) 240,000			(60,000)		
Retained earnings—Johnson 1/1/X7		(580,000)	(EL) 464,000	(NCI) 35,000		(142,500)		
			(D1) 2,000					
			(A2) 2,500					
			(A3) 4,000					
Sales	(1,100,000)	(425,000)			(1,525,000)			
Costs of goods sold	470,000	170,000			640,000			
Other expenses	250,000	100,000	(A2) 6,250					
			(A3) 10,000					
					366,250			
Dividend income	(24,000)		(CY₂) 24,000					
Dividends declared	50,000	30,000		(CY₂) 24,000		6,000	50,000	
Total	0	0	1,895,750	1,895,750				
Consolidated net income					(518,750)			
To NCI					27,750	(27,750)		
To controlling interest					491,000		(491,000)	
NCI						(424,50)		(424,250)
Controlling retained earnings, December 31, 20X7							(1,806,000)	(1,806,000)
								0

Subsidiary Johnson Company Income Distribution

Equipment depreciation	$ 6,250	Internally generated net income	$155,000
Patent amortization	10,000		
		Adjusted income	$138,750
		NCI share	20%
		NCI	$ 27,750

Parent Payrol Company Income Distribution

Internally generated net income	$380,000
80% x Johnson Company adjusted income	111,000
Controlling interest	$491,000

Eliminations and adjustments:
(CV)   Convert from the cost to the equity method as of January 1, 20X7.
         [$580,000 January 1, 20X7 – $400,000 January 1, 20X5 = $180,000 x 0.80 = $144,000.]
(CY$_2$) Eliminate intercompany dividends.
(EL)   Eliminate subsidiary equities.
(NCI) Adjust NCI to fair value and.
 (D)   Distribute the excess cost as given by the determination and distribution schedule:
          (1) Decrease retained earnings by $10,000 for inventory sold.
          (2) Increase equipment $50,000.
          (3) Increase patents $100,000.
          (4) Increase goodwill $15,000.
 (A)   Record amortizations resulting from the revaluations:
          (1) No amortization necessary.
          (2) Record $6,250 annual increase in equipment depreciation for the current and past two years.
          (3) Record $10,000 annual increase in patent amortization for the current and past two years.

CHAPTER 9

PART 1

1.   F
2.   F
3.   T
4.   F
5.   T
6.   F
7.   F
8.   T
9.   T
10. F
11. F
12. F

PART 2

1.   D. Importing
2.   F. Anglo-Saxon accounting
3.   G. Foreign currency transaction
4.   E. Harmonization
5.   H. European Union
6.   C. IASC
7.   B. IFAC
8.   C. IASC
9.   I.   International Financial Reporting Standards
10.   J. U.S. GAAP

DERIVATIVES MODULE

PART 1

1. T
2. F Net settlement is allowed.
3. F An increase in value would occur if the forward rate is greater than the spot rate.
4. T
5. T
6. T
7. F No, just the opposite.
8. F There is no intrinsic value, on time value.
9. T
10. F It would be prudent if variable rate were to decrease relative to fixed rates.
11. T
12. T

PART 2

1. F Hedges on forecasted transactions are cash flow hedges.
2. T
3. T
4. F An options return profile is always asymmetric.
5. F Such changes are always recognized currently in earnings.
6. T
7. F A commitment to buy would have gained in value, not on to sell.
8. F Because the notional amount is the same, on would expect changes to be totally offset.
9. T
10. T
11. T
12. F No, it will be recognized when the transaction affects earnings.

PART 3

Without a swap the 20X5 interest expense would have been:	
6% x $500,000 x 12/12 year or	$30,000

With the swap the interest expense was as follows:	
First quarter interest expense (6% x $500,000 x 3/12 year)	$7,500
Second quarter interest expense (6% x $500,000 x 3/12 year)	7,500
Third quarter interest expense (5.6% x $500,000 x 3/12 year)	7,000
Fourth quarter interest expense (5.2% x $500,000 x 3/12 year)	6,500
Total 20X5 interest expense	$28,500

The swap reduced the interest expense by $1,500.

PART 4

Change in value of the firm commitment:
    First 30 days (100,000 x ($2.10 vs. $2.10)) $ 0
    Second 30 days (100,000 x ($2.10 vs. $2.07))   3,000 loss

Change in value of the derivative instrument:
    First 30 days:
        Change in value (100,000 x ($2.09 vs. $2.08))   1,000 gain
        Present value of change in value ($1,000 FV,
            $n = 1$, $i = 6\%/12$)   995 gain
    Second 30 days:
        Change in value (100,000 x ($2.09 vs. $2.07))   2,000 gain
    Present value of change in value $2,000
      Prior present value   995
    Change in present value   1,005 gain
    Total gain on forward contract $2,000 gain

PART 5

	July	August	September	October
Value of option at end of period	$2,300	$4,100	$3,000	N/A
Intrinsic value of option at end of period	2,000	4,000	3,000	N/A
Time value of option at end of period	300	100	0	N/A
Time value at beginning of period	700	300	100	
Change in time value	400	200	100	
Intrinsic value reported as OCI	2,000	4,000	3,000	$3,000
Portion of OCI reclassified into earnings	0	0	0	(1,800)
OCI balance at end of period	2,000	4,000	3,000	1,200
Ineffectivenes loss in earnings	400	200	100	

CHAPTER 10

PART 1

1. F If spot rate is greater than forward rate, forward contract is at a discount.

2. T

3. F There is no intrinsic value.

4. F The excess hedge is speculative.

5. F

6. T

7. F The gain on a hedge of a forecasted transaction is recognized as part of other comprehensive income.

8. F It is recognized when the transaction affects earnings.

9. F

10. F The resulting inventory account will be adjusted.

11. F They should be presented at their fair market value.

12. T

13. F It is recognized over the life of the contract.

PART 2

1. C. Strengthening dollar
2. G. Contract premium
3. D. Floating system
4. H. Indirect quote
5. B. Transaction loss
6. A. Other comprehensive income
7. E. Fair value hedge
8. B. Transaction loss
9. F. Weakening dollar
10. J. Cash flow hedge

PART 3

Income Effect as of April 30	Case A	Case B	Case C	Case D
Loss on purchase transaction [10,000 x ($0.60 – $0.66)]	$(600)	$(600)	$(600)	$(600)
Gain on forward contract [10,000 x ($0.66 – $0.62)]		400	400	
[10,000 x ($0.66 – $0.64)]				200
Gain on speculative hedge [5,000 x ($0.66 – $0.62)]			200	
Hedge of commitment: Gain on hedge [10,000 x ($0.64 – $0.63)]				100
Loss on commitment				(100)
Total	$(600)	$(200)	$ 0	$(400)

PART 4

Hedge A

Sales revenue (100,000 x $1.042)	$ 104,200
Cost of sales	(80,000)
Gross profit	24,200
Gain on hedge [100,000 x ($1.045 – $1.042)]	300
Net income effect	$ 24,500

Hedge B

Option gain ($3,800 – $3,000)	$ 800
Commitment loss	(800)
Net income effect	$ 0

Hedge C

Exchange loss on loan payable [384,000 x ($1.041 – $1.043)]	$ (768)
Interest expense (384,000 x 1% x $1.043)	(4,005)
Gain on forward contract [395,000 x ($1.0405 – $1.042)]	593
Net income effect	$ (4,180)

Hedge D

Gain on option ($2,100 – $2,000)	$ 100

PART 5

10/1/X8	Accounts receivable—FC	162,000	
	Sales—foreign		162,000
	To record sale to German company for 300,000 FC when 1 FC = $0.54		

11/1/X8	Forward contract receivable—$	160,500	
	Forward contract payable—FC		160,500
	To record contract to deliver 300,000 FC when forward rate is 1 FC = $0.535		

12/31/X8	Exchange loss	3,000	
	Accounts receivable—FC		3,000
	To accrue exchange loss at Jem Company's year end, when 1 FC = $0.53		

12/31/X8	Forward contract payable—FC	1,500	
	Unrealized gain on contract		1,500
	To record gain on forward contract when forward rate is 1 FC = $0.53		

1/31/X9	Foreign currency	156,000	
	Exchange loss	3,000	
	Accounts receivable—FC		159,000
	To record receipt of payment of 300,000 FC when 1 FC = $0.52		

1/31/X9	Cash	160,500	
	Foreign contract payable—FC	159,000	
	Unrealized gain on contract		3,000
	Foreign currency		156,000
	Forward contract receivable—$		160,500
	To record settlement of forward contract when 1 FC = $0.52		

PART 6

Under the alternative involving a forward contract, the company would have to spend $248,000 (400,000 FC x $0.62) in order to secure the 400,000 FC necessary to settle the exposed liability position.

Under the loan alternative, the balance due on the loan at maturity will be the equivalent of $243,200 [$240,000 + (240,000 x 8% x 60/360)]. In order for the company to receive the 400,000 FC necessary to settle the exposed liability position, the spot rate when the loan is settled must be 1 FC = $0.608 ($243,200/400,000 FC).

If the actual spot rate on July 31 is less than $0.62, the loan would be the more attractive alternative.

However, if the spot rate is more than $0.62, the forward contract would be more attractive. In the final analysis, the choice of the right alternative depends on what the actual spot rate is on July 31. This exercise emphasizes that the choice of a hedging strategy is dependent on one's estimate of how spot rates will change over time. For example, if one thought that the July 31 spot rate would be less than $0.608, then neither alternative would be preferable to not taking a hedged position.

CHAPTER 11

PART 1

1. F The objective is to reflect the economic effects of rate changes on an entity's cash flows and equity.

2. T

3. F The division is an integral component of the American company's operations. Its functional currency is the dollar.

4. F Functional currency statements must be prepared on the basis of U.S. generally accepted accounting principles before translation takes place.

5. F All assets are translated using the current exchange rate at the date of translation.

6. T

7. F Elements of income are translated at the exchange rates at the time of the actual transaction.

8.   F   A translation adjustment always exists due to rate changes since an entity's inception.

9.   T

10. T

11. F   The cumulative translation adjustment remains in other comprehensive income until the investment in the foreign entity is sold or substantially liquidated.

12. F   Eliminate after translation.

13. F   The tax effects are to be included, with the exchange gain or loss, in the cumulative translation adjustment.

14. T

15. T

16. F   The resulting elimination entry produces an additional translation adjustment.

PART 2

1.   Cost of goods sold for 20X6:

Beginning inventory, January 1, 20X6	30,000	FC
20X6 purchases	103,000	
Goods available	133,000	
Ending inventory, December 31, 20X6	52,000	
Cost of goods sold	81,000	FC

Translated value, assuming LIFO inventory method:

Date of Purchase	Amount		Rate		Value
November 1, 20X6	20,000 FC	x	$1.26	=	$ 25,200
October 1, 20X6	40,000		$1.25		50,000
June 1, 20X6	21,000		$1.22		25,620
Total cost of goods sold	81,000 FC				$100,820

2.   The translated value of the loss must be inferred, based on the following entry, to record the sale:

Cash (13,200 FC x $1.25)	16,500	
Accumulated depreciation (2,000 FC x $1.19)	2,380	
Loss	160	
Equipment (16,000 FC x $1.19)		19,040

3.   Liability to broker at December 31, 20X6, is measured as follows:

Foreign currency amount		Spot rate at		
of the forward contract	x	year end		
20,000 FC	x	$1.28	=	$25,600

PART 3

1.   d   500,000 x 0.75

2.   c   (900,000 x 0.62) + (600,000 x 0.61)

3.   d   5,500,000 x 0.70

4.   a

5.   b

6.   c   3,000,000 x 2 x 1.50

7.   c

8.   a   200,000 x 0.61

PART 4

1. c

2. c

3. d

January 1, 20X3 net assets multiplied by difference in exchange rates for the period, 2,000,000 FC x ($0.71 – $0.69)	$40,000
Net loss (decrease in net assets) multiplied by difference between average and year-end exchange rates (10,000 FC) x ($0.71 – $0.70)	(100)
Proceeds of stock issuance (increase in net assets) multiplied by difference in exchange rates between issuance date and year end, 50,000 FC x ($0.71 – $0.72)	(500)
20X3 translation adjustment	$39,400

4. d   100,000 B x 1.2 x 2.25; 50,000 B x 1.2 x 2.25

5. c

6. c   100,000 FCB x 0.67 FCA x $0.55

7. d   100,000 FCB x 0.67 FCA x $0.54 x 0.10

8. b   a = 0, b = (18,000), c = 5,000

9. a   (100,000 FCA x 0.48) < (95,000 FCA x 0.51) so value at cost (100,000 FCA x 0.48 x 1.05) = $50,400

PART 5

	20X8	20X9
Net assets owned by investor at beginning of year, multiplied by the change in exchange rates during year	$ 0[1]	$(102,200)[4]
Increase in net assets (excluding capital transactions) multiplied by the difference between the current rate and the average rate used to translate income	(33,200)[2]	(7,200)[5]
Increase in net assets due to capital transactions (including investments by the domestic company in stock and dividends declared) multiplied by the difference between the current rate and the rate at the time of the capital transaction	(82,800)[3]	15,000[6]
Translation adjustment	$(116,000)	$ (94,400)

[1] 0 x ($0.99 – $1.00) = 0.

[2] 830,000 x ($0.99 – $1.03) = (33,200).

[3] 3,780,000 x ($0.99 – $1.00) – 500,000 x ($0.99 – $1.02) + 1,000,000 x ($0.99 – $1.05) = (82,800).

[4] (3,780,000 + 830,000 + 1,000,000 – 500,000) x ($0.97 – $0.99) = (102,200).

[5] 720,000 x ($0.97 – $0.98) = (7,200).

[6] 500,000 x ($0.97 – $1.00) = 15,000.

PART 6

Analysis of Investment in Foreign Entity Account

	Balance (in U.S. dollars)
Initial investment	$2,900,000
Share of investee net income (25% of 9,000,000 FC x $0.54)	1,215,000
Share of investee dividend (25% of 1,800,000 FC x $0.58)	(261,000)
Share of investee translation adjustment ($3,144,000 x 25%) (See Note A)	786,000
Amortization of cost over book value related to depreciable assets (See Note B)	(32,400)
Balance in investment account	$4,607,600

Note A: [(138,000,000 x 0.62) + (59,000,000 x 0.54) − (110,000,000 x 0.62) − (68,000,000 x 0.54) − (20,800,000 x 0.50) + (1,800,000 x 0.58)] = translation adjustment of $3,144,000.

Note B:

Cost of investment ($2,900,000 ÷ 0.50)	5,800,000	FC
Book value of investment (20,800,000 x 25%)	5,200,000	
Excess of cost over book value	600,000	FC

600,000 FC ÷ 10 years x $0.54 equals amortization of $32,400.

CHAPTER 12

PART 1

1. T

2. F   Such liquidations should be recorded at estimated replacement cost.

3. F

4. F   Although permanent differences may in some cases not be recognized as a component of taxable income, they nevertheless influence the tax calculation. Furthermore, effective tax rates are expressed as a percentage of pretax income, including permanent differences.

5. F

6. F   Recognition is dependent upon whether the projected annual income is more likely than not.

7. T

8. F

9. F   The restated effective tax rate may only reflect the decision to discontinue. Allowing other items to be considered would result in accounting for changes in estimates on a retroactive basis.

10. F

11. F

12. T

13. T

14. T

PART 2

Second-quarter net income is computed as follows:

Revenue		$ 730,000
Cost of sales:		
Current quarter purchases (3,400 units x $150)	$(510,000)	
Liquidation of beginning inventory (600 units x $170)	(102,000)	(612,000)
Research costs (Note A)		(40,000)
Accrued vacations ($80,000 allocated over 4 quarters)		(20,000)
Net income before taxes		58,000
Income taxes (Note B)		(11,560)
Net income		$ 46,440

Note A: The entire research cost must be expensed by year end. Since its benefits extend beyond the current year, the amount may be amortized over the second, third, and fourth quarters. $120,000 ÷ 3 quarters = $40,000 per quarter.

Note B: The effective tax rate is computed as follows:

YTD income ($40,000 + $58,000)	$ 98,000
Projected income	70,000
Annual income	$168,000
Tax on income ($100,000 x 30%) + ($68,000 x 32%)	$ 51,760
Less: tax credits	(15,000)
Net tax	$ 36,760
Effective tax rate	22%

The YTD tax expense is $21,560 (22% x $98,000), of which $10,000 (25% x $40,000) was recognized in the first quarter. Therefore, the tax expense traceable to the second quarter is $11,560 ($21,560 – $10,000).

PART 3

	Case A	Case B	Case C	Case D
Estimated annual pretax income (loss)	$100,000	$ (15,000)	$ (60,000)	$(100,000)
Permanent differences	(10,000)	(10,000)	0	10,000
Taxable income (loss)	$ 90,000	$ (25,000)	$ (60,000)	$ (90,000)
Tax expense	$ 27,000			
Tax credit	(4,000)			
Net tax expense	$ 23,000			
Tax (benefit) of carryback		$ (5,000)	$ (8,000)	$ (8,000)
Tax credit carryback		(2,000)	0	0
Tax (benefit) of carryforward		N/A	0	(9,000)
Net tax (benefit)		$ (7,000)	$ (8,000)	$ (17,000)
Estimated effective tax credit*	23%	46.67%	13.33%	17.00%

*Note that the tax rate is expressed as a percentage of the estimated annual pretax accounting (versus tax) income or loss.

PART 4

	Ordinary Income	Total Income	Total Income (excluding nonordinary losses)	Total Income (excluding nonordinary gains)
Pretax income	$210,000	$80,000	$260,000	$30,000
Tax expense (benefit) after tax credits	61,000	15,500	78,500	

Incremental tax expenses (benefits) on:

Ordinary income	$ 61,000
Nonordinary loss (item A)	(63,000)[1]
Nonordinary income (items B & C)	17,500[2]
Total income	$15,500

[1] $15,500 – $78,500.

[2] This is a plug-in order to reconcile to the tax on total income.

Therefore, the tax benefit on item A is $63,000. However, the total tax expense of $17,500 traceable to items B and C must be apportioned between the items.

	Total Income		Total Income (excluding item B)	Total Income (excluding item C)
Pretax income	$80,000		$60,000	$50,000
Tax expense (benefit)	15,500		10,000	7,500

Incremental tax expense (benefit) traceable to:

Nonordinary item B (15,500 – 10,000)	5,500
Nonordinary item C (15,500 – 7,500)	8,000

Apportionment of tax expense traceable to nonordinary gains:

The $17,500 incremental tax expense traceable to all nonordinary gains is ratably apportioned to each individual gain category as follows:

	Each Gain Category		
	Incremental Expense	Percent	Apportioned Amount
Gain category B	$ 5,500	40.74	$ 7,130
Gain category C	8,000	59.26	10,370
	$13,500	100.0	$17,500

PART 5

1.

Sales to unaffiliated customers	$1,890,000
Intersegmental sales	110,000
Combined revenue	$2,000,000

Segmental revenue required to satisfy revenue criterion:
10% x $2,000,000 = $200,000

2.

Segment	Operating Profit	Operating Loss
A	$ 20,000	
B		$(22,000)
C	175,000	
D	60,000	
E		(8,000)
Total	$255,000	$(30,000)

Portion of absolute amount of the greater of operating profit or operating loss to satisfy operating profit/loss criterion:
  10% x $255,000 = $25,500

3.   Segment identifiable assets required to satisfy identifiable asset criterion: 10% x $2,200,000 = $220,000

4.   Summary:

Segment	Revenue ≥ $200,000?	Operating Results ≥ $25,500?	Identifiable Assets ≥ $220,000?	Segment Reportable?
A	Yes	No	Yes	Yes
B	Yes	No	No	Yes
C	Yes	Yes	Yes	Yes
D	Yes	Yes	Yes	Yes
E	No	No	No	No

CHAPTER 13

PART 1

1. d
2. c
3. c
4. a
5. c
6. c
7. c

PART 2

1.

	Profit Allocation			
	Hanyard	Robertson	Turman	Kelly	Total
Interest on capital	$ 5,000	$ 4,500	$ 2,000	$ 4,700	$ 16,200
Bonuses (Note A)	3,000	2,000	—	—	5,000
Salaries	20,000	10,000	—	—	30,000
Subtotal	$28,000	$16,500	$ 2,000	$ 4,700	$ 51,200
Remaining profit	13,450	13,450	13,450	13,450	53,800
Income	$41,450	$29,950	$15,450	$18,150	$105,000

Note A:
Bonuses = 5% (net income – bonuses)
105% Bonuses = 5% ($105,000)
105% Bonuses = $5,250
Bonuses = $5,000
Bonuses allocated 3/5 to Hanyard and 2/5 to Robertson.

2.

	Profit Allocation			
	Hanyard	Robertson	Turman	Kelly	Total
Interest on capital	$ 5,000	$ 4,500	$ 2,000	$ 4,700	$ 16,200
Bonuses (Note B)	—	—	—	—	—
Salaries	20,000	10,000	—	—	30,000
Subtotal	$ 25,000	$14,500	$ 2,000	$ 4,700	$ 46,200
Remaining profit	(21,550)	(21,550)	(21,550)	(21,550)	(86,200)
Income (loss)	$ 3,450	$ (7,050)	$(19,550)	$(16,850)	$(40,000)

Note B: Bonuses are only applicable if there is net income.

3.

	Hanyard	Robertson	Turman	Kelly	Total
			Profit Allocation		
Interest on capital	$ 5,000	$ 4,500	$ 2,000	$4,700	$ 16,200
Bonuses (Note C)	1,143	762	—	—	1,905
Salaries (Note D)	14,597	7,298	—	—	21,895
Income	$20,740	$12,560	$ 2,000	$4,700	$ 40,000

Note C:
Bonuses = 5% (net income – bonuses) .
105% Bonuses = 5% ($40,000)
105% Bonuses = $2,000
Bonuses = $1,905
Bonuses allocated 3/5 to Hanyard and 2/5 to Robertson.

Note D: Salaries are allocated based on 20,000/30,000 to Hanyard and 10,000/30,000 to Robertson.

PART 3

1.　c
2.　c
3.　b
4.　d
5.　a

PART 4

1.　b
2.　c
3.　d
4.　c
5.　b
6.　a

CHAPTER 14

PART 1

1.　F
2.　T
3.　F　The percentage interest in capital is multiplied by the sum of the book value of the old partnership and the new partner's investment.
4.　T
5.　T　Goodwill suggests an increase in value that would be implied only if a withdrawing partner was paid more than that partner's capital balance.
6.　T
7.　F
8.　T　This is the right-of-offset doctrine.
9.　F　Unsatisfied partnership creditors can attach to the net personal assets of any solvent partner.
10.　T
11.　F
12.　T

PART 2

1. $190,000 x 50% = $95,000.

2. $197,200 ($190,000 + $7,200)

Book value of new partnership ($190,000 + $100,000 + $150,000)	$440,000
Rogers' percentage interest	30%
Rogers' new capital balance	132,000
Rogers' contribution	150,000
Bonus from Rogers	$(18,000)
Gabriel's share of bonus (40% x $18,000)	$ 7,200

3. $125,000 ($375,000 – $250,000)

Adjusted capital of old partnership ($190,000 + $100,000 – $40,000)	$250,000
Interest in new partnership represented by above	66.67%
Total suggested value of new partnership	$375,000

4. $194,000

Gabriel's original capital	$190,000
Gabriel's share of overstatement (40% x $50,000)	(20,000)
Gabriel's share of goodwill [40% x (($150,000 ÷ 1/3) – ($190,000 + $100,000 – $50,000 + $150,000))]	24,000
	$194,000

5. $170,000 ($150,000 + $20,000)

Adjusted capital of original partners ($190,000 + $100,000 + $50,000)	$340,0000
Suggested value of new partnership ($340,000 ÷ 2/3)	$ 510,000
Suggested value of a 1/3 interest (1/3 x $510,000)	$ 170,000
Amount paid by Rogers	150,000
Implied goodwill	$ 20,000

PART 3

1. b
2. c
3. a
4. d
5. b
6. a
7. b
8. c

PART 4

1. $9,500 to Partner A

	A	B	C
Capital balances	$ 70,000	$ 72,000	$ 3,000
Maximum loss possible	(49,600)	(49,600)	(24,800)
Allocation of debit capital balance	(10,900)	(10,900)	21,800
	$ 9,500	$ 11.500	$ 0

2. Partner C's capital balance equals $0

	A	B	C
Capital balances	$ 70,000	$ 72,000	$ 3,000
Loss on sale	(8,000)	(8,000)	(4,000)
Contribution of capital			1,000
			$ 0

3. $7,000 to Partner A and $13,000 to Partner B

	A	B	C
Capital balances	$ 70,000	$ 72,000	$ 3,000
Right of offset	—	4,000	15,000
Maximum loss possible	(57,600)	(57,600)	(28,800)
Allocation of debit capital balance	(5,400)	(5,400)	10,800
	$ 7,000	$ 13,000	$ 0

4.

	A	B	C
Capital balances	$(30,000)	$(25,000)	$ (5,000)
Contribution of assets	36,000	20,000	4,000
	$ 6,000	$ (5,000)	$ 1,000

5. $15,000 to Partner A

	A	B	C
Capital balances	$ 80,000	$ 70,000	$ 10,000
Gain on disposal of assets	4,000	4,000	2,000
Distribution of assets	(20,000)	—	—
Maximum loss possible	(44,000)	(44,000)	(22,000)
Allocation of debit capital balance	(5,000)	(5,000)	10,000
	$ 15,000	$ 25,000	$ 0

PART 5

Schedule of Safe Payments

	Martini	Manhatton	Moskel	Total
Profit and loss percentage	40%	40%	20%	100%
January 15 distribution:				
Combined capital and loan balances before distribution	$ 52,000	$102,000	$ 26,000	$ 180,000
Estimated liquidation expenses	(6,000)	(6,000)	(3,000)	(15,000)
Balances	$ 46,000	$ 96,000	$ 23,000	$ 165,000
Maximum loss possible	(66,000)	(66,000)	(33,000)	(165,000)
Balances	$(20,000)	$ 30,000	$(10,000)	0
Allocation of debit balances	20,000	(30,000)	10,000	0
Safe payments	0	0	0	0

*Since cash is restricted for the amount of estimated liquidation expenses of $15,000, no cash is available for distribution to the partners.

February 28 distribution:

	Martini	Manhatton	Moskel	Total
Combined capital and loan balances before distribution	$ 46,000	$ 96,000	$ 23,000	$ 165,000
Estimated liquidation expenses	(6,000)	(6,000)	(3,000)	(15,000)
Balances	$ 40,000	$ 90,000	$ 20,000	$ 150,000
Maximum loss possible	(50,000)	(50,000)	(25,000)	(125,000)
Balances	$ (10,000)	$ 40,000	$ (5,000)	$ 25,000
Allocation of debit balances	10,000	(15,000)	5,000	0
Safe payments	0	$ 25,000	0	$ 25,000

May 15 distribution:

Combined capital and loan balances before distribution	$ 42,000	$ 67,000	$ 21,000	$130,000
Maximum loss possible	(30,000)	(30,000)	(15,000)	(75,000)
Safe payments	$ 12,000	$ 37,000	$ 6,000	$ 55,000

Installment Liquidation Statement

	Cash	Noncash Assets	Liabilities	Loans from Martini	Martini	Manhatton	Moskel
Beginning balances	20,000	$240,000	$ 60,000	$ 10,000	$ 50,000	$110,000	$ 30,000
Jan. 5, sale of assets	55,000	(75,000)			(8,000)	(8,000)	(4,000)
Balances	$ 75,000	$165,000	$ 60,000	$ 10,000	$ 42,000	$102,000	$ 26,000
Payment of liabilities	(60,000)		(60,000)				
Jan. 15, distribution	0				0	0	0
Balances	$ 15,000	$165,000	0	$ 10,000	$ 42,000	$102,000	$ 26,000
Jan. 20, sale of assets	25,000	(40,000)			(6,000)	(6,000)	(3,000)
Balances	$ 40,000	$125,000	0	$ 10,000	$ 36,000	$ 96,000	$ 23,000
Feb. 28, distribution	(25,000)					(25,000)	
Balances	$ 15,000	$125,000	0	$ 10,000	$ 36,000	$ 71,000	$ 23,000
May 6, sale of assets	60,000	(50,000)			4,000	4,000	2,000
May 10, payment of liquidation expenses	(20,000)				(8,000)	(8,000)	(4,000)
Balances	$ 55,000	$ 75,000	0	$ 10,000	$ 32,000	$ 67,000	$ 21,000
May 15, distribution	(55,000)			(10,000)	(2,000)	(37,000)	(6,000)
Balances	0	$ 75,000	0	0	$ 30,000	$ 30,000	$ 15,000
May 21, sale of assets	79,000	(75,000)			1,600	1,600	800
Balances	$ 79,000	0	0	0	$ 31,600	$ 31,600	$ 15,800
June 1, final distribution	(79,000)				(31,600)	(31,600)	(15,800)
Balances	0	0	0	0	0	0	0

CHAPTER 15

PART 1

1. T
2. T
3. T
4. T
5. F It does not include fixed assets or general long-term debt.
6. F The measurement focus is flows of financial resources.
7. F A transaction may require an entry in more than one fund or group.
8. T No depreciation expense is recorded in governmental funds. Therefore, no depreciation expense appears on the statement of revenues, expenditures, and changes in fund balances. Depreciation expense is, however, required for the government-wide statements and may be recorded in the general fixed assets account group.
9. F The serial bond payable is accounted for in the general long-term debt account group and in the government-wide attachments.
10. T

PART 2

1. A   Revenue
2. F   Borrowing transaction within the fund
3. B   Other financing sources
4. A   Revenue
5. A   Revenue
6. B   Other financing sources
7. C   Expenditures
8. D   Encumbrances
9. H   None of the above
10. C, G Expenditures, designation of the fund balance
11. C   Expenditures
12. E   Other financing uses
13. G   Designation of the fund balance
14. B   Other financing sources
15. C, B Expenditures, other financing sources
16. A   Revenue

PART 3

1.	Estimated revenues	375,000	
	Appropriations		300,000
	Estimated other financing uses		60,000
	Budgetary fund balance— unreserved		15,000
2.	Encumbrances	7,000	
	Fund balance—unreserved, undesignated		7,000
3.	Property taxes receivable—current	350,000	
	Allowance for uncollectible current property taxes		7,000
	Revenue		343,000
4.	Cash	21,200	
	Delinquent taxes receivable		20,000
	Revenue		1,200
	Allowance for uncollectible delinquent taxes	3,000	
	Revenue		3,000
5.	Cash	3,500	
	Tax liens receivable		3,500
	Allowance for uncollectible tax liens	2,000	
	Revenue	500	
	Tax liens receivable		2,500
6.	Cash	340,000	
	Property taxes receivable— current		340,000

7. Property taxes receivable—delinquent   10,000
    Property taxes receivable—
      current   10,000

    Allowance for uncollectible current
      property taxes   7,000
    Allowance for uncollectible
      delinquent taxes   7,000

    Tax liens receivable   12,000
    Property taxes receivable—
      Delinquent   12,000

    Allowance for uncollectible
      delinquent taxes   12,000
    Allowance for uncollectible
      tax liens   12,000

8. Due from state government   45,000
    Revenue   45,000

9. Encumbrances   23,000
    Fund balance—reserved for
      encumbrances   23,000

10. Fund balance—reserved for
      encumbrances   27,000
    Encumbrances   27,000

    Supplies inventory   15,000
    Expenditures   275,000
    Vouchers payable   290,000

11. Vouchers payable   290,000
    Cash   290,000

12. Expenditures   17,000
    Supplies inventory   17,000

    Fund balance—reserved for inventory   2,000
    Fund balance—unreserved,
      undesignated   2,000

13. Other financing uses   59,000
    Cash   59,000

PART 4

1.
(a)   Appropriations   475,000
     Budgetary fund balance—unreserved   50,000
        Estimated revenues   525,000

(b)   Revenues   500,000
       Expenditures   470,000
       Fund balance—unreserved, undesignated   30,000

     Fund balance—unreserved, undesignated   12,000
       Encumbrances   12,000

2.

Village of Victory
General Fund
Budgetary Comparison Schedule
For Fiscal Year Ended December 31, 20X8

	Budget	Actual Results	Variances— Favorable (Unfavorable)
Revenues	$525,000	$500,000	$(25,000)
Expenditures	475,000	470,000	5,000
Excess of revenues over expenditures	50,000	30,000	(20,000)
Fund balances, January 1, 20X8	140,000	140,000	—
Fund balances, December 31, 20X8	$190,000	$170,000	$(20,000)

3.

Village of Victory
General Fund Balance Sheet
December 31, 20X8

Assets			Liabilities and Fund Equity		
Cash		$ 55,000	Liabilities:		
Taxes receivable—delinquent	$30,000		Vouchers payable		$ 25,000
Less allowance for uncollectible			Fund balances:		
delinquent taxes	15,000	15,000	Reserved for encumbrances	$ 12,000	
Tax liens receivable	10,000		Unreserved, undesignated	158,000	170,000
Less allowance for uncollectible tax liens	5,000	5,000			
Marketable equity securities		120,000	Total liabilities and fund equity		$195,000
Total assets		$195,000			

PART 5

1. General fund:

Encumbrances	150,000	
Fund balance—reserved for encumbrances		150,000

2. General fund:

Fund balance—reserved for encumbrances	150,000	
Encumbrances		150,000
Expenditures	154,000	
Cash		54,000
Other financing sources		100,000

General fixed assets account group:

Equipment	154,000	
Investment in general fixed assets—general funds		154,000

General long-term debt account group:

Amount to be provided for payment of note payable	100,000	
Note payable		100,000

3. General fund:

Cash	15,000	
Other financing sources		15,000

General fixed assets account group:

Investment in general fixed assets—general funds	50,000	
Equipment		50,000

4. General fund:

Expenditures	50,000	
Other financing sources		50,000

General fixed assets account group:

Leased equipment	50,000	
Investment in general fixed assets—capital lease		50,000

General long-term debt account group:

Amount to be provided for payment of lease obligation	50,000	
Lease payable		50,000

5. General fund:

Expenditures	35,000	
Cash		35,000

General long-term debt account group:

Bonds payable	35,000	
Amount to be provided for payment of bonds payable		35,000

CHAPTER 16

PART 1

1. F   They are transferred to the debt service fund.
2. T
3. T
4. T
5. T
6. T
7. T
8. T
9. F   A capital projects fund is a governmental fund of a municipality.
10. F   They would be accounted for in a special revenue fund.

PART 2

1. d   Since construction is complete, there would be no balance in this fund.

2. b   The current portion is received in time to meet expenditures; the deferred portion is financed by issuing bonds.

3. a   Only if there is no potential liability to the city can the liability be excluded from the general long-term dept account group.

4. c   This fund uses business-type accounting methods.

5. d   This is an expenditure, similar to a payment to an outside vendor.

6. b   Assets are restricted or unrestricted.

7. b   The landfill enterprise fund should report closure and post-closure care expenses based on usage. The expense is calculated as $[(540,000 \div 1,000,000) \times \$2,000,000] - \$973,000 = \$107,000$

8. d   General long-term debt account group records liability. General fixed assets account group records change in source of funds. Debt service fund records payment. Capital projects fund records receipt of funds.

PART 3

1.a.	Estimated revenues	300,000	
	Estimated other financing		
	sources	1,000,000	
	Appropriations		575,000
	Budgetary fund balance—		
	unreserved		725,000
b.	Cash	990,000	
	Other financing sources		990,000
	General long-term debt account group:		
	Amount to be provided for		
	payment of bonds	1,000,000	
	Bonds payable		1,000,000
c.	Cash	300,000	
	Revenues		300,000
d.	Expenditures	45,000	
	Cash	45,000	
e.	Encumbrances	1,250,000	
	Fund balance—reserved for		
	encumbrances		1,250,000

f.	Encumbrances	30,000	
	Fund balance—reserved for encumbrances		30,000
g.	Fund balance—reserved for encumbrances	30,000	
	Encumbrances		30,000
	Inventory of supplies	35,000	
	Vouchers payable		35,000
h.	Fund balance—reserved for encumbrances	375,000	
	Encumbrances		375,000
	Expenditures	375,000	
	Contracts payable (or vouchers payable)		375,000
i.	Expenditures	23,000	
	Inventory of supplies		23,000
	Fund balance—unreserved, undesignated	12,000	
	Fund balance reserved for inventory of supplies		12,000
j.	Budgetary fund balance—unreserved		725,000
	Appropriations	575,000	
	Estimated revenues		300,000
	Estimated other financing sources		1,000,000
	Revenues	300,000	
	Other financing sources	990,000	
	Expenditures		443,000
	Fund balance—unreserved, undesignated		847,000
	Fund balance—reserved for encumbrances	875,000	
	Encumbrances		875,000
	General fixed assets account group:		
	Construction in progress	443,000	
	Investment in general fixed assets—capital projects funds		443,000
2. a.	General fund:		
	Other financing uses	320,000	
	Cash		320,000
	Debt service fund:		
	Cash	320,000	
	Other financing sources		320,000
	General long-term debt account group:		
	Amount available in debt service fund		250,000
	Amount to be provided for payment of bonds		250,000
	Total amount for principal and interest		320,000
	Less amount for interest payment (7% x $1,000,000)	70,000	
	Amount available for principal payment		250,000
b.	Debt service fund:		
	Expenditures	70,000	
	Matured interest payable		70,000
c.	Debt service fund:		
	Cash with fiscal agent	320,000	
	Cash		320,000
d.	Debt service fund:		
	Matured interest payable	70,000	
	Cash with fiscal agent		70,000

PART 4

1. a. Cash   1,000,000
        Interfund transfer from general fund
            (nonoperating revenue)   750,000
        Nonoperating revenues   250,000

    b. Buildings   700,000
        Cash   700,000

    c. Buildings   200,000
        Cash   200,000

    d. Restricted assets—tenants' deposits cash   20,000
        Tenants' deposits payable from restricted assets   20,000

    e. Cash   50,000
        Operating revenues   50,000

    f. Operating expenses   45,000
        Cash   45,000

    g. Restricted assets—tenants' deposits investments   9,000
        Restricted assets—tenants' deposits cash   9,000

    h. Operating expenses   45,000
        Accumulated depreciation—buildings   45,000
        (Annual depreciation is
          $900,000 ÷ 20 years, or $45,000.)

    i. Cash   1,500
        Nonoperating revenues   1,500

2.

City of James Bay
Public Housing Authority Enterprise Fund
Statement of Revenues, Expenses, and Changes in Net Assets
December 31, 20X7

Operating revenues:		
Rental income		$ 50,000
Operating expenses:		
Depreciation expense	$ 45,000	
Heat, light, and taxes	45,000	90,000
Operating income (loss)		(40,000)
Nonoperating revenues:		
Federal grant	250,000	
Interfund transfer	750,000	
Investment income	1,500	1,001,500
Net income		$ 961,500
Net assets, January 1, 20X7		0
Net assets, December 31, 20X7		$ 961,500

3.

City of James Bay
Public Housing authority Enterprise Fund
Balance Sheet
December 31, 20X7

Assets			Liabilities and Fund Equity	
Current assets:			Liabilities:	
Cash		$106,500	Current liabilities (payable from restricted assets):	
Restricted assets:			Tenants' deposits payable	$ 20,000
Tenants' deposits—cash	$ 11,000		Net assets:	961,500
Tenants' deposits—investments	9,000	20,000	Total liabilities and net assets	$981,500
Property, plant, and equipment:				
Buildings	$900,000			
Less accumulated depreciation	45,000	855,000		
Total assets		$961,500		

PART 5

1.	Cash	75,000	
	Additions—contributions		75,000
2.	Interest receivable on investments	130,000	
	Additions—investment income		130,000
3.	Deductions—benefits paid	74,000	
	Annuities payable		60,000
	Due to resigned employees		14,000
4.	Deductions—refunds paid	7,500	
	Cash		7,500
5.	Investments	10,500	
	Net increase in carrying value		10,500
6.	Investments fees	500	
	Cash		500
7.	Additions	215,000	
	Deductions		82,000
	Plan net assets		133,500

8.

Statement of Changes in Plan Net Assets
For the Period Ending December 31, 20XX

Additions:	
Contributions	$ 75,000
Investment income	130,000
Net increase in value of investments	10,500
Total additions	215,500
Deductions:	
Benefits	74,000
Refunds	7,500
Fees	500
Total deductions	82,000
Changes in plan net assets	$133,500

CHAPTER 17

PART 1

1. GASB Statement No. 34 mandates government-wide and fund-based statements.

2. Major funds are determined by comparing the size of the fund with others in the same category or with the government as a whole. To qualify as a major fund, a fund must have assets, liabilities, revenues, or expenditures/expenses of at least 10% of all funds in the category and at least 5% of all governmental and enterprise funds combined. In addition, management can designate any fund it wishes to highlight as major.

3. Governmental activities are accounted for using modified accrual in the funds-based statements and for using full accrual in the government-wide statements.

4. Management's discussion and analysis (MD&A) contains concise overview and analysis of the information in the financial report.

5. Budgetary information—including the original and final amended budget—is required supplementary information in the new model.

PART 2

As in all governments, the general fund is considered a major fund. Every other governmental fund must be examined to determine if it is at least 10% of all the governmental funds and at least 5% of all government and enterprise funds combined. Every enterprise fund must also be examined to determine if at least 10% of all the enterprise funds and at least 5% of all the government and enterprise funds combined. The size tests are based on assets, liabilities, revenues, and expenditures/expenses. Internal service funds are not considered major funds. In addition, management may need to be interviewed to determine if there are funds that they wish to disclose in a separate column in the fund statements because they are of particular interest or convey unique information, even though they do not meet the size text.

PART 3

Governmental Fund Statement of Revenues, Expenditures, and Changes in Fund Balance

General Fund	DSF	CPF A	CPF C	Other Governmental Funds	Total

Proprietary Fund Statement of Revenues, Expenses, and Changes in Net Assets

Enterprise Fund D	Enterprise Fund E	Other Funds	Total	Total Internal Service Funds

PART 4

1. b
2. a
3. b
4. c
5. a
6. b
7. b
8. b
9. b
10. b
11. b
12. c
13. b
14. c
15. b

CHAPTER 18

PART 1

1. T
2. F   Fixed assets are accounted for in the plant fund.
3. F   The loss is recorded as a loss.
4. T
5. F   At the time of receipt of interest payment, a portion of the interest equal to the premium amortization is retained as principal of the endowment. Only the portion recognized as revenue is unrestricted.
6. F   A full accrual basis is used.
7. T   Only VHWOs are required to present a statement of functional expenses.
8. F   Contributions of property are valued at their market values at the time of receipt and are classified as contributions in the appropriate net asset class.
9. F   The donation is classified as a temporarily restricted contribution.
10. T
11. F   Both the contribution and the rent expense should be recorded at the amount that normally would be charged for rent.
12. T
13. F
14. T
15. T

PART 2

1. current unrestricted fund, current restricted fund
2. current restricted fund, plant fund, endowment fund, custodian fund
3. unrestricted net assets, unrestricted net assets—designated
4. principal, investment revenue
5. revenue

PART 3

Lakeside Nature Center
Statement of Activities
For Year Ended May 31, 20X5

	Unrestricted	Temporarily Restricted	Permanently Restricted	Total
Public support and revenue:				
Public support:				
Contributions	$190,000	$ 94,000		$284,000
Special events support (net of direct costs of $1,200)	3,800			3,800
Legacies and bequests	75,000		$ 12,000	87,000
Total public support	$268,800	$ 94,000	$ 12,000	$374,800
Revenue:				
Membership dues	$ 75,000			$ 75,000
Investment revenue	13,000	$ 6,500		19,500
Net increase in carrying value of investments			$ 20,000	20,000
Gain on sale of investments	1,200			1,200
Total revenue	$ 89,200	$ 6,500	$ 20,000	$115,700
Net assets released from restriction:				
Satisfaction of program restrictions	$ 63,400	$(63,400)		
Satisfaction of equipment acquisition restrictions	13,700	(13,700)		
Total net assets released from restriction	77,100	(77,100)		
Total public support, revenue, and other support	$435,100	$ 23,400	$ 32,000	$490,500
Expenses:				
Wildlife preserve program	$ 84,400			$ 84,400
Children's activities	113,300			113,300
Planting program	153,900			153,900
Management and general services	16,600			16,600
Fund-raising services	3,700			3,700
Membership development services	2,000			2,000
Total expenses	$373,900			$373,900
Change in net assets	$ 61,200	$ 23,400	$ 32,000	$116,600
Net assets, June 1, 20X4	56,000	54,600	160,000	270,600
Net assets, May 31, 20X5	$117,200	$ 78,000	$192,000	$387,200

CHAPTER 19

PART 1

1. F Revenue is recognized at public universities when cash is received and at private universities when the condition is met.
2. F The fair market value of noncash property pledged is recognized as revenue.
3. T
4. T
5. T
6. F Private universities are required to recognize depreciation on fixed assets.
7. T
8. F All governments now account for investments at fair value.

PART 2

1. c
2. c
3. c
4. b
5. a

PART 3

1.	CUF	Estimated revenues	1,000,000	
		Estimated expenses		750,000
		Unallocated balance		250,000
2.	CUF	Pledges receivable	25,000	
		Revenues—unrestricted pledges		25,000
3.	CUF	Accounts receivable	900,000	
		Revenues—student tuition and fees		500,000
		Revenues—governmental appropriations		100,000
		Revenues—state grants		200,000
		Revenues—other income		100,000
		Expense—institutional support	10,000	
		Allowance for uncollectibles—student accounts receivable		10,000
4.	CUF	Accounts receivable	75,000	
		Revenues—auxiliary enterprises		75,000
5.	CUF	Cash	965,000	
		Accounts receivable		965,000
6.	CUF	Cash	25,000	
		Pledges receivable		25,000
7.	CUF	Inventory of materials and supplies	65,000	
		Accounts payable		65,000
8.	CUF	Expenses—student aid	7,500	
		Cash		7,500
	CUF	Reclassification out—temporarily restricted	7,500	
		Reclassification in—unrestricted		7,500
9.	CUF	Expenses—instruction	250,000	
		Expenses—research	50,000	
		Expenses—student services	25,000	
		Expenses—operation and maintenance of plant	50,000	
		Expenses—student aid (scholarships)	40,000	
		Expenses—auxiliary enterprises	70,000	
		Expenses—academic support	200,000	
		Cash		685,000
10.	CUF	Interfund transfer for additions to plant	10,000	
		Transfers for principal payment	20,000	
		Cash		30,000
11.	CUF	Expenses—instruction	25,000	
		Expenses—student services	20,000	
		Expenses—auxiliary enterprises	15,000	
		Inventory of materials and supplies		60,000
12.	CUF	Interfund transfer to loan fund	75,000	
		Cash		75,000
13.	CUF	Interfund transfers for principal payment	35,000	
		Cash		35,000
14.	CUF	Cash	200,000	
		Revenues—expired term endowments		200,000
15.	CUF	Cash	30,000	

		Revenues—temporarily restricted contributions		30,000
16.	CUF	Cash	5,000	
		Revenues—temporarily restricted endowment income		5,000
17.	CUF	Expenses—research	25,000	
		Expenses—academic support	4,000	
		Cash		29,000
	CUF	Reclassification out—temporarily restricted	29,000	
		Reclassification in—unrestricted		29,000
18.	CUF	(a) Unallocated balance	250,000	
		Estimated expenses	750,000	
		Estimated revenues		1,000,000
		(b) Revenues—auxiliary enterprises	75,000	
		Net assets—unrestricted	10,000	
		Expenses—auxiliary enterprises		85,000
		Revenues—unrestricted pledges	25,000	
		(c) Revenues—student tuition and fees	500,000	
		Revenues—government appropriations	100,000	
		Revenues—state grants	200,000	
		Revenues—other income	100,000	
		Revenues—expired term endowments	200,000	
		Expenses—institutional support		10,000
		Expenses—instruction		275,000
		Expenses—research		50,000
		Expenses—student services		45,000
		Expenses—student aid (scholarships)		40,000
		Expenses—academic support		200,000
		Expenses—operation and maintenance of plant		50,000
		Net assets—unrestricted		455,000
		(d) Net assets—unrestricted	140,000	
		Transfers for principal payment		140,000
19.	RCF	Reclassification in—unrestricted	36,500	
		Revenues—temporarily restricted contributions	30,000	
		Revenues—temporarily restricted endowment income	5,000	
		Net assets—temporarily restricted	1,500	
		Expenses—student aid		7,500
		Expenses—research		25,000
		Expenses—academic support		4,000
		Reclassification out—temporarily restricted		36,500

PART 4

1. Loan fund:

a.	Cash	85,000	
	Revenues—temporarily restricted contributions		10,000
	Interfund transfer		75,000
b.	Investments	35,000	
	Cash		35,000
c.	Loans receivable	45,000	
	Reclassification out—temporarily restricted	45,000	
	Cash		45,000
	Reclassification in—unrestricted		45,000
d.	Expenses—institutional support	1,500	
	Loans receivable		1,500
e.	Cash	27,000	
	Loans receivable		25,000
	Revenues—unrestricted other investment income		2,000

2. Endowment and similar funds:

a.	Cash	40,000	
	Revenues—quasi-endowment		40,000

b.	Investments	250,000	
	Revenues—term endowment		250,000
c.	Cash	40,000	
	Revenues—unrestricted endowment income		40,000
d.	Cash	46,000	
	Loss on investment—term Endowment	4,000	
	Investments		50,000

3. Annuity and life income fund:

a.	Cash—annuity	150,000	
	Annuities payable		120,000
	Revenues—temporarily restricted contribution		30,000
b.	Investments—life income	100,000	
	Revenues—life income from contributions		100,000
c.	Actuarial adjustment of annuities payable	9,600	
	Annuities payable		9,600
	Annuities payable	10,000	
	Cash		10,000
d.	Cash	12,000	
	Revenues—temporarily restricted income on investments		12,000

4. Plant fund:

a.	Cash	60,000	
	Revenues—temporarily restricted contributions		60,000
b.	Cash	210,000	
	Revenues—temporarily restricted contributions		210,000
c.	Cash	485,000	
	Bonds payable		485,000
d.	Construction in progress	255,000	
	Contracts payable		255,000
e.	Construction in progress	240,000	
	Contracts payable		225,000
	Cash		495,000
f.	Library books	50,000	
	Cash		50,000
g.	Reclassification out—temporarily restricted net assets	50,000	
	Reclassification in—unrestricted net assets		50,000
h.	Expenses	45,000	
	Cash		45,000

PART 5

1. T

2. T

3. F They are shown as a reduction of gross revenues. Only net revenue is displayed on the financial statements.

4. T

5. F Although the indirect method is acceptable, the audit guide encourages the use of the direct method.

PART 6

1.	Accounts receivable	345,000	
	Patient service revenue		320,000
	Other operating revenue		25,000
	Provision for uncollectibles	12,000	
	Contractual adjustments	8,000	
	Allowance for adjustments and uncollectibles		20,000
2.	Cash	300,000	
	Allowance for adjustments and uncollectibles	15,000	
	Accounts receivable		315,000
3.	Nursing services expense	100,000	
	Other professional services expense	200,000	
	General services expense	25,000	
	Fiscal services expense	30,000	
	Administrative services expense	10,000	
	Cash		365,000
4.	Notes payable	20,000	
	Interest expense	31,000	
	Mortgage payable	40,000	
	Cash		91,000
5.	Reclassification out—temporarily restricted—satisfaction of program restrictions	90,000	
	Reclassification in— unrestricted—satisfaction of program restrictions		90,000
6.	Property, plant, and equipment	150,000	
	Accounts (or vouchers) payable		150,000
7.	Depreciation expense	18,000	
	Accumulated depreciation		18,000
8.	Cash	10,000	
	Investment income—unrestricted	10,000	

PART 7

Grand Rapids Hospital
Statement of Cash Flows
For Year Ended July 31, 20X6

Cash flows from operating activities and nonoperating revenue:	
Cash received from patients and third-party payors	$ 4,280,950
Cash received from flower shop	258,850
Cash received from unrestricted gifts	81,750
Cash received from endowment income	80,000
Cash paid to employees and suppliers	(3,675,500)
Cash paid to physicians consultation service	(100,000)
Cash paid for interest	(73,500)
Net cash provided by operating activities and nonoperating revenue	$ 852,550
Cash flows from investing activities:	
Purchase of operating room equipment	$ (250,600)
Net cash outflow for purchase of equipment	$ (250,600)
Cash transfer to assets whose use is limited	(114,000)
Net cash used by investing activities	$ (364,600)
Cash flows from financing activities:	
Cash paid for retirement of indebtedness	$ (300,000)
Cash paid to First Bank for payment of long-term note	(121,150)
Net cash used by financing activities	$ (421,150)
Net increase in cash	88,300
Cash at beginning of the year (August 1, 20X5)	137,950
Cash at end of the year (July 31, 20X6)	$ 204,750

Grand Rapids Hospital
Reconciliation of Excess of Revenues over Expenses
To Net Cash Provided by Operating Activities and Nonoperating Revenue
For Year Ended July 31, 20X6

Excess of revenues over expenses	$731,650
Adjustments to reconcile excess of revenues over expenses to net cash provided by operating activities and nonoperating revenue:	
Depreciation	216,250
Increase in liability for estimated malpractice costs	6,150
Unrestricted gain from sale of investments	(8,750)
Increase in patient accounts receivable	(113,700)
Decrease in supplies inventory	5,900
Increase in accounts payable	15,050
Net cash provided by operating activities and nonoperating revenue	$852,550

CHAPTER 20

PART 1

1. F
2. T
3. T   Certain real property may be exempt along with assets included in the homestead or family allowance.
4. F   The debts of an estate are recorded when paid by the estate fiduciary.
5. T
6. T
7. T
8. F   The tax basis of the inherited property is equal to the fair market value of the item used for estate tax purposes. This value is most often different from the decedent's tax basis.
9. T   A reduction of income for depreciation and/or depletion would help to preserve the value of the estate principal.
10. F
11. T
12. T

PART 2

1. B
2. J
3. D
4. G
5. H
6. F

PART 3

1. c   Under a testate distribution, a legatee receives personal property while a devisee receives real property.

2. d   The formula to be used is: the annual exclusion from gift tax x number of years x number of gift recipients. The data for the last term in the formula have not been provided. Thus the answer is not determinable.

3. a   Carlotta should sell the stock in order to establish a capital loss for income tax purposes and donate the proceeds. By donating either cash or the shares directly, the capital loss would not be established.

4. c   Since the alternative valuation date was not applicable, Julio's basis is market value on the date of death—$20,000.

5. a   It is only availabe to decedents who are married at the time of their death. Option (b) is not correct since gifts should be considered in all estate planning. Option (c) is incorrect since it is the surviving spouse who receives the assets of the deceased, increasing total property that one day may be subject to estate tax. Option (d) is incorrect since those estates are not subject to estate tax.

6. b   A general legacy does not specify the source of funds from which the legacy is to be paid. It would be a specific legacy if it read, "I leave my friend Chien Yang the $10,000 in Account 720-0335 at Valley National Bank in Tucson, Arizona."

7. d   The taxable estate is increased by any taxable gifts made after 1976.

PART 4

Estate of Pete Mitchell
Change and Discharge Statement
For the Period February 28, 20X7, to December 31, 20X7

As to Principal

I charge myself with:

Assets per original inventory	$185,000	
Assets subsequently discovered	25,000	
Total charges		$210,000

I credit myself with:

Loss on realization of principal assets	$ 5,000	
Funeral and administration expenses	10,000	
Debts of decendent paid	25,000	
Legacies distributed	10,000	
Devises distributed	15,000	
Total credits		65,000

Balances as to estate principal,
consisting of:

Cash—principal	$ 45,000	
Corporation stock	100,000	
		$145,000

As to Income

I charge myself with:

Estate income		$34,000

I credit myself with:

Expenses chargeable against income	$ 4,000	
Distribution to income beneficiaries	5,000	
Total credits		9,000

Balance as to estate income, consisting of:

Cash—income		$25,000

PART 5

		Would Affect		
		Principal Only	Income Only	Principal and Income
1.	Recording of the original assets of the estate	X		
2.	Sale of capital stock in the original estate at a gain	X		
3.	Recording receipt of interest (partly accrued at date of death) on bonds in original estate			X
4.	Recording assets subsequently discovered	X		
5.	Purchase of bonds at a premium along with accrued interest	X		
6.	Receipt of first interest check on bonds in 5.			X
7.	Payment of property taxes on a rental apartment		X	

CHAPTER 21

PART 1

1. T
2. T
3. T If the total of all payments made under the restructuring is less than the basis of the debt, no interest expense is recognized because the payments are considered to be reductions of the principal balance of the debt.
4. T Interest expense under a Chapter 11 reorganization is based on a market rate of interest. An effective rate of interest is used in other instances.
5. T
6. F
7. F Both reorganizations and liquidations may be either voluntary or involuntary.
8. F The creditors must represent at least two-thirds of the dollar amount due.
9. F
10. T
11. F
12. T

PART 2

1. c An $80,000 gain on restructuring plus a $120,000 gain on the realized appreciation of the assets.
2. b
3. d
4. d The total interest to be recognized is $171,011 based on a market rate of 7%. The first year's interest expense is $30,029 (7% x $428,989).
5. a The total consideration received in satisfaction of the debt is $610,000 [$220,000 + ($78,000 x 5)]. Because this amount exceeds the $600,000 basis of the debt, no gain is recognized.
6. c
7. a The decrease in value of the equipment of $150,000 ($700,000 – $550,000) is added to the previous deficit of $320,000. This total deficit of $470,000 requires a reduction in common stock at par of $70,000. Therefore, the balance in common stock must be adjusted to $130,000 for 20,000 shares ($200,000 ÷ $10 par/share) or a par value of $6.50 ($130,000 ÷ 20,000).

PART 3

1. c
2. b The only fully secured creditor is the $40,000 account payable.
3. b The partially secured creditors are as follows:

	Secured	Unsecured
Equipment payable	$350,000	$ 10,000
Business loan payable	80,000	100,000
	$430,000	$110,000

4. d The realizable values of assets are as follows:

	Cost	Realizable Value
Cash	$ 12,000	$ 12,000
Receivables (net)	100,000	80,000
Receivables (net)	180,000	150,000
Inventory	40,000	44,000
Inventory	30,000	32,000
Plant assets (net)	340,000	350,000
	$702,000	$668,000

Fully secured and partially secured claims total $40,000 and $430,000, respectively. Therefore, $198,000 ($668,000 − $40,000 − $430,000) of free assets are available to unsecured creditors.

5. c   Of the unsecured creditors, $30,000 due the officer and $10,000 due employees have priority. After satisfying these claims, $158,000 ($198,000 − $30,000 − $10,000) of assets will be available to satisfy the $180,000 ($220,000 − $30,000 − $10,000) of Class 7 unsecured creditors ($158,000 ÷ 180,000 = 88%).

PART 4

1. a   The statement of affairs stresses the amount to be realized and its potential distribution.

2. d   By definition, goodwill is the present value of future excess profits over a normal rate of return. It is likely to have no realizable value if the company is in financial difficulty.

3. d   One purpose of a quasi-reorganization is to eliminate a deficit, which results in the corporation's retained earnings account's having a zero balance immediately after recording the reorganization.

4. c   For Class 7 unsecured creditors to receive any payment, Classes 1 through 6 must be paid in full.

5. c   Interest expense will be recognized if the net present value of future cash payments is less than the carrying value. This is possible even if the total of all payments exceeds the carrying value.

6. c   The amount realized in excess of a lien is assigned to cover unsecured debts.

PART 5

1. Claims of Classes 1 through 6:

Wachs (Class 1)	$1,500
Income taxes (Class 6)	3,500
Total unsecured claims with priority	$5,000

2. Computation of dividend to Class 7 unsecured claims:

Total expected amount to be realized for unsecured (given)	$70,000
Amount needed to cover Classes 1 through 6 (from question 1)	5,000
Amount available for Class 7	$65,000

Total Class 7 claims: $105,000 − $5,000 = $100,000.

$$\text{Dividend to Class 7: } \frac{\text{Amount available for Class 7}}{\text{Total Class 7 claims}} = \frac{\$65,000}{\$100,000} = 65\% = \$0.65 \text{ per dollar}$$

3.

Creditor	Expected Amount to be Realized
(a) Wachs	$1,500 x 100% = $1,500
(b) Bart	$1,060 x 65% = $ 689
(c) Gamble	$2,400 x 100% = $2,400
	600 x 65% = 390
	$3,000 $2,790 (93%)
(d) Land	$1,530 x 100% = $1,530
(e) Income taxes	$3,500 x 100% = $3,500